UNIVERSITY OF NOTRE DAME

LITURGICAL STUDIES

VOLUME II

Liturgical Studies

LITURGICAL COMMITTEE OF THE UNIVERSITY OF NOTRE DAME

Liturgical Piety
REV. LOUIS BOUYER (OF THE ORATORY)

Church Building and Furnishing
REV. J. B. O'CONNELL

•

IN PREPARATION

The Psalter as a Christian Prayer Book
REV. BALTHASAR FISCHER

The Primitive Liturgy
REV. JOSEF A. JUNGMANN, S.J.

The Bible and the Liturgy
REV. JEAN DANIELOU, S.J.

Liturgy and Western Culture
REV. HERMAN SCHMIDT, S.T.

The Prayer Life of the Church
REV. BONIFAAS LUYKX, O.PRAEM.

Aphikomen: The Key to the Last Supper
EUGENIO ZOLLI

The Missionary Value of the Liturgy
REV. JOHANNES HOFINGER, S.J.

The Sacred Scripture and the Spiritual Life
VERY REV. MSGR. FRANCIS H. DAVIS

Church Architecture for Our Time
HERMANN BAUR

CHURCH BUILDING

AND FURNISHING

Liturgical Studies

CHURCH BUILDING AND FURNISHING:

THE CHURCH'S WAY

A Study in Liturgical Law

BY

J. B. O'CONNELL

UNIVERSITY OF NOTRE DAME PRESS

NOTRE DAME, INDIANA

IMPRIMI POTEST: THEODORE J. MEHLING, C.S.C.,

PROVINCIAL

NIHIL OBSTAT: EUGENE P. BURKE, C.S.C.,

CENSOR DEPUTATUS

IMPRIMATUR: ✠ LEO A. PURSLEY,

APOSTOLIC ADMINISTRATOR, DIOCESE OF FORT WAYNE

OCT. 13, 1955

The Lord gave Moses this message: "Bid the Israelites bring me gifts in kind. . . . I mean them to build me a sanctuary, so that I can dwell among them; this dwelling and the appurtenances to be used in it must be of the pattern which I will now shew thee. . . . Look well, and make everything in due accord with the pattern which has been shewn to thee on the mountain."

Exodus 25. 2, 8, 40.

EDITOR'S PREFACE

THE original manuscript of *Church Building and Furnishing* by Rev. J. B. O'Connell of Builth Wells, Wales, Great Britain, first entitled *The Church's Way,* was the basis of this author's lectures in the Liturgy Program in the 1953 Summer Session of the University of Notre Dame.

There have been many important books written about various aspects of church building, decoration and furnishing; and although it is true that Father O'Connell has also written his book from the special point of view of liturgical law, yet this feature touches practically all phases of the construction of a Church. Liturgical law is basic because it shows how and why worship in a Catholic church dictates the requirements laid down by the Church.

Moreover, these requirements have for their object not merely to prevent the construction of churches that are not properly effective for Catholic worship, but primarily to free talent to make them more effective. Besides, these laws and directives, along with a proper commentary, are not easily accessible to architects, artists, craftsmen and, sometimes, even patrons. Accordingly, the Notre Dame Liturgical Committee feels that Father O'Connell has rendered a genuine service by his book.

This American edition of Father O'Connell's work has been supplemented by a number of plates selected under the guidance of Professor Francesco Montana, head of the Notre Dame Department of Architecture, which should prove of value to architects and pastors, not so much by suggesting models for them necessarily to imitate, as by demonstrating how wide is the range of technical solutions open to those who wish to build in accordance with the mind of the Church. As these diverse illustrations make very clear, the tradition and rubrics governing the building and furnishing of churches have been established to free, rather than constrain, those who obey them. So long as they do not transgress against these and the principles of sacred art, architects and pastors may meet the requirements laid down by the Church in any way that local conditions and their own ingenuity make possible.

Since the selection of the plates for this American edition was not made by Father O'Connell, he is, of course, not to be held in any way responsible for it.

For the privilege of reproducing them, we wish to make grateful acknowledgment to the following: *L'Art d'église; L'Art sacré; Christliche Kunst; Katholiek Bouwblad;* and *Liturgical Arts.*

MICHAEL A. MATHIS, C.S.C.
Editor, Liturgical Studies

University of Notre Dame,
January 6, 1956

FOREWORD

T H E Church summarizes her laws about the building and furnishing of churches in two short canons of the Code of Canon Law,
canons 1164, § 1, and 1296, § 3. These canons declare that tradition
is to be the chief guide in the building of a church, the rubrics in its
furnishing, while "the laws of sacred art" are to direct both.

I have endeavored in this book to explain the meaning of these
two canons, and to give some account of the vast amount of knowledge that is resumed in the seemingly simple terms "ecclesiastical tradition," "liturgical prescriptions" and "the laws of sacred art." I
have tried to set forth the mind of the Church regarding the making
and furnishing of her places of divine worship, and so I call this book
The Church's Way. It does not deal with ecclesiastical architecture
except incidentally; nor with sacred art as such, but only in so far as
this is affected by the Church's law. The book confines itself—and I
emphasize this—to a study of *liturgical law* in regard to the building,
decoration and furnishing of a Catholic church.

Art has been defined by St. Thomas Aquinas as *recta ratio facti-
bilium,* right (ordered) thinking applied to making. This book aims at
helping towards this right thinking in regard to church building and
furnishing, and defines it as the thought of the Church, on the subject,
set forth in her laws—her laws about her Liturgy, that creation of reverence and piety, of the spirit of order, and of tradition.

A church is something not only in which but with which to honour
God, and promote man's salvation. Its planning, erection and decoration, and furnishing are themselves acts of worship; the pencil of
the architect, the spade, trowel and hammer of the artisan, the chisel
of the sculptor, the shuttle of the weaver, all contribute their acts of
worship. But this labour needs the Church's guidance, if its fruit is to
be flawless. A church should be a building well and truly designed
and constructed for its sublime purpose, but it should also be—as far

as possible—a thing of beauty. A faithful compliance with the Church's law will secure the former, and will go far to create the latter also.

Disregard of liturgical prescriptions, of sound tradition and of the norms of sacred art by architects and artists, and their patrons, has resulted in some churches and oratories which are defective in plan, poor in design, tawdry in decoration and incorrect in furnishing. Too often the accessory has become the principal, the sham has ousted the genuine, quantity seems to count for more than quality, and one is shocked to see high altars that are unclothed and uncanopied, tabernacles unveiled, "an unreasonable multiplicity of pictures and statues"[1] that are often "second-rate and for the most part stereotyped."[2] All this is alien to the mind of the Church. There is need to restore to some of our churches that "sanctity and dignity of the temple" that St. Pius X wrote of in his famous *Motu Proprio, Tra le Sollecitudini* (1903) on church music. "This is a fearsome place, it is the house of God," sings the Church in the Mass for the dedication of a church.

This holiness and dignity will be restored by good taste—which respects truth, loves beauty, appreciates simplicity of design and ornamentation—but especially by an exact compliance with the Church's law in regard to the decoration and furnishings of a church.

The Church has very definite and detailed laws concerning the setting of the "divine mysteries"—the great drama of the celebration of the Mass, and the administration of the sacraments and sacramentals. She does not leave this to be regulated by local ecclesiastical authority, much less by the piety of private individuals according to *their* ideas of what is reverent, becoming and attractive.

For each item of church furniture I have given a brief account of its liturgical history, based on the best modern authorities available to me. Dates must, usually, be regarded as approximate only. Many usages—arising often from convenience and from aesthetic considerations, sometimes from symbolism—originated in different places, at different periods, and only later became general and codified. For statements in the historical sections I do not give authorities. This

[1] Pius XII, *Mediator Dei* (1947), § 189.
[2] Instruction of the Holy Office on Sacred Art (1952), § 19.

would unduly prolong and complicate the text; and readers who desire to delve more deeply into history are referred to the Bibliography (p. 255). Each historical section is followed by a statement of the law now in force, and this is fully documented.

In the opening chapters I have tried to deal with the complex and, in some respects, obscure subjects of "Christian tradition" and the "laws of sacred art," but *only from the limited standpoint of liturgical law*. Some of what I write there will, probably, be unacceptable to certain modern artists. It may arouse controversy and provoke contradiction. So much the better. This will stimulate thought and promote the search for truth. I am well aware that the artistic directives that result from liturgical law are necessarily vague and general, and their application in concrete cases uncertain and difficult. None the less, these directives enshrine sound principles, expressing the Church's mind in all that concerns church building and furnishing.

In a book such as this that must needs deal with a multitude of details, it would be too much to hope that there are no errors or inaccuracies. I shall be sincerely grateful to any reader who will be kind enough to point them out to me.

I cordially thank those who were good enough to supply me with photographs of high altars for this book and for permission to reproduce them.

J. B. O'CONNELL

Builth Wells, Wales

Contents

PART I

THE CHURCH AND ITS PARTS

PART II

THE ALTAR

PART III

Church Furniture

Illustrations

DIAGRAMS

SECTION OF PHOTOGRAPHS BEGINNING PAGE 265

Sources

Caeremoniale Episcoporum (typical edition 1886)

Decreta Authentica Congregationis Sacrorum Rituum (1588-1926)

Instructio Clementina (1731)

Memoriale Rituum Benedicti XIII (typical edition 1920; first edition after the typical 1950)

Missale Romanum (typical edition 1920; sixth edition after the typical 1954)

Pontificale Romanum (typical edition 1888)

Rituale Romanum (typical edition, 1952)

Motu Proprio *Inter Pastoralis Officii Sollicitudines* of St. Pius X, 1903

Constitutio Apostolica *Divini Cultus Sanctitatem* of Pius XI, 1928

Encyclical Letter *Mediator Dei* of Pius XII, 1947 (Vatican Library Translation—National Catholic Welfare Conference)

Instruction of the Supreme Sacred Congregation of the Holy Office on Sacred Art, 1952

Directives of the Bishops of Germany on Church Building, Fulda, 1932[1]

Directives of the Bishops of France regarding Sacred Art, 1952

[1] See p. 245.

PART ONE

THE CHURCH BUILDING

AND ITS PARTS

Chapter I

What Is a Church?

T H I S question can receive a reply both from the point of view of
Canon Law and from that of the Sacred Liturgy, and might get yet
another answer from an architect or an artist.

I. A Church in Canon Law

"A church is a sacred building dedicated to divine worship primarily that it may be used by all the faithful for the public exercise
of divine worship" (C.J.C., canon 1161).

"An oratory is a place destined for divine worship not, however,
primarily that it should be at the disposal of all the faithful for the
public practice of religion" (canon 1188, § 1).

A church is "sacred" intrinsically, and not merely because sacred
acts take place within it, or because it houses the Blessed Sacrament.
It is permanently and exclusively set aside by consecration or solemn
blessing for divine worship, and so made "sacred."[1] A church differs
from an oratory, not by its size or importance but in that its primary
purpose is for the use of *all* the faithful to take part therein in public
worship. An oratory serves a determined body of the faithful and is
"sacred" only if consecrated or solemnly blessed. An oratory is *public*
if, although it is erected chiefly for the convenience of a determined
body of persons, all the faithful have a right (legitimately established)

---

[1] This sacred character is celebrated (in the case of a consecrated church) by an
annual feast of high rank.

to enter it, at least during the hours of divine worship. It is *semi-public* if it is erected for the convenience of some community or body of the faithful and admission to it is not open to everyone. It is a *private* or *domestic oratory* if it is erected in a private house for the convenience of some private person or family.[2] A public oratory is regulated by the same laws as a church,[3] and in it—provided that it has been set aside, by the authority of the Ordinary, for the public worship of God by (solemn) blessing or consecration—all sacred functions may take place, unless the rubrics determine otherwise.[4]

History

In the first centuries Christian worship took place in private houses, occasionally in catacombs or in cemeteries (e.g., in a *memoria* erected over the grave of a martyr), but churches were built in the 2nd and 3rd centuries even in times of persecution, which was local and spasmodic. After the Edict of Milan (313) the great basilicas of Rome were built by the Emperor Constantine, and a multitude of churches arose throughout the Roman Empire. At first these were in cities and towns, but, later (6th and 7th centuries), churches were erected even in country places. Side by side with these were the domestic chapels in the private houses of important people and, in the country, built on the great estates. Gradually, however, these too became parish churches (8th and 9th centuries). With the progress of monasticism (from the 6th century in the West) chapels and oratories came into being in religious houses. These grew larger and more important as more and more monks became priests (from the 7th century).

By degrees laws were enacted—in the 4th and 5th centuries in the East and in Africa, later in Rome itself, and in England—forbidding the celebration of Mass in private houses, or at least requiring the bishop's permission for it.

From the classical[5] and Byzantine[6] styles of the earliest centuries

[2] C.J.C. 1188.
[3] C.J.C. 1191, § 1.
[4] C.J.C. 1191, § 2.
[5] Building according to the models of Greek and Roman antiquity—the period of the basilica, but which included also some round and octagonal churches—which reached its apogee in the 5th and 6th centuries.
[6] To Greco-Roman architecture the Byzantine style added oriental elements. This

Christian church architecture in the West developed into the various styles of the Romanesque period (10th-12th centuries). Then came the Gothic age, which reached its peak in the 13th century, to be succeeded, in its turn, by the Renaissance (neo-classical) period (15th-16th centuries). One form of Renaissance architecture, the Flamboyant, produced the Baroque (in vogue in the 17th and 18th centuries), and an exaggerated form of this was the Rococo (18th century). Finally came what has been called the Neo-Gothic age (18th-19th centuries).[7]

II. Conditions for the Building of a Church or Oratory

For the building of a new church or public[8] oratory: (1) the express consent of the Ordinary of the place, given in writing, is required,[9] and the Ordinary should approve of the site;[10] (2) the foundation stone must be blessed and laid, by the Ordinary of the place (or by the Major Superior for exempt clerical Religious) or by a priest delegated by him;[11] (3) the building must be in accord with the forms received from the Christian tradition and the laws of sacred art;[12] (4) after its construction a church, or oratory, must be dedicated to divine worship by consecration or blessing before the Sacred Liturgy is celebrated in it.[13]

III. The Consecration of a Church

Canon Law directs that cathedrals be consecrated, and, as far as possible, collegiate, conventual, and parish churches.[14] A public

style flourished especially in the East from the 4th to 15th centuries—its apogee being from the 6th to 8th centuries.

[7] The dates given above indicate broadly the period at which a particular style flourished. In fact, these periods overlapped one another, and there were specimens of each style of architecture in almost every century.

[8] A semi-public oratory may not be erected without the leave of the Ordinary. This he may not give until he has first satisfied himself that the oratory is properly equipped. To have a private oratory does not require leave, but Mass may not be celebrated there without due permission. (C.J.C. 1192, 1195).

[9] C.J.C. 1162, § 1.

[10] Rubric of P.R. (part II) in the rite of blessing and laying the foundation stone. Cf. C.J.C. 1162, § 4.)

[11] C.J.C. 1163, 1156. This is an obligation of liturgical law, assumed by canon 1163. A bishop follows the rite of P.R. for the ceremony; a priest that of R.R. (IX, ix, 16).

[12] C.J.C. 1164, § 1. See infra, pp. 41, 32.

[13] C.J.C. 1165, § 1.　　　　　　　　　　[14] C.J.C. 1165, § 3.

oratory may be consecrated,[15] and so may even a semi-public oratory[16] (when it is permanent). A church or oratory built of wood or
metal may not, however, be consecrated,[17] but may, and should be,
solemnly blessed. A church constructed of brick or concrete may be
consecrated provided that the twelve spots where the walls are
anointed are of stone, and also the spot on each jamb of the principal
door where it is anointed with chrism.[18]

If a church is to be consecrated it should stand free on all sides, as
the bishop who consecrates it must be able to pass right around the
church for the sprinkling of the exterior walls. If he is partly impeded
in doing this, because the church does not stand detached on every
side, the church may still be consecrated;[19] but if he is totally impeded
by the position of the church, recourse must be had to the Holy See.[20]

The altar—which will normally be the high altar—that must be
consecrated at the same time as the dedication of the church must
stand well away from the wall of the apse, so that the bishop and the
incensing priest can pass freely around it during the ceremony of
the consecration.

Part of the rite of the consecration of a church—indeed the chief
part—is the anointing of the walls with chrism at twelve different
spots.[21] These anointings must be made on stone,[22] and so if the
church is built of other material, such as brick or concrete, stone slabs
must be inserted into the walls to receive the anointings. The rubric
of the Roman Pontifical directs that the anointing be made at three
places on each of the four walls (not on a column); but, by almost
universal practice, the anointings are done in two places near the
altar within the sanctuary, in two places near the main door, and the
remaining eight anointings are done on four places on each side wall.[23]

15 Cf. C.J.C. 1191, § 1.
16 Cf. S.R.C. 4025[5]. A semi-public oratory is not usually consecrated; indeed it
need not even be solemnly blessed (cf. C.J.C. 1196, § 2).
17 C.J.C. 1165, § 4.
18 S.R.C. 4240.
19 S.R.C. 1321[1]; cf. 3852.
20 S.R.C. 3687.
21 These anointings date from at least the 8th century; the crosses are not mentioned until later (13th century).
22 S.R.C. 4240.
23 This avoids the inconvenience of having one anointing over the high altar and
one over the main door.

This practice has been sanctioned by a decision of S.R.C.[24]

The twelve places of the anointing must be permanently marked by twelve crosses, of any design and colour,[25] which serve as a memorial of, and a testimony[26] to, the consecration of the church. The crosses may be painted on the walls, or carved, or done in mosaic and similar work, or may be of metal affixed to the walls. The crosses should not be of wood or any fragile material. If they are painted they must be repainted when they wear away; if they are affixed they must be renewed if they become detached.[27] The crosses should be plainly visible in the church. In a small church a good position for the crosses is some seven feet above the floor, so that the consecrating bishop can conveniently reach the spot for the anointing without having to mount a ladder or platform. In a large church they may have to be higher.

Over each cross, as the rubric of the Roman Pontifical prescribes,[28] or under (as is the common practice), must be a sconce—e.g., in wrought iron, or in carved wood—to hold the twelve candles that are lighted before the crosses during the ceremony of the consecration, and also during the divine offices on each anniversary of the consecration. These sconces may be detachable, and can then be kept stored away until needed for use.

The rite of consecration includes the anointing of the entrance of the church[29] outside. This means that each jamb of the main door is anointed with chrism.[30] This anointing must be made also on stone, and[31] so if the jambs are not of stone, a stone must be inserted in each —some four or five feet above the ground—for the anointing. The two places of the anointing must be permanently marked with a cross. The best way of doing this is to have a cross sculptured on each stone.

IV. A Church in the Sacred Liturgy

From the liturgical point of view a church is a building erected pri-

[24] 31574.
[25] The traditional colour is red, and the cross usually stands in a circle.
[26] Cf. S.R.C. 3545, 3584, 3651.
[27] S.R.C. 31574, 3498; 3545; 35841,2.
[28] Obviously this is the better position at the ceremony of the consecration.
[29] P.R.
[30] S.R.C. 33646.
[31] S.R.C. 4240.

marily for the celebration of the Sacred Liturgy, i.e., "the whole public worship of the Church, the Mystical Body of Jesus Christ, Head and members."[32] In the second place, a church is built to enshrine the Blessed Sacrament, and as a house of prayer. It is God's House and the house of God's people.[33] The church is a sacred place—set apart from its surroundings and from all other buildings—made so by consecration or solemn blessing, by its symbolism, and by what takes place within its walls, the celebration of the Sacred Mysteries and the worship of the faithful. Apart from the sacramental presence of our Lord, the church is a holy place, filled with the Divine Presence—more so than the Temple of the old[34] ever was. It is itself an act of worship —as its planning, building and furnishing were acts of worship—it is prayer in stone. We worship with a church as well as in it. The church is the physical embodiment of the spiritual edifice, the Church of Christ. The material building and its contents flow from, and are an expression of, the faith, the hope and the love of God of those who erected it. Accordingly, the church is a place of awe and majesty, the tabernacle of God among men.[35] "This is a fearsome place, it is the House of God, the gate of heaven; it shall be named the palace of God."[36] Unlike the buildings around it, the church is something permanent and not ephemeral—has something of the eternal embodied in it. A church by its very appearance should proclaim its character and the grandeur of its high and enduring purpose. It should not only be a church but look one; it must not be distinguished from the town hall, or the factory, or the cinema theatre merely by the cross on its roof top. "Sacred architecture, although it may adopt new styles, may not in any way be equated with profane[37] building, but must always perform its own office, which concerns the House of God, and the House of Prayer."[38] The church should have its own peculiar atmosphere, an atmosphere that is holy,

[32] *Mediator Dei* (Pius XII, 1947), § 20.
[33] Cf. the first great consecratory preface (Vere dignum . . . adesto precibus nostris) at the consecration of a church (P.R., part II).
[34] Cf. Exodus 25.22, 40.32; II Paralipomenon 7.2.
[35] Cf. Apocalypse 21.3.
[36] Introit of the Mass of the dedication of a church.
[37] I.e., building which is not sacred.
[38] Instruction of the Holy Office, June 30, 1952 (n. 11).

hieratic, mystical, inspiring. Such an atmosphere will be created if the church is built and furnished in *full* harmony with the Church's mind, i.e., if it is built in accordance with liturgical law, Christian tradition and the laws of sacred art.[39] Fidelity to the mind of the Church—as set forth in the rubrics and enshrined in Christian tradition—will secure the sacred character of the church, and its perfect adaptation to the needs of the Sacred Liturgy and to the comfort of those who worship in it. The observance of the laws of sacred art, in addition, will ensure that all this is done with due regard to the claims of beauty. The result will be an edifice worthy of its high purpose, with that atmosphere of holiness, dignity, majesty, nobility, reverence, calm, peace and joy that befits the perfect House of God.

The Purpose of a Church

The remote purpose of a church is to give glory to God and his saints, to edify and sanctify the people who worship in it, to enlighten and attract those who are not of the household of the faith. Its immediate purpose is to provide all that is necessary for the due performance of the Sacred Liturgy, for the worthy custody of the Most Holy Sacrament, for the needs of the faithful who take part in the public worship of the Church, or come there for private prayer. Accordingly, the planning and building of a church is governed not only by the laws of sound and beautiful construction, but also by certain rules proper to a church as distinct from all other buildings.[40] Account has to be taken of: (*a*) the special needs of the ceremonial of the Roman rite; (*b*) symbolism (e.g., orientation, the unity of the altar); (*c*) the practical needs of a congregation supposed to take an active part in the Sacred Liturgy (e.g., visibility of the altar, free access to the altar rails). All these requirements are dealt with in the rubrics, supplemented by tradition and practical experience. They form the subject matter of this book.

[39] C.J.C. 1164, § 1; 1296, § 3.
[40] See pp. 22, 50.

Chapter II

The Parts of a Church or Oratory

F ROM the liturgical point of view there are three classes of buildings for public worship: the small church (or oratory), the parish or
conventual church, the cathedral or abbatial church.

I. Kinds of Churches

1. *The Small Church or Oratory*

A church or chapel, however small, should—when possible—have
these parts: (*a*) a sanctuary or chancel, large enough not only for its
daily services but also for an occasional function on a larger scale;
at least one extra chapel, if the liturgy of Holy Week is carried out,
or the Forty Hours' Prayer takes place each year; (*c*) a place for an
organ or harmonium; (*d*) a confessional or confessionals; (*e*) two
sacristies (one being a working sacristy and store-room). A chapel of
Religious may need a place set aside for the laity and a tribune for
the infirm. A seminary chapel will need a spacious chancel and, possibly, stalls.

2. *A Parish Church*

This will comprise: (*a*) a chancel, spacious in proportion to the
size of the church, and giving ample room for the proper accomplish-
ment of liturgical functions;[1] (*b*) a narthex or porch, in which to
carry out the preliminary rites of baptism, churching and some cere-

monies of Holy Week (and so it must be large enough to accommodate a number of persons and be free of draughts); (c) at least one side chapel, and more than one if more than two altars for Mass are needed; (d) a baptistery; (e) a mortuary chapel; (f) a pulpit and, perhaps, ambones;[2] (g) an organ and a place for singers; (h) confessionals; (i) at least two sacristies. A conventual church may also need stalls in the chancel. A large parish church will have such additions as a belfry, a meeting-room, a priest's reception room or office, a parking space, possibly a crypt,[3] but there are no liturgical rules, generally speaking, about these.

3. A Cathedral

A cathedral will have in addition to a very spacious[4] sanctuary, numerous side chapels, sacristies, etc.: (a) the Bishop's throne—a permanent feature—in the chancel; (b) a special chapel of the Blessed Sacrament,[5] (c) stalls for the canons; (d) a secretarium[6] (with places for the canons); (e) a Chapter-House; (f) provision (e.g., in a crypt or along the side walls) for the tombs of bishops.

In planning a church suitable spaces for (a) the fourteen Stations of the Cross, and (b) for the twelve consecration crosses (if the church is to be consecrated) should be provided.[7]

II. THE CHANCEL

In the liturgical books the part of the church reserved for the high altar and for the clergy is called *chorus* or *presbyterium*.[8] "Chorus" is also used for (1) the clergy[9] who occupy the chancel and are the singers of the Divine Offices, and (2) for the *schola cantorum* of lay singers.[10] The entire presbyterium is called in English the "chancel"

[1] E.g., a parish church will need ample space on the Gospel side for a throne, etc., on the occasion of the Bishop's visits.
[2] See p. 79.
[3] This may be essential for extra Masses in a populous parish and very useful for catechism classes, etc. It will have its own separate entrance.
[4] This is needed for ceremonies like Ordinations, the consecration of Holy Oils and the like.
[5] C.E. I, xii, 8, 17.
[6] C.E. I, xii, 15; II, viii, 2.
[7] P.R.
[8] Cf., e.g., C.E. I, xiii.
[9] C.E. I, xviii, 7.
[10] In the early centuries the presbytery was often behind the altar and sometimes

(the part of the church marked off by *cancelli* or railings). In large churches the east end of the chancel—nearer the altar—is called the "sanctuary," the west end the "choir." In smaller churches the entire chancel is generally called the "sanctuary."[11]

From early days—there was local legislation as far back as the 4th century—entrance to the chancel, except momentarily, on certain occasions, was forbidden to the laity. This legislation is embodied in C.E. (I, xi, 12; xiii, 13) and in some fifteen decisions of S.R.C. The sanctuary is cut off as a place specially sacred,[12] and reserved to the clergy, between whom and the laity there is a distinction of divine origin. The clergy are by ordination the representatives of God and set aside for the carrying out of liturgical worship *within the sanctuary*. Laics are admitted to a part of this only out of necessity, and are, for the purpose, temporarily regarded as clerics and wear clerical dress (cassock and surplice). On the other hand the congregation is supposed to take an *active* part in the Liturgy, which is not merely a spectacle "for detached and silent onlookers,"[13] but a community act. Accordingly, in a correctly built church the congregation is not cut off from the clergy by formidable barriers (like rood screens), and contact is maintained between the two by the dialogue (sung or spoken) of the Sacred Liturgy.

The sanctuary is usually raised above the level of the nave, but there should not be too many steps leading to the high altar, rendering ceremonial more difficult and cutting off the altar unduly from the people;[14] nor should there be different levels within the chancel, which is inconvenient for ceremonial movement. It is most important that the chancel should be spacious to allow of the dignified performance of the sacred ceremonies—spacious in proportion to the size and dignity of the particular church.[15] A wide, rather than deep, chancel

still is; and the schola on the west side of the altar. Later the presbytery moved to the west side.
[11] The word "sanctuarium" does not occur in the rubrics.
[12] As the Holy Place and the Holy of Holies was in the Temple at Jerusalem.
[13] Pius XI, in *Divini cultus sanctitatem* (1928).
[14] There must be a proper balance between a desirable prominence and a reverent seclusion of the altar and its setting.
[15] E.g., there should always be sufficient room on the Gospel side to erect a throne on the occasion of the Bishop's visit.

is desirable; it is more suitable for the ceremonial and does not divorce the congregation from the liturgy.

III. THE COMMUNION RAIL

History

From about the 4th century the clergy were separated in church from the people by a low barrier (*cancelli, septum, transenna*) in stone, wood or metal; and the *schola cantorum,* near the altar and west of it, was sometimes cut off from the congregation by a similar enclosure. *Cancelli* were also used to protect shrines, relics, etc., and in due time some of them developed into great ornate screens (*pergula, jube*). Up to the 15th or 16th century the *cancelli* were a mere barrier; after that they developed into the Communion rail. In the early centuries Holy Communion was received standing,[16] and this lasted until the 13th century in England (the period when Communion under the form of wine died out); it was not received kneeling at an altar rail until the 15th or 16th century, or even later in England. The clergy still communicate at the altar itself, and so do laics sometimes (e.g., the server at Mass). Although lay folk normally receive Holy Communion at the Communion rail, they are supposed to be receiving the Body of Christ *from* the altar of sacrifice,[17] and so it is preferable to think of the Communion rail rather as a prolongation of the altar than as a Communion table (it is the table of the *altar* that is really this). Hence the ideal is to construct the rail to resemble somewhat the altar (the same material, style, decoration, etc.).

Law

There is nothing whatever in the rubrics about an altar rail; it is nowhere prescribed. It is purely utilitarian, to protect the chancel from irreverence (especially in a crowded church);[18] but it has become a necessity for the giving of the Holy Communion in large churches. If there is a fixed rail, it must have gates sufficiently wide

[16] It is still so received by a bishop at his consecration and by the deacon and subdeacon at a Papal Mass.
[17] Cf. the prayer *Supplices* of the Canon of Mass ("ut quotquot . . .").
[18] In a small church an ornamental cord suffices to mark off the chancel.

to allow for processions into the nave, and capable of being securely fastened if people kneel before them for Communion. The height of the rail should be from, say, 2 feet 3 inches to 2 feet 6 inches; and it should have a flat top, some 9 inches to 12 inches wide, on which the Communion cloth rests,[19] and which sometimes supports candle-sticks.[20] The Communion rail should not have more than one step, and this a good deep step, and fairly high, that old and infirm people may kneel easily on it. It is a good thing to have cushions, upholstered in leather (preferably green), rubber or other easily cleaned material, laid along the step. The rail will need studs at intervals along the inner side, on to which the Communion cloth can be fastened.

In small churches or oratories a *movable* rail—strongly made in timber, well balanced, moving on ball castors and capable of accom-modating two, three, or four persons side by side—is very useful. Apart from the time of Communion it can be put aside altogether, leaving an uninterrupted view of the chancel, and extra chancel space can be made available on the occasion of a big ceremony. The grow-ing modern tendency to remove all barriers between the altar and the people—except what is strictly necessary—is in keeping with the earlier usage of the Church.

IV. SIDE CHAPELS

In many churches to which a number of priests are attached, in addition to the high altar other altars will be needed. As the altar in any church, because of its symbolism, should be *one* only—this unity is traditional,[21] a symbol and pledge of the oneness of the Catholic faith—these extra altars should not be, normally, in the main building, but in side chapels[22] or in a crypt. Even the smallest church or ora-tory will need one side chapel—and this of sufficient size to allow of the celebration of High Mass[23]—if the Holy Week liturgy, even in its simple form of the *Memoriale Rituum,* is carried out, or the Forty

---

[19] It is no longer held by the communicants for whom a plate is used.
[20] P. 213.
[21] See p. 164.
[22] The practice of placing two side altars one at each side of the high altar, in the chancel, is quite incorrect.
[23] Hence it should be so placed that a ceremony in it can be seen by as many as possible of the congregation in the church.

Hours' Prayer. In very large churches a side chapel may be used, instead of the high altar, when the congregation is not large (e.g., at early Mass on a week day), or for some special function (e.g., a wedding). In larger churches, an important side chapel is the mortuary chapel. This is best placed at the west end of the church (say at the south-west corner, facing the baptistery) and should, if possible, have a separate entrance. It may be in the crypt, should there be one. It should, when possible, be large enough to hold at least a small group of mourners; and must always be spacious enough to permit of the carrying out of the Absolution of the dead, which requires the presence of a crossbearer and two acolytes, and the free movement of the priest and his two assistants around the coffin. The permanent furniture of this mortuary chapel comprises: (1) a bier or trestles on which the coffin is placed;[24] (2) a pall;[25] (3) tall standing candlesticks—four or six is the usual number—made in dark metal or wood, containing candles of unbleached (yellow) wax; (4) a small table to hold the lustral water, incense boat, etc.

[24] See p. 239.
[25] See p. 241.

CHAPTER III

The Position of a Church and Its Title

1. THE CHURCH SITE

FROM the liturgical point of view, the position of a church is affected by (1) the needs of the rite of its consecration or blessing, (2) ceremonial convenience, (3) the tradition of orientation, (4) certain decisions of the Church on some minor points.

1. *The Site and the Dedication of a Church*

During the ceremony of the consecration or of the solemn blessing of a church, the Bishop goes right around the building sprinkling the outer walls with lustral water. Hence, the edifice should stand free on all sides and, if possible, have a path leading all around it.[1]

2. *Ceremonial Convenience*

When space permits it is very useful to have a courtyard, or some open space, before the building, cutting it off somewhat from the noise and dust of the streets, and providing a suitable space for processions and other occasional outdoor functions.

3. *Orientation*

By the orientation of a church nowadays is meant that its longitudinal axis lies east-west, so that the apse, with the altar, is at the east end, the main entrance at the west end.

Facing eastwards for worship and prayer was at first, probably,

---

[1] This is also suitable sometimes for processions.

derived from Jewish and pagan practice, and seems to have been well established by the 3rd century. It was based for Christians on the symbolism of the rising sun—the symbol of the Messiah, coming from the east and thence departing—the symbol also of the risen Christ.[2] Originally—especially at the period of the foundation of the great basilicas of Rome (4th-5th centuries)—the orientation of a church meant that *the celebrant* of the Sacred Liturgy,[3] when at the high altar, was facing east, and also faced the congregation and the main entrance of the church. It was later on (about the 9th and 10th centuries, earlier in some places) that the opposite idea of orientation prevailed; i.e., that the congregation too faced east and that the altar was at the east end. This came about when the congregation had changed its position so as to be behind the celebrant, and the high altar had been withdrawn more and more into the apse, so that now it was necessary to have the latter at the east end.[4] By the 11th century this second idea of orientation—the one that still prevails—had established itself. It was confirmed when, about the same period, or somewhat later, the position of the Bishop's throne was changed from the apse to the Gospel side of the chancel, in a position partly between the congregation and the altar. Gradually, mainly because of practical difficulties, the tradition of the orientation of a church became less and less familiar in the Western Church—especially as this tradition was not primitive and had not been either constant or universal. There is no law requiring that a church be now orientated, but when this can be done without difficulty it is becoming to conform to the old tradition, with its wealth of symbolism.

4. *Some Laws about a Church Site*

A church should be so placed, when possible, or built in such a fashion that the interior is not visible from outside. From the church

[2] Cf. Ezechiel 43.2; Zacharias 6.12; Malachy 4.2; Matthew 24.27; Apocalypse 7.2; Psalm 67.33 (used in the liturgy of Ascension Day). The west was regarded as the region of darkness, and a catechumen used to face westwards when renouncing the devil in the baptismal rite.
[3] Including the Bishop at his throne in the apse, which was at the West end of the church.
[4] C.E. II, viii, 44, supposes the high altar to be at the east end of the church when it directs the subdeacon holding the book for the singing of the Gospel by the deacon to stand with his back to the north.

no door or window may open into the house of *lay folk*.[5] No room immediately under or over the church itself may be used for *merely profane* purposes.[6] Thus a room under the church may not be used for, e.g., storing wine,[7] or as a theatre[8] or cinema, but may be used as a school, or library, or assembly room for confraternities and the like. There may not be a bedroom immediately over a church, or over an altar where the Blessed Sacrament is reserved.[9]

II. THE FOUNDATION STONE OF A CHURCH

The rubrics of the Roman Pontifical suppose the blessing and ceremonial laying of a foundation stone for every church or public oratory.[10] This is carried out by the Bishop of the place (or by the major superior[11] of an exempt clerical religious Order), or by a priest delegated by him.[12] Some ceremonial blessing of a foundation stone is referred to as early as the 9th century; earlier than that the rite was incorporated in that of the dedication of the church. The present rite of the Pontifical was drawn up by Durandus in the 13th century. Whatever may be the material of the church the foundation stone must be a real, natural stone. The rubrics suppose it to be small (say a cubic foot), so that it can be easily handled in the course of the rite. If it is a very large and heavy stone it must be hung on a derrick over the place where it is to be laid. It should be square and angular.[13] On each of its six sides a cross is (in practice) incised beforehand. On its front face—especially if this will be visible after the stone has been laid—a suitable inscription is carved, giving the particulars of its laying. Often nowadays—though nowhere ordered in the rubrics—a cavity is made in the stone, and a glass or lead tube containing a parchment giving a report of the proceedings

[5] C.J.C. 1164, § 2.
[6] Ibid.
[7] S.R.C. 3157[5].
[8] S.R.C. 3546[1]. A crypt—but not the sacristy—does form part of a consecrated church.
[9] S.R.C. 756, 2812, 3460, 3525[2], 4213[3].
[10] Cf. C.J.C. 1163; 1191, § 1.
[11] C.J.C. 488, § 8.
[12] C.J.C. 1163; 1156. The rite is contained in P.R. (part II), and in R.R. IX, ix, 16 (for a priest delegated for the function).
[13] Christ is described in Ephesians 2.20 as the chief corner-stone (*summus angularis lapis*).

is put into it, with some coins of the period. There must be a small stone slab to cover this cavity and this is cemented on by a mason in the course of the ceremony.

Position of the Stone

No law fixes what the precise position of the stone is to be. In theory it is the first stone of the foundations, but, in practice, it is laid overground, when the walls have risen to some height from the ground. Rubricians recommend that the stone be laid on the Gospel side of the chancel, where the apse joins the transept.[14] It is not fixed by any rubric whether it should be in an outer or inner wall. In practice, it is preferable to place it in an outer wall, on ground level, or a little over ground level, where the inscription on it can be read without difficulty. Once the stone has been ceremonially fixed in its place, it must not be moved, so that all that is necessary to fix it permanently should be at hand for the ceremony.

III. THE TITLE (TITULAR) OF A CHURCH

Each consecrated or solemnly blessed church has its Title or Titular,[15] i.e., the person, mystery or sacred object, in whose name the church has been founded, in whose honour it is dedicated and after whom it is called.[16] Every church or oratory is dedicated to God, but it may be dedicated also *in honour* of another. This has been the Church's practice from the 4th or 5th century. The Title is named by the Bishop when laying the foundation stone of the church, and is irrevocably constituted[17] when the church is consecrated or solemnly blessed.[18] In this rite—as at the laying of the foundation stone—the Title is mentioned in the prayers and in the Litanies of the Saints, and Mass is celebrated in his honour. His name is also mentioned in the attestation of the consecration. Once the Title has been fixed by the consecration or solemn blessing of the church, it may not be changed

[14] Schulte, *Consecranda*, pp. 4, 5, gives other suitable positions for the stone.
[15] C.J.C. 1168, § 1; S.R.C. 3752¹.
[16] Cf. S.R.C. 3048. The Title must not be confused with the Patron of a place (country, diocese, town).
[17] The Title may, then, be changed between the time of the laying of the foundation stone and the consecration or blessing.
[18] R.R. IX, ix, 17.

without Apostolic indult.[19] If a church was first solemnly blessed and later on consecrated, the Bishop may *add* (not substitute) another Title at the consecration.[20]

Choice of Title

In general, any person, mystery or sacred thing that may be the object of public veneration may be chosen as Title, and so (1) the Blessed Trinity, or one of the Divine Persons,[21] our Lady under any title, the angels, or any named angel; any canonized saint[22] mentioned in the Roman Martyrology, or in the approved calendar of any diocese or religious Order; or (2) any mystery (e.g., the Incarnation, the Blessed Eucharist);[23] or (3) a sacred object (e.g., the Holy Cross) or event (e.g., the Conversion of St. Paul) may be chosen as Title. A church may have more than one Title—whether the feast is celebrated on the same date or on a different date—and each Title will have the same liturgical privileges.[24]

Liturgical Honours to a Title

The Jews celebrated the dedication of their Temple with a feast lasting seven days, and from the 4th century (beginning at Jerusalem) the Liturgy has celebrated the feast of the dedication of any church and has had a special Mass for it from the 8th century. The feast of the Title is now a double of the first class, to be celebrated by the clergy attached to the church or oratory.[25] If the Title is our Divine Saviour, its feast will be the Transfiguration[26] (August 6). If the Titular be our Lady under a title that has no special feast, the Titular feast is celebrated on the feast of the Assumption.[27] The feast of the Title of the cathedral of a diocese—which is a primary feast[28]—is

[19] C.J.C. 1168, § 1; S.R.C. 2719[2], 2853[1].
[20] Cf. S.R.C. 2619[3], 2853.
[21] Not, however, to God the Father, since there is neither feast, Mass nor office of the First Person (cf. Nabuco, II, 153, n. 30).
[22] S.R.C. 3876[5], 4335. Not a *beatus;* not any saint of the Old Testament (cf. S.R.C. 1978); not the Souls in Purgatory.
[23] S.R.C. 3157[3].
[24] S.R.C. 2619[4], 3289[1], 3417[3], 3469[2], 3622[1].
[25] C.J.C. 1168, § 2.
[26] S.R.C. 2439[4], 2721[2].
[27] S.R.C. 2529[1,2]. If the Title is our Lady of Sorrows, the feast is the one on Sept. 15.
[28] S.R.C. 4249[2].

celebrated throughout the diocese as a double of the first class.[29] The name of the Title is mentioned in the *A cunctis* prayer.

Loss of Title

The Title is lost if the consecration or blessing of the church is lost (i.e., if the church be destroyed in great part or execrated).[30] If the church is reconstructed the old Title should be retained, in such a case a new Title may be added when the church is newly consecrated or blessed.

[29] *Rub. Gen. Breviarii Rom. (Addit.)*, IX, 2. S.R.C. March 23, 1955, II, 11.
[30] C.J.C. 1170.

CHAPTER IV

The General Plan of a Church

F ROM the liturgical point of view there are certain general principles that should govern the planning of a church. These are derived from the nature of a church as a sacred place, as the shrine of an altar and of a baptismal font, and as the scene of the worship of the community.

1. THE SANCTITY OF A CHURCH

A church is a sacred place—dedicated by solemn consecration or blessing to divine worship.[1] Its general purpose is the glory of God and the sanctification of men. It is not merely a building in which sacred actions are performed, it is the dwelling-place of God, itself sacred[2]—quite independently of what takes place in it, or of the abiding presence of our Lord in the Holy Eucharist—a sacramental. This inherent sacredness is expressed in almost every text of the Mass for the Dedication of a church, and is commemorated each year by a feast of high rank in memory of the church's hallowing and its permanent sacred character. The material building is the very habitation of God, the shrine of the Blessed Sacrament, the place where the Sacred Liturgy is to be duly accomplished, and an auditorium for sacred purposes. It may take, architecturally, many forms. The term "formae a traditione christiana receptae" of the Canon Law[3] gives

---

[1] Cf. C.J.C. 1161.
[2] More so even than the Tabernacle or the Temple of the Old Law, sanctified by the indwelling of the Divine Presence (cf. Exodus 24, 25, 40; II Paralipomenon 7).
[3] Canon 1164, § 1. See *infra*, pp. 141 *sqq*.

wide scope, and can be reasonably interpreted as meaning any form that fulfils the requirements of the Sacred Liturgy, complies with liturgical law, and is in accordance with the Church's conception of a church. The building should proclaim aloud—by its very form, its dignity, its beauty—its inherent sanctity and its sacred purpose. It should not only be a church, but look like one; the visible edifice is itself a symbol of the supernatural organism, the Church, the Mystical Body of Christ.

This sacred character of a church, and the majesty and dignity that should flow from it, exclude the profane, the bizarre—extravagant and undignified forms are contrary to Christian tradition—the superfluous, the unworthy. The tawdry, the trivial, the false, the pretentious should find no place in the ideal church. Truth and respect for materials are elements of beauty, and for her Liturgy the Church prescribes natural stone, precious metals, fair linen, olive oil, pure wax.[4]

In planning a church the requirements of the Sacred Liturgy, the prescriptions of liturgical law, are paramount. "The Church," wrote St. Pius X in his *Motu Proprio* on church music (1903), "has always recognized and favoured the progress of the arts, admitting to the service of worship everything good and beautiful discovered by genius in the course of the ages, always, however, with due regard to liturgical laws." After the requirements of the Liturgy come the needs and comfort of the worshippers.[5] But perfect adaptation to material needs is not sufficient, beauty is an element in worship, and so the church plan must not neglect the claims of the aesthetic. These, however, are the province of the architect, the artist and the craftsman, not the primary concern of the liturgist.

II. The High Altar and Baptistry, the Focal Points of a Church

A Catholic church is built primarily to house an altar; a church

[4] "There ought to be nothing in a church which might trouble or lessen the devotion and piety of the faithful, nothing that might give a reasonable cause for distaste or scandal; above all, nothing which might offend against the propriety and sanctity of the sacred functions, and so be unworthy of the House of prayer and the majesty of God" (St. Pius X, *Motu Proprio* on sacred music).
[5] *Infra*, p. 25.

cannot exist without an altar, nor may it be consecrated unless an altar (normally, the high altar) is dedicated at the same time.[6] The church is, as it were, built about its high altar.[7] This altar is the optical and architectural centre of the church—as it is the spiritual centre of its liturgical life—and so "all possible emphasis should be given to it by architectural skill in its setting; uninterrupted floor space, sufficiently ample for the due performance of ceremonial, should provide dignity; and colour—which in itself is a medium of emphasis—should be concentrated on the altar before being applied to its surroundings."[8] "The altar is, so to speak, the very soul of the church and its *raison d'être*. It is the culminating spot in the entire edifice, and in a well-designed church all matters of proportion, design, furnishing and decorating are subordinate to the altar, towards which the soul of the worshipper is directed through eye and mind by means of the lines in the building, the curves of its arcades and groining, and the forms of its transept, chapels and apse. . . . Upon the altar, as the stage whereon are daily enacted the sacred mysteries of the Last Supper and Calvary, all attention must be focused."[9]

It follows that in planning a church the high altar must be clearly visible—if at all possible—from every point of the building. It should dominate the church, stand out unmistakably by its position, structure, ornamentation and lighting.[10]

The second focal point of a parish church is the baptistery—placed, normally, near the main entrance, and at the far end from the high altar (for the Christian proceeds from the font, where his Christian life begins, towards the altar). In the ideal parish church the liturgical focal points—the high altar and the baptistery—will be indicated even externally; the baptistery visible as a distinct part of the building, the altar clearly marked as the chief part of the church by being, e.g., surmounted by a dome or tower, so that the *architectural and the litur-*

[6] C.J.C. 1165, § 5.
[7] When the foundation stone is laid, a cross is set up at the spot where the high altar will be placed.
[8] Geoffrey Webb, *Post-war Church Building*, p. 107.
[9] E. J. Weber, *Catholic Church Buildings*, p. 197. "The interior elevation should lead the eye to the high altar without conscious effort" (G. Webb, *op. cit.* p. 108). The lines of pillars in the great basilicas do this.
[10] See pp. 65, 158, 187.

gical points of the church coincide[11] (an excellent example of this is the Duomo of Florence, Santa Maria del Fiore).

III. The Active Participation of the Worshippers

A third principle that affects the plan of a church from the liturgical angle is the necessity of providing for, and encouraging in every way, the *active participation* of the worshippers in the Sacred Liturgy, and the fostering of the community spirit of worship. While lay folk are excluded from the chancel by the laws of the Church—out of reverence and to mark the distinction, of divine origin, between the clergy and the laity—the Church desires the closest co-operation between the sacred ministers at the altar and the congregation. Hence the people should not be cut off from the altar by its distance from them—a long narrow church with the altar far away is undesirable, it is destructive of liturgical unity—or by any barriers (such as a rood screen), or obstacles (a multitude of columns, hiding a clear view of the altar, should be avoided). The altar should be plainly visible[12] in a raised position, but not so raised as to be unduly detached from the congregation. The sacred ministers should be both visible and audible when at the altar or in the pulpit, the choir so placed[13] as to be a link between them and the people.

IV. Provision for Ceremonial

The plan of a church must be adapted to the needs of ceremonial. Artists and architects must have "both the skill and the will to find in religion the inspiration and methods and plans best adapted to the exigencies of divine worship."[14] The needs of ceremonial will vary greatly according to the type of church—the greater functions of the Liturgy take place normally in cathedrals, in collegiate or conventual churches, in the chapels of seminaries, and not in smaller parish churches or convent oratories—but even the smallest church requires:

(1) A chancel with *ample* space[15] for the *due* performance of any

[11] Cf. H. A. Reinhold, *Speaking of Liturgical Architecture*, p. 3.
[12] In larger churches a sloping floor might be found desirable.
[13] See p. 93.
[14] Pius XII, *Mediator Dei*, § 196.
[15] See remarks on a movable altar rail, p. 13.

sacred function that is likely to occure in it, nothing so much detracts from dignified ceremonial as the want of proper space.

(2) Full freedom of movement—ensuring order, dignity and due quietude—obtained by passages of sufficient width to allow of easy movement between the sacristies and the chancel, the main door and the chancel, the congregation and the chancel (so that the people may easily approach one way and return by another when going to Holy Communion, or to receive blessed ashes, or kiss a relic, etc.). Free access to the baptistery from the narthex is, obviously, essential; and proper room for the celebrant and his assistants to go around the church at the Asperges and when making the Way of the Cross.

(3) A porch or narthex, with sufficient space for the preliminary ceremonies of baptism, churching, etc.

(4) At least one side chapel—large enough to allow of the celebration of High Mass—if the liturgy of Maundy Thursday or the Forty Hours' Prayer takes place in the church.

(5) A mortuary chapel—at least in larger churches—with sufficient space to carry out properly the Absolution of the dead.

(6) A baptistery, in a parish or succursal church.

(7) Doors at the main entrance, and leading from the sacristy to the chancel, wide and high enough to allow people in procession (two or even three abreast), or a mitred bishop, or bearers of a canopy to pass through without difficulty.

A very important thing in every church is the number and position of doors (giving entrance and exit). Doors should be sufficiently numerous—a large church will need many,[16] but even a small church should have at least two, for safety's sake—roomy, easily opened from the inside (if possible outwards, in case of panic). Traditionally, the main door is at the west end of the church, facing the high altar, but a large church will have, perhaps, other doors at the west end too, and also several doors on both sides. Some of these should be well up the church, though for reverence sake not too close to the sanctuary. In a crowded church with Masses following one another quickly, it is obvious that, if order is to be preserved, some doors

---

[16] And the possibility of draughts must be considered and dealt with. Cross currents are, on the other hand, valuable for ventilation.

should be used as *entrances only*, others as *exits only*. The best plan seems to be to make the door(s) at the west the exits(s),[17] and the door(s) well up the church the entrances(s). This means that the people enter the church—on both sides—well up its length, towards the altar. They can see more easily where there is room, and it prevents them avoiding the front seats and crowding at the back of the church (sometimes even blocking up the exits). It also penalizes the late-comer.[18]

V. The Hierarchical Element in Church Planning

In the designing of a church "it is necessary to work not only a structural plan but also a well thought-out plan of artistic expression which will be theologically and pedagogically correct . . . an ensemble of the theme of our holy faith . . . with a certain completeness . . . in significant proportions and with the right placing of accent."[19]

This hierarchical element in a church plan, the difference in importance of the various parts of the building, the different emphasis to be laid on certain features, applies to the relation of the parts (e.g., the high altar and the baptistery are the principal parts of a church; the non-liturgical furnishings, such as Stations of the Cross, are the least important and should receive less prominence), to the position of altars, images, etc., to the decoration,[20] and even to the lighting.

VI. Symbolism

Even Christian symbolism has a certain bearing on a church plan, e.g., the high altar being one[21] in each church and representing Christ; the main door, a symbol of the portal of heaven; the baptistery at the north-west corner, below floor level,[22] the confessionals placed, when possible, near the church doors.[23]

---

[17] On special occasions (e.g., the Bishop's visit) entry for a procession could be by the main west door.
[18] Cf. Reinhold, *Speaking of Liturgical Architecture*, p. 21.
[19] "Directives for Shaping the House of God" (edited by Fr. Theodor Klauser), issued by the Liturgical Commission of the German Bishops (*Orate Fratres*, Dec. 1949), § 18.
[20] See p. 59.
[21] See p. 164.
[22] See p. 24.
[23] See p. 73.

Chapter V

The General Law of Church Building and Furnishing

1 Canons 1164 (§ 1) and 1296 (§ 3) of the Code of Canon Law

THE general law of church building and furnishing is set forth in two canons of the Code of Canon Law: "Ordinaries, having, if necessary, taken counsel with experts, are to take care that in the building or repair of churches the forms received from Christian tradition[1] are preserved and the laws of sacred art[1] observed" (canon 1164, § 1). "Regarding the matter and form of sacred furnishings, liturgical law, ecclesiastical tradition, and also, as far as possible, the laws of sacred art are to be observed" (canon 1296, § 3).[2] From these two canons certain general conclusions follow: (1) As a church is a sacred place, all that concerns its building and adornment is under the control of the Ordinary (the Bishop or major superior).[3] This does not destroy the liberty of the artist,[4] but regulates it. (2) Ordinaries are advised —they are directed in canon 1280, which deals with the restoration of valuable works of art—to consult experts in regard to church building (these experts are architects, artists and liturgical scholars). St. Pius X ordered[5] for the direction of ecclesiastical music the setting up of diocesan musical commissions, while a circular of the Secre-

---

[1] See p. 41.
[2] There are special laws about images (pp. 99).
[3] Cf. C.J.C. 198, § 1; 1261.
[4] See pp. 51, 54. By "artist" in this book is meant anyone who contributes his work to the building or adornment of a church, the architect, sculptor, painter, glass or metal or textile worker, etc.
[5] *Motu Proprio*, 1903 (VIII, § 24).

tariate of State to the bishops of Italy (September 1, 1924) suggested that regional or diocesan commissions on Sacred Art be established, and a central commission was instituted in Rome to help ecclesiastical superiors. The Instruction of the Holy Office, June 30, 1952, on Sacred Art says (§ 4):[6] "If there are lacking experts on the diocesan Commission, or doubts and controversies arise, let the local Ordinaries consult the Metropolitan Commission, or the Roman Commission on Sacred Art"; and the Holy Office added (§ 17), "Works of painting, sculpture and architecture should be entrusted for their execution only to men who are outstanding for their technique and who are capable of expressing sincere faith and piety, which is the purpose of any sacred art." (3) Both canon 1264, § 1, and canon 1296, § 3, refer to tradition, "Christian" and "ecclesiastical." The Church links sacred art, in all its forms, with the past, as she links her faith and her Liturgy. This traditional attitude arises from the fidelity of the Church to her supernatural origin and her abiding identity all through the vicissitudes of nearly two thousand years. "Forms received from Christian tradition" does not mean the external appearances of any work of art, or the technique of its production, but rather refers to the ideas, the spirit, that gave the great works of art of the past their special character (p. 41). (4) Both canons refer to the "laws of sacred art." Evidently there are, then, (a) laws of *sacred* art as distinguished from art in general, (b) laws that affect church building in addition to liturgical law and tradition. The Church has not set forth in detail these laws, but they may—it would seem—be deduced from the nature of sacred art,[8] the directives of ecclesiastical authority[9] (Popes, the Holy Office, etc.) and the teaching of recognized experts on this art. (5) Canon 1296, § 3, refers to the prescriptions of liturgical law in regard to church equipment.[10] Obviously, this law, as far as it goes, is paramount. Where liturgical law gives express directions it is of obligation. This law is to be found chiefly in the Code of Canon Law, in the rubrics of the

[6] Cf. I.H.O. § 15(4).
[8] See *infra*, pp. 31 *sqq.*
[9] See *infra*, p. 34.
[10] There is no reference to these in canon 1264, § 1, because there is no explicit law about church *building*.

liturgical books and in the decisions of S.R.C. and other Roman tribunals. Liturgical law on church furnishings is not all-embracing, and so it is supplemented—and interpreted—by local law, by ecclesiastical tradition[11] (from which we can learn the mind of the Church) and by the laws of sacred art.[12]

II. SACRED ART

By sacred (Christian) art is meant art directly and in due manner devoted to divine worship and the service of the Church. It is art in and for a church (or oratory). By "sacred" is meant that set apart for, dedicated to some religious purpose, and so made holy by association with God, or with any other object of worship (in its general meaning of veneration). Sacred art is dedicated—proximately or remotely—to divine worship,[13] and is, almost in its entirety, part of the Sacred Liturgy, which integrates the arts into the service of God. It is part of external (visible or audible) worship, representing religious ideas by means of perceptible and lovely forms. It is art concerned with a religious subject, serving religion, inspired by religion, providing serviceable and beautiful things for divine worship. Sacred art is in contact with the supernatural—it reaches into the next world and touches on the infinite—art used for the honour of God and in the service of the Mystical Body of Christ.

Sacred art is a subdivision of religious art, from which it differs not only by the character and inspiration of the artistic effort, but more especially by its purpose.[14] Sacred art has two main divisions, liturgical art and non-liturgical art. The former is either (1) an integral part of the Sacred Liturgy (the prose and poetry of the sacred texts, ceremonial, music), or (2) immediately connected with the Liturgy (the church, the altar and all the other accessories of divine worship), or (3) remotely connected with the Liturgy (e.g., images which are objects of veneration). Non-liturgical art is sacred art which does not directly serve any special liturgical purpose, but is

---

[11] Pp. 43 *sqq.*
[12] Pp. 32 *sqq.*
[13] Cf. Pius XII in *Mediator Dei* (cited as M.D.), § 196.
[14] "As a craft, sacred art does not differ from profane art; but it differs essentially from it in its content, in the requirements of the Liturgy, and in the formal dignity with which this content must be expressed" (Costantini, *Fede et Arte, Preface*).

merely decorative (e.g., wall paintings in a church, statues decorating the exterior of a church).

Sacred art, therefore, embraces all the arts when "they put themselves at the service of our churches and sacred rites." It[15] includes architecture, sculpture, painting, glass and metal work, textiles.

The Purpose of Sacred Art

The purpose of sacred art is a spiritual one, and this purpose enters into the very nature of any work of this kind (even a Venus de Milo or an Apollo Belvedere would not do in a church). "It is the function and duty of sacred art, by reason of its very definition to enhance the beauty[16] of the house of God and to foster the faith and piety of those who gather in a church to assist at the divine offices and to implore heavenly favours."[17] "Sacred Christian art, which originated with Christian society, possesses its own ends, from which it may never diverge, and its proper function which it may never desert."[18]

The chief purpose of sacred art is to honour God by the homage of beauty—of which he is the exemplar and source (Wisdom 13.3)— by the fitting adornment of his temple, and by the provision of a worthy setting, and all that is necessary or useful, for the due performance of the Sacred Liturgy. Sacred art is also to promote the salvation of souls by moving men to true interior worship, raising their minds from the beauty of sight and sound to beauty of thought; by fostering faith and arousing sentiments of piety and devotion,[19] by aiding recollection and prayer. Sacred art should help to create, encourage, intensify all those sentiments of religion which are the true soul of worship. "One of the essential characters of art consists in a certain intrinsic affinity of art with religion which makes artists in some way interpreters of the infinite perfections of God, and particularly of their beauty and harmony. The function of every art consists in breaking through the narrow and sad enclosure of the finite, in

[15] M.D. § 196.
[16] *Decor*, not *pulchritudo*, is the word used. Sacred art demands an austere and spontaneous beauty.
[17] Instruction of the Holy Office on Sacred Art of June 30, 1952 (cited as I.H.O.), § 1.
[18] Ibid., § 8.
[19] Cf. ibid., § 10.

which man is immersed while he is living here below, and opening a window to his spirit aspiring to the infinite."[20] Sacred art is a form of Christian apostolate; the Church uses the arts, consecrating them to God's service, precisely because they contribute so powerfully to the furtherance of the work of the Incarnation and Redemption.

III. The "Laws of Sacred Art"

The Code of Canon Law, canons 1164, § 1, and 1296, § 3, speaks of the "laws of sacred art." "Laws" in English suggests a written code of regulations. This is not the meaning of "laws" in canons 1164 and 1296.[21] It means, apparently, certain qualities of sacred art, certain standards or norms to which artists who work for the Church, and who create sacred art, must conform. Sacred art—in which one seeks the artistic equivalents of spiritual qualities—has its own characteristics, its own norms, over and above those of good religious art. These are derived from the very nature and purpose of sacred art and its relation to divine worship,[22] and guidance about them must be sought in Canon Law (especially liturgical law), in the directives of ecclesiastical authority (papal pronouncements, decisions of the Holy See or local Ordinaries), in Christian tradition, and from recognized experts on this particular form of art.

The "laws" of sacred art are, necessarily, of a general character; their application in any particular case is left to the judgment of the Ordinary.[23] These norms are few, but their spirit is all pervading. Their general purpose is—in an age that is largely pagan and profane —to secure reverence for what is sacred (for sacred persons, places, things), and the exclusion of the unworthy from the service of the Church; to safeguard the dignity and decorum of the church and the Sacred Liturgy, and prevent scandal and the disedification of the worshippers, or offence to their religious feelings. And so the recent Instruction of the Holy Office on Sacred Art cites (§ 2) the words of St. Pius X in his *Motu Proprio* on sacred music:[24] "Nothing should

[20] Pius XII to exhibitors at the sixth Roman Quadriennale (April 8, 1952).
[21] The commentators on the Code are very coy in their treatment of these canons. They say little or nothing at all about the "laws of sacred art."
[22] See pp. 34 *sqq.*
[23] Cf. C.J.C. 1164, § 1.
[24] *Tra le Sollecitudini,* Nov. 22, 1903, Introduction.

have place in the church which disturbs or even merely diminishes the piety and devotion of the faithful, nothing which might reasonably be considered in bad taste or cause scandal, nothing above all which . . . might be unworthy of the house of prayer and the majesty of God."[25] In § 4 the Instruction cites the Council of Trent[26] on iconography: "Let bishops exercise such diligence and care concerning these matters that nothing disordered may meet the eye, nothing distorted and confused in execution, nothing profane and unbecoming, since sanctity befits the house of God." In the Instruction the Holy Office draws attention to the canons of the Codex which have a bearing on sacred art, and nearly all of them are concerned with the sanctity of the church and the reverence due to it.[27] It adds (§ 10): "This supreme sacred Congregation, deeply anxious to preserve the faith and piety of the Christian people through sacred art, has decreed that the following rules [which the Instruction then sets forth] should be recalled to the attention of Ordinaries throughout the world, in order that the forms and principles (*rationes*) of sacred art may fully correspond to the beauty (*decor*) and holiness of God's house."[28]

Accordingly, sacred art must be:

(1) *Orthodox,* in complete conformity with dogmatic truth, the teaching of the church, for sacred art is pictorial, apologetic, teaches, interprets, and should aid the Catholic formation of worshippers. Hence it must not lead into error or foster superstition.[29]

(2) *In conformity with the moral law,*[30] "not an immoral art, which professedly lowers and enslaves the soul's spiritual powers to the passions of the flesh. After all the words 'art' and 'immoral' are in flagrant contradiction."[31] The purpose of sacred art is to elevate and edify, not to degrade and shock.

(3) *Holy,* sacred art is art used in a sacred place for a sacred pur-

---

[25] "It is the duty of our brothers in the episcopate . . . to see that the important provisions of the Code [on sacred art] be obeyed and observed, and that nothing, wrongly calling itself art, shall intrude to offend against the sanctity of the church, and of the altar, and disturb the piety of the faithful" (Pius XI when inaugurating the Vatican Picture Gallery, Oct. 28, 1932).
[26] Session XXV.
[27] Especially canons 485, 1161 (defining a church as a sacred place), 1178.
[28] Cf. also M.D. (Pius XII, 1947), § 196.
[29] Cf. C.J.C. 1279, § 3.   [30] Ibid.
[31] Pius XII to the first International Congress of Catholic Artists in Rome (Sept. 5, 1950).

pose and so must be characterized by the note of holiness that shuns the impious and the profane, rejects the sensual, the worldly, the theatrical, the bizarre, the fantastic. Sacred art needs a spiritual quality, it is a vehicle of divine grace—not a mere ornament—it is a language speaking to men's souls through eye and ear.[32] Accordingly, the Instruction of the Holy Office (§§ 5, 15) declares that, in conformity with canons 485 and 1178, "Ordinaries should see to it that everything is removed from sacred buildings which is in any way contrary to the holiness of the place and the reverence due to the house of God."[33]

(4) *In full accordance with liturgical law.* As sacred art is part of external worship, and liturgical art is part of the Sacred Liturgy, what the artist makes for the church—from the building itself down to the smallest requisite of worship—must be fully adapted to its purpose and in entire accordance with liturgical law. This conformity to liturgical law, when complete, goes a long way to procuring, almost automatically, a worthy artistic form. It is the failure to observe the prescriptions of liturgical law, *in their entirety,* in many of our churches, which often accounts for their aesthetic failings. "Artists and architects," writes Pius XII in *Mediator Dei,*[34] must have "both the skill and the will to find in religion the inspiration of methods and plans best adapted to the exigencies of divine worship."

(5) *Sacred art is subsidiary and subject to ecclesiastical control.* This follows at once from the purpose of sacred art. When art enters the church, it must accept control other than that of mere aesthetics, because it is no longer a question of beauty alone or of personal experience, but of a religious message which must be authentic. And so: (*a*) canon 1164, § 1 directs Ordinaries to control the work of building churches (canon 1296, § 3, deals with their furnishing), taking counsel with experts when necessary. Canon Law supposes Ordinaries to have a diocesan Commission on sacred art (as St. Pius X ordered such a Commission for church music in every diocese),[35] and the Instruction of the Holy Office on Sacred Art says (§ 18): "If there are lacking experts on the diocesan Commission, or doubts or controver-

---

[32] Cf. the blessing of a sacred image in R.R. (IX, ix, 15).
[33] Cf. also St. Pius X in his *Motu Proprio* on music; the Apostolic Constitution *Divini Cultus Sanctitatem* of Pius XI (1928); and Pius XII, M.D. § 195, 188.
[34] § 196.   [35] *Motu Proprio* (1903), § VIII (n. 24).

sies arise, let the local Ordinaries consult the Metropolitan Commission or the Roman Commission on Sacred Art." (*b*) Pius XII writes in *Mediator Dei* (§ 195): "On condition that these modern arts, architecture, sculpture, painting, steer a middle course between an excessive naturalism on the one hand and an exaggerated symbolism on the other, and take into account more the needs of the Christian community than the personal taste and judgment of the artist, they should be allowed full scope if, with due reverence and honour, they put themselves at the service of our churches and sacred rites." And (§ 196) the Pope directs the bishops "to enlighten and direct the artists and architects who will be charged with the task of restoring and rebuilding churches." (*c*) Pius XI, in his Apostolic Constitution[36] on the Sacred Liturgy, spoke of the arts as "very noble handmaids in the service of divine worship." Accordingly, the Holy See and Ordinaries have taken a strong stand against unsuitable art,[37] and "reprobated corrupt and errant forms of sacred art."[38]

(6) *Sacred art is social in character,* it is art in the service of the community, for the people's house of prayer, and so it must be: (*a*) *Universal* in its appeal (as St. Pius X laid down for church music).[39] Sacred art is not intended merely for a coterie of aesthetes, but for the public. It must not be individualistic, nor must the merely subjective element of beauty be the prevailing feature in it. Sacred art has a teaching office,[40] is interpretative of the mind of the Church (not merely of the feelings of the artist) and commemorative, and so needs to be correct, clear and intelligible. Pius XII in *Mediator Dei* (§ 188) teaches that one of the qualities demanded by all that pertains to the Liturgy is "a universality which, while respecting legitimate local customs, manifests the unity of the Church." (*b*) "Sacred art must be *intelligible;* it must not be esoteric. It should give its message clearly and quickly. It must have an expressive value, lacking which it ceases to be true art. To say as much is not superfluous in our day when all too often, among certain groups, the work of art is not sufficient in itself to render the thought, to externalize the feelings, to

[36] *Divini Cultus Sanctitatem* (1928).
[37] See *infra,* pp. 38 *sqq.*
[38] I.H.O., § 8.   [39] *Motu Proprio,* §§ 1, 2.
[40] "The painter by his art does for religion," wrote St. Basil, "what the orator does

lay bare the soul of its author. Yet the moment it needs to be explained in verbal terms, it loses its value as a sign and serves only to afford the senses a physical joy rising no higher than their own level, or else it affords the mind merely the pleasure of subtle and useless play."[41] "When artists work in the sanctuary, they must remember that they are not working in a locked cenacle, and so their work must be capable of being understood by the body of the faithful, without the necessity of long and learned explanations."[42] "Art is not an enigma to be solved . . . it ought to know how to make itself understood quickly and give pleasure."[43] "Christian art which is not intelligible is neither Christian nor is it art; not Christian because the Church is universal, not art because it has refused to declare itself, in the terms of its medium, for exactly what it is, whether pattern or representation—or comprehensible combination of both—so that it may be judged."[44]

IV. THE CHURCH WELCOMES GOOD ART

Down through the ages the Church has been the greatest patron of art, and has welcomed the art of every period, of every country, of every school, provided that it has the qualities that are essential to sacred art. In our own day Pius XI, when inaugurating the new Vatican Gallery of Paintings (October 27, 1932), having declared that corrupt and errant forms of art may not be admitted into churches, used these words: "Open wide the portals and tender sincere welcome to every good and progressive development of the approved and venerable traditions, which in so many centuries of Christian life, in such diversity of circumstances and of social and ethnic conditions, have given stupendous proof of their inexhaustible capacity of inspiring new and beautiful forms, as often as they are investigated or studied and cultivated under the twofold light of genius and faith."[45] St. Pius X had written[46] in his *Motu Proprio* on church music

by his eloquence."
[41] Pius XII to First International Congress of Catholic Artists (Sept. 5, 1950) (*Liturgical Arts,* Nov. 1950).
[42] Directives of the French Bishops on Sacred Art (April 28, 1952), n. V.
[43] Cardinal C. Costantini in *Osservatore Romano* (June 10, 1951).
[44] William Justema in *Liturgical Arts,* Nov. 1951, p. 32.
[45] These words are cited in the Instruction of the Holy Office (1952), § 8.
[46] § II, 5.

(1903): "The Church has always recognized and promoted the progress of the arts, admitting to the service of worship everything good and beautiful that men's genius has created throughout the centuries, provided that it was in conformity with liturgical law." Pius XI in his Constitution on the Liturgy (1928) spoke of "the arts contributing, as is fitting, to divine worship like very noble handmaids." And he added: "The arts suffer nothing by being used in the church; rather their use in sacred places enhances their dignity and splendour." Pius XII in *Mediator Dei*[47] (1947) wrote: "It is easy to understand that the progress of the fine arts, especially architecture, painting and music, have also had great influence in shaping and determining in various ways the external features of the Liturgy." The Church does not reject modern art. Pius XII in *Mediator Dei*,[48] having spoken of the admission of modern pictures and statues into the church, provided they conform to the requirements of sacred art, added: "Thus modern art, too, may lend its voice to the magnificent chorus of praise which great geniuses throughout the ages have sung to the Catholic faith." And later on:[49] "Drawing their inspiration from heaven these human arts will then shine with heaven's clear light, and contribute not only to the progress of civilization but also to the glory of God and the salvation of souls." "The Roman Papacy, heir of universal culture, has never ceased to esteem art, to surround itself with its works, to make it a collaborator—within due limits—of its divine mission, preserving and elevating its purpose, which is to conduct the soul to God."[50] The bishops of France in their "Directives" regarding sacred art (§ II), dated April 28, 1952,[51] noted with satisfaction that some of the most famous artists of the day had been invited to work for the Church and had willingly accepted the invitation.

The Church shows her care of works of art in her legislation to prevent their alienation (C.J.C. 1281, § 1), and to secure their preservation: "Precious images, namely those of special value because of their beauty, artistic or cultural value, must not—should they need repair—be restored without the written consent of the Ordinary, who, before

[47] § 56.
[48] § 195.
[49] § 196.
[50] Pius XII to the exhibitors at the Roman Exhibition (April 8, 1952).
[51] *La Croix,* May 18, 1952.

he gives permission, is to consult prudent experts" (C.J.C. 1280).

The Church's Control of Sacred Art

Because of the nature and purpose of sacred art the Church has the right and the duty to control the work of the artist and to reject and refuse admission into churches of unsuitable art. She is bound to ensure reverence for what is sacred, to safeguard the dignity and holiness of the church and of divine worship, and to prevent any disturbance of or offence to the religious sentiments of the faithful. This is all the more necessary in a materialistic age, insensitive to the things of the spirit, when many artists are no longer inspired or guided by the Christian faith and tradition. Accordingly, the Church rejects worthless and degraded art.

V. The Church Rejects Worthless Art

The Church demands that sacred art be worthy of its high purpose and be of permanent value, not the plaything of passing fashion, and she orders that competent expert opinion be obtained in all matters pertaining to the building and furnishing of churches.[52] Expert opinion means that of competent architects, artists, liturgists. Each diocese is supposed to have a Commission on sacred music and art,[53] and a metropolitan Commission is to be available for further consultation, as well as the central Art Commission in Rome.[54] Ecclesiastical authorities are sometimes obliged to tolerate inferior so-called "art" in churches, but the Church frowns on this factory rubbish. "Let Ordinaries," says[55] the Instruction of the Holy Office (1952), "severely forbid second-rate and for the most part stereotyped statues and pictures to be multiplied, and improperly and absurdly exposed to the veneration of the faithful on altars themselves or on the adjoining walls of chapels." The French bishops in their "Directives" on sacred art (April 1952) wrote:[56] "It goes without saying that the Commission gladly recognizes that the collection of poor art[57]—lacking life and dignity—which is so often the shame of our churches, should be

[52] C.J.C. 1164, § 1 (cited in I.H.O. § 13); I.H.O. §§ 18, 21, 22.
[53] Motu Proprio of St. Pius X (§ 24); M.D., § 109.   [54] I.H.O. §§ 4, 18.
[55] § 19.   [56] § X.
[57] "Toute une production de mièvrerie" is difficult to express adequately in English.

more and more excluded from them." Cardinal Celso Costantini, an authority on sacred art, writing in *Osservatore Romano* (June 10, 1951), denies with vigour that approved sacred art means "cheap reproductions of painted plaster statues and all the industrial rubbish that has invaded so many churches." He adds: "We must dispose of the very common misconception that because certain forms of modern sacred art are condemned,[58] we approve and uphold as the ideal these banal reproductions. Nothing is further from the truth."

Degraded Art

The Church does not reject what is modern in art—the use of new materials and of a new technique, new ideas, new forms[59]—and gives great freedom to the artist[60] who undertakes a work of sacred art, but she does emphatically reject degraded art (which for convenience sake we term here "modernistic art," using "modern" for good contemporary art). This art—which is over subjective, often bizarre and extravagant, sometimes coarse or even barbaric, the product of undisciplined sentimentalism and mere ephemeral whim, idiosyncratic—desires to pass off as beautiful the deformed and the grotesque and "loses itself in the wild forest of cubist and abstract art."[61] This errant art arises from false ideas about originality, modernity and progress. True modernity, based on the honest desire to make the arts more effective in the service of religion, makes use of diversity of style and fashion without becoming its slave, employs the living art and the living creative intelligence of our own day as the great artists of the past used the art and intelligence of their day. True modernity means "efficacy and freshness of expression, means living and popular language, but this must be correct and intelligible, not esoteric and repulsive."

Pius XI in his discourse[62] at the opening of the new Vatican Art Gallery (October 28, 1932) spoke of "so many works of art, indisput-

---

[58] See *infra*, pp. 40 *sqq.*
[59] Cf. p. 36. The Commission recognizes that, "like every art, and perhaps more so than others, sacred art is a living thing and that it must correspond to the spirit of the times, as well as to its technique and materials" ("Directives" of the French Bishops, § I).   [60] Cf. pp. 51, 54.
[61] Cardinal C. Costantini in *Osservatore Romano* (July 23, 1942). Cubist art, it seems, has faded out of fashion.   [62] *Acta Apostolicae Sedis* (1932), p. 356.

ably and for ever beautiful . . . which bring to mind, by a well-nigh irresistible force of contrast, certain other so-called works of art, that seem to recall the sacred, only to distort it to the point of caricature, very often of real profanation. An attempt to defend this is made on the plea of the search for the new, and of rational craftsmanship. The new represents no true progress if it is not at least as beautiful and as good as the old."[63] This same enlightened Pontiff declared: "This so-called modern art in religion must not disfigure the House of God. Sacred art has no foundation or reason for its existence unless it represents spiritual ideals. Works of art that are *foreign to the Christian tradition* must not be admitted into places of prayer."[64]

On February 25, 1947, Archbishop G. Costantini, president of the Central Art Commission in Rome, circulated to the bishops of Italy a warning about degraded art that the Holy Office—following an exhibition held in one of the art galleries of Rome—had issued (December 10, 1946). It spoke of "the fashion of the deformed and grotesque," arousing "disgust and reprobation," and the necessity of saving Christians who were scandalized, and of safeguarding "the dignity of worship and of sacred places, as well as the proper meaning of sacred art, i.e., to create in Christians sentiments of piety and devotion." Pius XII in *Mediator Dei* (November 1947) wrote:[65] "We feel bound . . . to deplore and condemn certain modern pictures and statues which are a disfigurement and degradation of genuine art, and are sometimes openly in conflict with Christian decorum, modesty and piety, and lamentably offensive to true religious sentiment; they must be barred[66] and ejected from our churches, and likewise, in general, anything that ill-beseems the sacred character of the place."

The 1952 Instruction of the Holy Office on Sacred Art (§ 8) declares: "Recently the Apostolic See reprobated corrupt and errant forms of sacred art. Of no moment are the objections raised by some

---

[63] Previously, an article in *Osservatore Romano* of July 7, 1932 (signed "T"—the usual signature of the editor, Count Della Torre) had vigorously denounced and condemned certain works of art that had been shown in an exhibition at Essen of contemporary German Catholic art.
[64] *Liturgical Arts*, Nov. 1950, p. 18.
[65] § 195. Cited in I.H.O. § 9.
[66] Pius XI had declared this also in his discourse cited above.

that sacred art must be adapted to the necessities and conditions of the present day. For sacred art, which originated with Christian society, possesses its own purpose, from which it may never diverge, and its proper function, which it may never desert."[67] The French bishops in their "Directives" on sacred art (April 28, 1952) declared (§ IV): artists "must be convinced that when there is question of sacred persons or religious subjects, no one has the right, in the execution of a work of art, to present deformations that would run the risk of shocking the faithful, and of appearing to the profane as unworthy of the persons or mysteries they represent, or even insulting to them."[68]

VI. "FORMS RECEIVED FROM CHRISTIAN TRADITION"

Canon 1164, § 1, of the Code of Canon Law says that in the building of churches "forms received from Christian tradition" are to be followed, and the 1952 Instruction of the Holy Office on Sacred Art cites this canon.[69] The canon is new legislation in the Code and has not yet received a standardized interpretation.[70] It cannot mean that new forms of building are excluded, for the Church has never prescribed any special style of architecture, and the text of the Instruction itself speaks of sacred architecture adopting "new styles,"[71] and cites[72] the words of Pius XI welcoming "every good and progressive development of the approved and venerable traditions which ... have given such great proof of their inexhaustible capacity of inspiring new and beautiful forms." And modern forms of architecture are being used in Rome itself. Not infrequently the newer form brings a fresh approach to the problem of church building, corrects some of the defects of older forms (e.g., their failure to conform to liturgical law) and, by the use of modern technique, can achieve desirable re-

[67] In a number of articles in *Osservatore Romano* (Feb. 2, 1949; June 10 and 18, 1951; July 23, 1952) Archbishop (now Cardinal) Celso Costantini had vigorously denounced and condemned "modernistic art."
[68] The bishops add a number of remarks about the necessity of temperate and enlightened criticism of modern works of art ("Directives," §§ VI, VII, VIII, IX. *L'Art Sacré,* mai 1952).
[69] The translation given in the English version of the Instruction is "traditional Christian styles of architecture." This appears to have been derived from Bouscaren, *Canon Law* (1951), p. 650, and does not seem correct. The Italian retains *forme* and the French *formes.*
[70] The commentators on the Code—with very few exceptions—say nothing whatever about the expression.
[71] § 11.   [72] § 8. The words of the Pope are given on p. 36.

sults that hitherto were unattainable. The Church, then, does not reject modern styles of architecture, provided they are in keeping with her laws, but she does insist that church architecture differs from secular building: "Sacred architecture, although it may adopt new styles, must not in any way be equated with profane building."[73]

There is a certain traditional idea of a church, based on its purpose and its needs, which has gradually taken shape and been handed down. It is quite a general idea—a broad concept—of certain fundamental features or characteristics which are common to all Catholic churches, whatever the material or style in which they are built. To this general idea any particular style of architecture (e.g., Gothic) adds certain individual notes and precisions—certain details of design and decoration—which label the building as belonging to a defined historical architectural form, and differentiate it from buildings of a different style. Thus every church has: (1) a certain general external form that marks it off from secular buildings (even its doors and windows have a traditional form); (2) a certain general internal plan, with a certain proportion and certain relations between its parts— necessitated by its purpose as the place of the Sacred Liturgy; (3) certain qualities of restrained and dignified beauty that make the building, however simple, worthy of its high purpose, the promotion of God's honour, a fitting place for divine worship, and a help to the devotion of the worshipper. It is with this general traditional idea of a Catholic church that canon 1164, § 1, seems to be concerned. Preserving the "forms received from Christian tradition" means that a church must be the kind of building which, externally and internally, fully responds to the liturgical and social exigencies of a Catholic place of worship.[74] These *formae*—unlike styles of architecture, which change in time and place—are a permanent, unchanging feature of church construction. The Church, while no enemy of real progress, is by its nature prudent and wisely conservative. So are the people in matters of religious

[73] I.H.O. § 11. "It would be a mistake to plan the exterior structure of a church in its outlines and spatial proportions, in its structural members and its decoration, according to the style of the profane architecture of the time and of the surroundings: lest the attractiveness of the church building be merely that of this world" (Directives of the German Episcopate on church building. See *Orate Fratres*, Dec. 1949, or more conveniently the appendix to this book, Conc. 3, p. 247). [74] Cf. Wernz-Vidal, *Jus Canonicum* (1934), IV, n. 555; Beste, *Introductio in*

practice. The insistence of the Church on traditional forms is a check on sudden and violent changes—often springing from an undue love of modernity and the foolish quest after supposed progress—which militate against the dignity and calm of the ideal church, and disturb the faithful. The Canon Law and the Holy Office Instruction insist that art in a church is a *sacred* thing, with its own "laws,"[75] its own traditional "forms."

VII. CHRISTIAN TRADITION

In her laws on church building and furnishing the Church lays down (C.J.C. 1164, § 1; 1296, § 3) that "the forms received from Christian tradition" are to be preserved in the construction of a church, that "ecclesiastical tradition" is one of the norms to be followed in the furnishing of one.

What is Tradition?

Tradition in general means handing on something from generation to generation. Sometimes it means the belief, practice or thing that is handed down (*a* tradition, tradition*s*), sometimes the organ or mode of transmission. In the case of the Catholic Church this latter means a current of life (e.g., of liturgical, of artistic life) and truth (the handing down of revealed truth) under the direction of the Church, guided by the Holy Spirit. Tradition plays a great part in the teaching of religious truth—the thought of the Church (*mens Ecclesiae*) is essentially traditional—and also in the Sacred Liturgy or worship of the Church, which is of its very nature traditional, and is religious truth in action. And as sacred art is art in the service of worship[76] tradition plays a part in this also. There is an artistic (including a musical) tradition in the Church; a tradition of beauty in the service of God and of souls, derived in part from the Old Testament.

What Christian Tradition is Not

The fidelity to Christian tradition in art which the Church demands does *not* mean:

Codicem (1944), p. 557; Costantini, *Fede ed Arte* (1946), II, p. 32, and in *Osservatore Romano* (July 30, 1952).   [75] Cf. pp. 31 *sqq.*   [76] P. 30.

(1) Mere copying[77] of past works of art, for the Church welcomes new forms, new inspiration, as well as the use of new materials and new technique.[78] She welcomes these when they are good and definitely an improvement on what preceded them. It is thus that the defects of the past are eliminated, and greater care taken to observe the prescriptions of liturgical law.

(2) It does not mean "archeologism," stagnation, fossilization, an adoption or retaining of the old merely because it is old. The Church is an organism; her Liturgy and her art are vital. "An ancient custom is not to be considered better," wrote Pius XII of liturgical usages,[79] "either in itself or in relation to later times, just because it has the flavour of antiquity." The Church in her art assimilates—slowly, it is true, never in a hurry—what is good from the spirit of the times, because it is something better, not because it is up to date. And so today, in keeping with what is really good in modern ideas, church builders are now, for example, showing greater appreciation of the value of plain surfaces and of the right use of colour, and dislike of the superfluous, the over-ornate, the fake, the tawdry and the pretentious.

(3) Fidelity to tradition does not mean the adoption of any one style of architecture, as if there were one or more special styles that are exclusively religious or Catholic.[80] As the Church has never canonized any one system of theology or philosophy (despite her marked predilection for that of St. Thomas Aquinas), or adopted exclusively any one rite or one style of music (while, again, favouring the Roman rite and plainsong), neither does she impose any one style of architecture, or other sacred art. It is quite permissible to invent new styles, but they must be based on, and have a link with, Christian tradition. Cardinal Costantini, commenting on the 1952 Instruction of the Holy Office, wrote:[81] "All styles are admissible, provided they are conformable to this fundamental principle that a church must be, and must appear to be, the house of God and the

---

[77] Yet even copying may sometimes be a virtue. It was St. Pius X who said of the new churches in Rome itself: "Better reproduce the old ones on a larger or smaller scale than waste time in devising ugly novelties of an eccentric or undefined style."
[78] See pp. 39 *sqq.*
[79] *M.D.*, § 61.
[80] See pp. 36, 41.
[81] *Osservatore Romano* (July 30, 1952),

ladder to heaven. . . . Nowadays one can see churches whose construction was inspired by a new style—for one can truly say today that there is a new architectural style—and which fully satisfy the requirements of worship, of a fresh appreciation of artistic beauty, and of an enlightened economic sense."

(4) Fidelity to tradition does not impose any *unreasonable* restraint on the legitimate liberty of the artist,[82] on his originality or inventiveness; it does not exclude the modern,[83] provided it is good and suitable for sacred art. It does not, e.g., require the adoption of the naturalistic as opposed to the stylistic treatment of forms, nor exclude abstract art. It does not ignore or eschew national forms of sacred art,[84] for taste in sacred art varies in different places as it varies in different times, provided they conform to the "laws of sacred art."[85] "The Church's purpose, when it seeks to adapt to ecclesiastical needs the art already existing in each country, is evident and quite simple. It is an expression of the Church's catholicity, and is to convince the people whom we wish to convert that the Catholic religion is from above, not from abroad."[86]

The Nature of Christian Tradition

In general it is tradition animated, enlightened, inspired by the Catholic faith, and guarded and directed by the Church—an unrivalled guide in virtue of her divine and permanent character and her artistic experience of nearly two thousand years.

Respect for tradition in the matter of sacred art means:

(1) A worthy and conscious fidelity to the supreme canons that have governed good sacred art through the ages; respect for an understanding of *the spirit* that inspired the great Christian artists of the past and was embodied in their superb work; a deep regard for and sensitiveness to the masterpieces of sacred art.

[82] Pp. 54 *sqq.*
[83] P. 41.
[84] E.g., in a letter to Cardinal C. Costantini, then Inter-Nuncio in China, and a promoter of Christian Chinese art, the S. Congregation of Propaganda warmly commended the success achieved in China by Christian art "understood in a truly Catholic spirit, and not as an occidental importation" (*Osservatore Romano,* Oct. 19, 1952).
[85] P. 32.
[86] Letter of the Prefect of the Propaganda Congregation to Archbishop Costantini in China (Dec. 21, 1934).

(2) Imitation—not mere servile copying—of past great works of sacred art (since they are the best examples of the realization of the principles of this art), by the use of living creative art, employing the artistic ideas and means of the day. There is nothing unworthy in such imitation. Pius IX when inaugurating the new entrance to the Vatican Museums, on December 7, 1932, took occasion[87] to show how much of the vague searching after new art-forms comes from a foolish contempt for all imitation. "At the root of all this lies a vulgar confusion between imitating and copying, as though imitation excludes all inspiration. If this were true, Dante, by imitating Virgil, forfeited all claim to original genius." Was it not Ruskin who wrote: "It is no sign of deadness in a present art that it borrows or imitates, but only if it borrows without paying interest, or if it imitates without choice"? To learn from the past is wisdom. Are not the experience, the technical education, the taste of the artist largely acquired from tradition? Not everything new is necessarily good, and the chief aim of the artist in a work of sacred art is not to produce something new, but to create—guided by Christian ideas—something beautiful and fully fitted to its purpose of suggesting the spiritual by the sensible.

(3) Fidelity to tradition means adapting and developing—"in the light of genius and truth" (Pius XI)—what the past has to teach. Learning from the failures as well as the successes of the past the Church has unrivalled experience of what is good in sacred art and what best suits her purpose in admitting it within her buildings. "The salvation of sacred architecture will be secured by turning to tradition, not to copy forms that have passed away, but only to recover the elements that have always persevered through all the styles and make them flourish again and be clothed with new life, life that beats in unison with the life of today. Not copies of old buildings, but old elements—that are the very stuff of architecture—reinvigorated with new life."[88] "We are traditionalists, not in the sense of a literal return to antiquity in order to copy and remake the works of the masters of the past, but in the sense of looking to tradition as a guide towards using with intelligence the conquests made by our predecessors, and

---

[87] *Osservatore Romano*, Dec. 8, 1932.
[88] Costantini, *Fede ed Arte*, II, p. 34.

going forward along the path of art to fresh stages of progress. Tradition is a starting-point and not a goal. We must indeed pass on the torch . . . but we must ourselves run and not stand still. Great art, like life, renews itself by disregarding worn-out and stale elements, and assimilating new ones. But life preserves physiological unity and continuity. Tradition is for us a kind of physiological equilibrium. We want modern, but not modernistic work."[89]

(4) Fidelity to tradition in sacred art means ordered and reasonable evolution, gradual development, continuity of ideas—not necessarily of forms—avoiding a violent and sudden break with the past. It means progress along certain defined lines, progress aware of and not ignoring the past. It is a dynamic and continuing force in sacred art.

Some Notes on Tradition

(1) Tradition is the source of certain general principles of sacred art. It passes on certain truths—certain norms—not put down in definite terms, but set forth in practice. It tells us what the Church has, in the past, accepted or rejected as sacred art. It guides us in the creation of "the atmosphere" of a Catholic church.

(2) Tradition is a protection against all extremes in religious art, against the bizarre and the degraded. It exercises a restraining influence on *undue* modernity and originality—on the thirst for the new at any price, for the sensational—and fosters a reasonable conservatism. It helps towards the expression of authentic religious thought and feeling, not merely the personal reactions of the artist.

(3) Tradition in sacred art is partly embodied in the rubrics—to which it is prior logically and in time—supplements them, and throws light on them.

(4) Tradition is quite different from traditions—which it transcends. Traditions are born (often in a negative way, by the Church not intervening to terminate some usage), change, die. They may be good or bad, genuine or false. They may be general or merely national. Traditions are often dated; the beauty and craftsmanship inspired by Tradition are perennial.

[89] Cardinal C. Costantini, *Arte Sacra e Novecentismo* (1925).

VIII. CHURCH BUILDING FROM THE LITURGICAL ANGLE

If an architect is to plan a perfect Catholic church he must know and take account of certain liturgical principles:

(1) The high altar—because of its importance and symbolism—is the focal point of the church.[90] The architect must, by the size and proportions of the altar, by its position and its setting (decoration of the apse, use of a canopy, etc.), by the spacing of the sanctuary, by the correct use of colour, by sufficient suitable lighting, and all the rest, direct the eyes and minds of the worshippers to the altar.

(2) Consequently, he should aim at the elimination of the unnecessary (e.g., gradines on the altar, statues in the sanctuary) and of all that would confuse the minds of the worshippers and distract their attention from the high altar (e.g., side altars not recessed, elaborate retables, Stations of the Cross in too prominent a position).

(3) The traditional principle of the unity of the altar should be maintained,[91] and so necessary side altars must never be placed within the sanctuary, nor—if possible—in the main area of the church, but in side chapels or be, at least, recessed.

(4) It is desirable, when it is feasible, that the architectural and liturgical focal points should coincide.

(5) The parts of a church, the different furnishings, have a quite different value. Thus the most important part of the church is the sanctuary because of the high altar (and the important aspect of this is the table of sacrifice, and not the requirements of Exposition). After the altar[92] in importance comes the baptistery (which is often a neglected and gloomy corner of the church, and sometimes even used for storage purposes), and then come the pulpit and confessionals, because of their liturgical use. Such non-liturgical features of a church as statues, shrines, Stations of the Cross are entirely secondary and subsidiary, and should be treated as such.

(6) A Catholic church is a place of ceremonial movement, not only for the sacred ministers and their entourage in the sanctuary (for whose convenience must be planned a sanctuary of suitable size, comfortable steps, etc.) but also for the people. Hence the architect must

[90] See p. 23.   [91] See p. 164.
[92] And, of course, after *real* side altars, if the church needs them.

plan for the free movement between the places of the worshippers and the sanctuary (so as to allow of *orderly* approach for Holy Communion, reception of blessed ashes, etc., and return to their places), between the narthex and the baptistery for baptisms, a suitable space and route for processions (from the sacristy, around the church, etc.) and the like (p. 26).

(7) It is for the architect to solve the delicate problem of the intimate connection of the worshippers with the altar[93] (by its prominence, visibility, etc.), so that they may take an *active* part in the Sacred Liturgy, combined with their exclusion from the sanctuary (by, at least, a token barrier of rope) to safeguard the dignity and tranquility of divine service, and preserve the sacred character of the precincts of the altar and the hierarchical character (by divine institution) of Catholic worship.

(8) Traditional symbolism (e.g., of the church,[94] of the altar) plays a part in the planning of a church—e.g., the unity of the altar,[95] its clothing,[96] the descent to the baptismal font[97] and the architect must have a knowledge of it.

(9) The correct construction and adornment of an altar and of a tabernacle are matters requiring no small rubrical knowledge,[98] necessary for the architect of a Catholic church.

(10) The internal planning of a church is also affected by the situation of the baptistery,[99] the places for consecration crosses[100] (if the church is to be consecrated), the correct position of confessionals,[101] of statues and of the Stations of the Cross,[102] of the sacrarium, of lustral water stoups, alms boxes, etc.

From all this it is evident that a church architect needs very special training over and above his formation as a competent architect. If he undertakes to plan Catholic churches, and oversee their erection,

[93] For some Catholic congregations—especially in large churches—it is necessary to break down the psychological barrier that separates them from the sacred action of the Mass, and makes them regard the sanctuary as another world in which they have no place, the Sacred Liturgy a drama in which they have no part to play.
[94] Cf., e.g., the Office and Mass for the Dedication of a Church (and altar).
[95] Cf. p. 164.
[96] Cf. p. 192.
[97] Cf. p. 124.
[98] They are dealt with at length in this book (p. 142 and p. 187).
[99] P. 124.　　　　[100] P. 6.
[101] P. 73.　　　　[102] P. 114.

he needs a sound knowledge of liturgical principles and liturgical prescriptions. If his education has not comprised the study of the Sacred
Liturgy, then he must be guided in his planning by a competent liturgist. He cannot afford to be ignorant of, or worse still, pay no
attention to the Church's law on church building and furnishing.

IX. THE CHURCH ARCHITECT

The task of the architect of a Catholic church is indeed a very special one, requiring a quite peculiar competence. "A church is a
building having exactly defined requirements, to be exactly, econom-
ically and beautifully supplied."[103]   A church is the product of the
useful, the symbolic and the beautiful. Its functional requirements
are paramount; but the physical comfort and aesthetic satisfaction of
the worshippers require due attention. "Sacred architecture, although
it may adopt new styles, cannot in any way be equated with profane
building, but must always perform its own office, which regards the
house of God and the place of prayer. In addition, in building
churches care should be taken about the convenience of the faithful,
so that they can take part in the divine offices with a better view and
more intimately. Let new churches, too, be distinguished by the
beautiful simplicity of their lines, eschewing sham ornamentation; but
avoiding likewise anything that savours of a neglect of art or of due
care."[104] A church architect must, then, plan and oversee the erection
of a building that will be not merely sound in construction—using the
best materials[105] and technique available—duly ventilated, heated,
lighted, acoustically satisfactory and all the rest, but also a building
that will be perfectly adapted to its purpose as a church. It must, in
addition, be as beautiful as circumstances permit—beautiful in construction (in its lines and surfaces, its proportions, etc.) and in adornment (with the right use of colour, correct emphasis, and all those
qualities that conspire to make a beautiful building).

A church has its own special requirements: (1) as the place
wherein the Sacred Liturgy is to be duly carried out; many of the
churches built in the past were defective in this respect, they were not

[103] H. S. Goodhart-Rendel in *Pax* (Winter 1945, p. 154).
[104] I.H.O. § 11.   [105] As the dignity of a church and true economy demand.

properly planned in accordance with liturgical law, and the liturgical revival of this century is profoundly affecting church building in its insistence that the plan of a church be examined and approved by a liturgical expert. (2) As a building with a traditional symbolical character (e.g., symbolism determines the orientation of a church, the position of the baptistery). (3) Even as an auditorium the church is not a mere hall but must have special features to meet the needs of a congregation that should take an active part in the Sacred Liturgy (and so, e.g., have a link with the altar and sanctuary wherein it stands), and that moves about (hence, e.g., the provision for free movement within the building). The kind of church the building is to be—whether cathedral, conventual, parochial; whether, e.g., a place of pilgrimage,[106] or a mere domestic oratory—will also affect the plan.

One of the tasks of the church architect—when he is allowed to perform it—is to harmonize the arts employed in the construction and adornment of the edifice, integrating them all into one complete structural plan.

The Freedom of the Architect[107]

In preparing his plans for a Catholic church the architect is given a large measure of freedom, but not by any means complete freedom. Apart from the wishes of his client, he is free to choose any "style" of architecture.[108] No special form of architecture is prescribed by liturgical law, and (pace Pugin) there is no one exclusively religious architectural style, though it must be confessed that the clergy are biased in favour of certain traditional styles of church building, because these are familiar and their especial appropriateness and practical utility have been proved by long experience. Even in Rome itself new forms of architecture are coming into use. Modern technique and new materials have made certain forms of construction, which were hitherto impossible, quite feasible. The need for economy has also had its influence on architectural designs. There is plenty of scope for modern ideas and technique—the solving of old

[106] Such a church, e.g., would need an ambulatory.
[107] See infra, pp. 54 sqq.
[108] Different styles of architecture suit different countries and climates, and the tastes and traditions of different peoples.

problems in new ways—provided the new is found superior to the old. But the freedom of the architect (or of his client) is not unlimited. He is bound by the prescription of liturgical law to preserve "the forms received from Christian tradition," and observe "the laws of sacred art."[109] "In what style shall a sacred edifice be built?" ask Archbishops Celso and Giovanni Costantini, no mean authorities on sacred art, in their book *Fede ed Arte* (1946),[110] and they reply: "In that style which the artist wishes, provided that the laws laid down by ecclesiastical authority through the centuries be observed, and provided that the sacred edifice truly appears as such, that it be a real house of God and as worthy as possible a place of prayer. The style is the language in which the artist gives expression to his thought. As the *Our Father* recited in any tongue gives praise to God, so a church —provided it be a real church—may be built in any style. The history of the development of the style of religious architecture is the most clear proof of the freedom allowed to the artist, provided that he creates a building that reveals itself at once as a real church by the dignity of its form and by its propriety."

X. THE CHRISTIAN ARTIST

By "artist" in this context is meant anyone who designs or executes anything for the service of the Church. Not every artist—even a great one—is capable of designing or executing a work of sacred art. It is a special, very special craft, demanding certain outstanding qualities.[111] Of the moral qualities needed *faith* is the chief, for sacred art concerns the sacred, and is art in contact with the supernatural. The French Episcopal Commission on Liturgy in their "Directives" on sacred art declared that it desired that artists who work for churches "should know how to steep themselves in the Christian spirit, otherwise they are unfitted for their task." "What work of sacred art,"[112] they con-

---

[109] C.J.C. 1164, § 1; 1296, § 3. The limitations thus imposed on the architect of a Catholic church are not a handicap or an unreasonable or injurious limitation of artistic freedom. They help to produce the true "atmosphere" of a church; the solemn, dignified, consecrated religious surroundings that direct one's thoughts to the supernatural.

[110] Vol. II, p. 32.

[111] "Artistic genius, religious inspiration—born of religious feeling and culture—and moral discipline, these three great qualities make the Christian artist" (Costantini, *Fede ed Arte*, I, p. 23).   [112] § III.

tinue, "could claim to be perfect of its kind without the inspiration of the Faith?" The Instruction of the Holy Office on sacred art demands[113] that those who serve on diocesan Commissions on sacred art should be "not only experts in art but also firmly adhere to the Christian faith, have been brought up in piety, and gladly follow the definite prescriptions of ecclesiastical authority." And while the Instruction does not expressly exclude non-believing artists, it does order[114] that "works of painting, sculpture and architecture should be entrusted for their execution to men who are outstanding for their technique, and who are capable of expressing sincere faith and piety, which is the purpose of any sacred art." "We have need for the Church," wrote Pere Régamey, O.P., a great advocate of modern art forms, "of artists whose personal life is Christian, whose culture is religious, authentic and deep, and whose touch is sure,"[115] while Valentine Reyre wrote: "To reform a Christian art, one must get rid of prejudice and false ideas about art and beauty, and become more deeply, more dogmatically, more vitally Christian."[116]

Allied with the faith of the true Christian artist, and springing from it, are the necessary virtues of reverence and humility. The artist must grasp what "the sacred" is and must have a deep reverence for all that is sacred,[117] realizing that when he undertakes the execution of a work of sacred art he ventures into the realm of the supernatural, he essays to create something perfect of its kind (perfect in performance, perfect in beauty)—as far as this be humanly possible—for the highest purpose, the honour of God and the welfare of souls; something, too, that is destined for the edification of the many in a public edifice; something intended to last, not for a few years, but perhaps for centuries. The Christian artist needs deep humility. Not primarily for his own glory or gain (though these might quite legitimately result from it) does he plan and execute a work of sacred art. He works for and under the direction of the Church. This may involve the sacrifice of some of his own ideas, put a curb on his own desire for self-expression,

[113] § 21.   [114] § 22.
[115] *L'Artisan Liturgique* (1948), p. 198.
[116] *L'art et la Liturgie* in *Ecclesia*, p. 684.
[117] Including due respect for ecclesiastical authority on questions of sacred art. If an artist does not wish to submit to this authority he may execute a work of religious art but not a work of *sacred art* (cf. p. 34).

in obedience to the higher dictates of truth and morality, all under the guidance of the Holy Spirit. By a preliminary theological and liturgical formation the true Christian artist must learn "the mind of the Church" on sacred art, and strive to be in perfect harmony with it, working under the Church's inspiration. He must know and respect Christian tradition,[118] and "the laws of sacred art,"[119] and be loyal to the letter and the spirit of liturgical prescriptions.[120] He will also need a competent knowledge of traditional Christian symbolism and iconography and the laws of each.

The Freedom of the Christian Artist

The artist who works for the Church enjoys an immense measure of freedom—of initiative and invention, of choice of materials and of design, etc.—but not unlimited freedom; that would be licence, not liberty. "Speak the language of your day," declared the late Cardinal Faulhaber of Munich to artists,[121] "provided it be language that is true and worthy of a sacred place. . . . Only one thing is essential— and this marks the limits within which ecclesiastical authority may concede every freedom to the artist—he must never forget the holy purpose for which he works, the *honour of God and of His saints,* and consequently the salvation of souls." In his circular letter to the bishops of Italy (February 25, 1947), Archbishop Giovanni Costantini, President of the Central Commission of Sacred Art, wrote:[122] "The Church has always given great liberty to artists regarding the means of expression, different techniques, various stylistic tendencies." "But," added his brother,[123] Cardinal Celso Costantini, "when art wishes to enter churches with sacrilegious deformations, then ecclesiastical superiors have the duty of safeguarding the purity of faith and morals." The same authority on sacred art had previously written:[124] "The artist retains the freedom to compose and express his own artistic conception, provided these are dignified; he also retains the choice of his own technique, provided this does not offend the sanctity of his

[118] Pp. 43 *sqq.* [119] Pp. 32 *sqq.*
[120] Cf. C.J.C. 1164, § 1; 1296, § 3.
[121] Walter Rothes, *Arte Sacra,* p. 386.
[122] *Documentation Catholique,* 1947 (1609).
[123] *Osservatore Romano,* July 30, 1952.
[124] Ibid., June 10, 1951.

subject. But the artist has not the right to deform the character of reverence, the theological thought, and the liturgical rôle of sacred representations."[125] The Christian artist is not free, then, to violate truth or morality, to be in conflict with the legislation of ecclesiastical authority, or to offend or shock the Christian conscience. The spontaneity of the artist is not destroyed by the ecclesiastical control of sacred art. It was not fettered in the great Christian artists of the past.

The Christian Artist and his Patron

The patron of a Christian artist (usually, nowadays, a bishop or priest) and the artist himself have this in common: the desire to procure the best possible (and this does not necessarily mean the most modern) work of art for God's glory and the pleasure and good of men. The artist is in a certain sense the priest of Christian beauty. It is a matter of opinion whether the artist who is not a believing Christian, can produce a work of sacred art.[126] What is certain is that the artist who wishes to create a work of sacred art needs, as part of his education, as a necessary element of his remote preparation for the vocation of a Christian artist, a theological and liturgical training— a religious culture—to enable him to understand the Catholic outlook and be acquainted with the Church's ideas and laws regarding art[127] (e.g., he needs a knowledge of Christian iconography). By his own study and from his patron he must learn "the mind of the Church" and acquire a sense of sacred things.[128] This is where the task of his clerical patron comes in, to coach him in these things, if he be willing to learn.

The clergy, on the other hand—who are, ordinarily, the artist's clients—need a training in sacred art, that they may be knowledgeable, discriminating in judgment and have good taste; that they may not only command but inspire good sacred art. Both Canon Law and the

[125] Cf. also the words of Pius XII (M.D. § 195), cited on p. 34.
[126] See pp. 52 *sqq.* regarding the Instruction of the Holy Office and the Directives of the French Episcopate on this point.
[127] Modern artists complain that they do not receive commissions from the clergy. This sometimes arises from lack of means to pay for an original work of art. More often it is because the clergy doubt if some of these artists—however distinguished —can produce a work of *sacred* art.
[128] This knowledge is—and was always in the past—part of the life of the clerical or monastic artist; it is indeed part of Catholic tradition. The artist must acquire it, as he acquires "local colour" for a commission.

Instruction of the Holy Office[129] ordain that the patrons of art consult, if necessary, expert opinion, such as the diocesan Commission for sacred art or the Central Commission in Rome, and direct that "aspirants for sacred Orders in schools of philosophy and theology be educated in sacred art and formed to its appreciation, in a way adapted to the ability and age of each, by masters who reverence what our ancestors cherished and established and comply with the prescriptions of the Holy See."[130] The clergy should, in matters of art, exclude from their churches all forms of modern art that do not conform to the definition of sacred art, or that fail to comply with the church's prescriptions. With equal resolution they should banish from their churches the rubbish that is neither art nor sacred, and is unworthy of a place in God's temple.

The creation of a worthy work of sacred art is a difficult task, demanding much from both the artist and his patron. But it is not impossible. The great works of sacred art of the past were born of the intelligent and friendly co-operation of patron and artist. These must work together in an atmosphere of mutual respect, understanding and sympathy. It is for the patron to brief his artist clearly—to set the theme, to recall the traditional principles and liturgical law that concern sacred art, to explain the "mind of the Church." It is for the artist to interpret all this in a worthy manner by his genius, and to do this he must be given all *due* liberty. He cannot, however, be given unlimited freedom if he is to create a work of *sacred* art; and his briefing and the prescriptions of ecclesiastical law do not unduly fetter his creative capacity. He will find them not a hindrance but a help and inspiration.[131] He needs God's blessing on his task. "Here is the name of the man I have appointed to help thee, Beseleel," said God to Moses.[132] "I have filled him with My divine spirit, making him wise, adroit, and skilful in every kind of craftsmanship." An artist—especially a Catholic—should deem it an honour and privilege, as did the greatest artists of the past, to work for God's glory and the spiritual good of his fellow-men.

[129] § 21.
[130] I.H.O., § 23.
[131] Cf. pp. 51 *sqq.*
[132] Exodus 31.2.

Chapter VI

The Decoration of a Church

T H E decoration of a church is both permanent and temporary (this latter depending on, and being graded by, seasons and feasts, places and persons).[1] The permanent decoration of a church derives from painting, sculpture, mosaic and similar arts, stained glass, metal work, textiles. There are no detailed laws about this permanent decoration. Canon Law (canons 1164, § 1, and 1296, § 3) does give a general directive about regard for the teaching of tradition, obedience to liturgical law and the observance of the "laws of sacred art";[2] and there is quite a body of law about images in the Code (canon 1279) and in decisions of S.R.C.[3] Certain general principles can, however, be deduced from the nature and purpose of sacred art,[4] from liturgical law about church furnishings, and from the general canons of decorative art, to aid the architect or artist who has to deal with the difficult problems of church decoration.

I. The Meaning and Purpose of Decoration

To decorate means to adorn, embellish, complete and enhance the existing harmony and beauty of a building, or of its furniture. The purpose of decorating a church is to add beauty and dignity to God's

[1] C.E. I, xii, deals with this temporary adornment of a church.
[2] See pp. 32 *sqq.*
[3] See p. 96.
[4] Pp. 30 *sqq.*

house, to the increase of His glory and that of His saints, to provide a fitter setting for the performance of the Sacred Liturgy. It is to create a milieu ever more apt for public worship, by creating for the people the "atmosphere" of a church, that atmosphere of austere dignity, of calm recollection in which they may find repose and peaceful contentment which will lead them to a deeper understanding of the mysteries of the faith, and raise their minds to the contemplation of spiritual things.[5]

The decoration of a church should be a silent sermon, emphasizing the sacred character and divine purpose of the edifice, speaking to the worshippers' faith, and elevating their thoughts and affections to the supernatural.

II. Decoration Is Part of the Architectural Plan

The permanent decoration of a church is part of the whole architectural scheme—is all part, really, of the Sacred Liturgy, flowing from this and in complete harmony with it. It should follow a carefully thought out plan—devised with theological correctness, a due sense of harmony and proportion, an appreciation of what is appropriate—of a competent and liturgically trained architect or artist, or both. This plan should be based on sound principles concerning the liturgical purpose of a church and its parts, so that the finished church may be in full accord with "the mind of the Church" and effectively give its message to all who enter it.

III. Some General Principles of Decoration

Writing about design,[6] Pugin said: "The two great rules for design are these: (1) that there should be no features about a building which are not necessary for convenience, construction or propriety; (2) that all ornament should consist of enrichment of the essential construction of a building." Isn't this second norm another way of saying that a builder may ornament construction but never construct ornament? "Let new churches," says[7] the Instruction of the Holy Office on

---

[5] Cf. the Council of Trent on the purpose of the ceremonial of the Mass (Sess. 22, Cap. V).
[6] *True Principles of Pointed or Christian Architecture*, p. 1.
[7] § 11.

Sacred Art, (1952) "be resplendent for the beauty of their lines, abhorring all deceitful ornament." "The secret of beauty is in logical construction, namely in the exact proportion and perfect harmony of the parts among themselves, and in their correspondence with the whole and with the function of the sacred edifice."[8] "Care must be exercised not to nullify the potentialities of the architectural design, and not to conceal or falsify the construction by the decorative ornamentation. The scheme should be so conceived that a grand harmony of line and colour is effected for the whole edifice, so that nothing can be added or taken away without producing a discordant note that would ruin the effect of the whole. The general scheme of colour decoration must be one that co-ordinates with the architectural style of the surroundings, and emphasizes the strength of pier and wall, the rhythm of line and proportion, and the character of leaf and chevron, capital and moulding."[9]

There is much beauty in plain surfaces and good lines (both vertical and horizontal), and these should not be broken up, as they freqently are by fussy "ornament."[10] "Lines and surfaces are two component parts of a fine perspective," wrote Mgr. Nabuco, "the more one breaks them, the more architecture loses. Give me lines that I can see through, surfaces where my eye can rest."

In general church ornamentation should be strong—a simple and bold design tells best when viewed at a distance—purposeful, sober and clear (not enigmatic). It should be centered on the high altar and have its source there.

IV. THE QUALITIES OF CHURCH DECORATION

A study of the "laws of sacred art" and of the prescriptions of the Church regarding ecclesiastical equipment suggests that church decoration should have these qualities:

(1) *Dignity*, befitting the church as a *sacred* edifice dedicated to the Triune God, the place of sacrifice, the abode of the Blessed Sacrament, the house of prayer. There is no place in church ornamenta-

[8] Costantini, *Fede ed Arte*, II, p. 97.
[9] Weber, *Catholic Church Buildings*, p. 246.
[10] Scattering crosses about in profusion does not make a building or object any more sacred, and it tends to lessen respect for the sacred emblem.

tion for the trivial, the petty, the tawdry, the vulgar, the theatrical, the worldly.

(2) *Sincerity and truth,* all pretence (so suggestive of theatrical "props") must be rigorously excluded, no more imitation "marble," imitation "candles" (souches), artificial flowers and all the rest. "All vulgar tawdriness, every hint of imitation or deception, and all useless profusion of white marble, must be strictly eschewed. Onyx and lacquered brass[11] should be used sparingly, while cheap, tinselly and gaudy effects in white and gold should be rigidly barred."[12]

Traditionally the decoration of a church is graded, being, naturally, more splendid in greater churches, simpler in smaller churches and chapels (and so the pretentious is excluded). It is also graded within the church itself, and, normally, it is the sanctuary—the setting of the high altar, the focal point of the church—the chapel of the Blessed Sacrament[13] (when distinct from the sanctuary), the baptistery and, because of their liturgical function, the ambons that should be the most ornate. The decoration of the sanctuary should be the most sumptuous of the whole church and, normally,[14] Christocentric, with special reference to the Mass. In medieval times the decoration of the apse was concerned chiefly with the Divine Persons, the Second Person throned in majesty as a ruler of all (*Pantocrator, Majestas*), surrounded by adoring angels and worshipping apostles and other saints (including the Titular); the First and Third Persons depicted by their symbols. Another favourite design was the Etimasy (*Hetoimasia,* i.e., an empty throne surmounted by a cross; it was the iconographic symbol of the Last Judgment). For the Lady Chapel our Lady enthroned (*Panagia*), having on her knee her Child and surrounded by angels and saints, is the most suitable theme. Obviously, symbols of the Blessed Eucharist are most fitting as elements of ornamentation in the sanctuary. "The architecture and the decoration of the sanctuary should be so designed that the eye will not be distracted but rather drawn to the altar and to the action of the Eucharistic

---

[11] A poor modern substitute for gold.   [12] Weber, *op. cit.,* p. 245.
[13] C.E. I, xii, 8, speaks of it as "praecellentissimus ac nobilissimus omnium locus in ecclesia."
[14] The scheme of decoration may also be centered on the Titular of the church and high altar.

sacrifice. Where figured paintings or mosaics adorn the sanctuary, these should represent ideas drawn from the Canon of the Mass, i.e., from the *Sursum corda* to the final doxology. . . . The terminal wall should not be adorned with figured paintings that bear no direct relation to the Eucharistic sacrifice or to the theme of the total liturgical year. . . . In all cases the representation should not be of historical events[15] but of static motives."[16] "While this implies the perfectly correct solution of leaving out all figurative decoration behind the altar, even to the degree of complete emptiness, in order to throw the liturgy into its all-important focus, it leaves the alternative of right decoration: a subsumption of the totality of the sacred cycle of the Church year, but not episodes from sacred history or lives of saints."[17] In side chapels (or in other parts of the church outside the sanctuary) a suitable source of inspiration for decoration may be found in the life of the saint in whose honour the church or chapel is built. Decorative motifs drawn from non-liturgical sources (e.g., from the titles of our Lady in the Litany of Loreto) are less suited for the decoration of the sanctuary itself.

For the baptistery there is a treasure house of ideas for decoration in St. John's rebirth imagery and St. Paul's resurrection symbolism concerning Baptism, and in the liturgical text of the rite of baptism and the hallowing of the baptismal water on Easter eve. The mortuary chapel—the scene of so much grief—can, by the theme of its decoration, bring consolation to the mourning: that death does not mean extinction, but transformation and glorification by entry into life eternal: *vita mutatur non tollitur*.[18]

V. COLOR IN CHURCH DECORATION

Colour is, obviously, a very important element in church decoration. Its correct use in creating the "atmosphere" of a Catholic church—joyous, calm, austere yet splendid—with the right emphasis on its significant parts (the high altar and the baptistery), and the proper degree of restraint, is a task for the expert. The liturgical

[15] Unless required by the Title of the church, e.g., the Nativity, the Assumption.
[16] Directives of the German Episcopate on church building (edited by Fr. Theodor Klauser; see *Orate Fratres*, Dec. 29) and in appendix of this book.
[17] Rev. H. A. Reinhold in *Liturgical Arts*, Feb. 1950.   [18] Preface of the Dead.

aspect of colour is, however, often overlooked. Quite a simple building can receive a wealth of lovely colour, which will vary and so will never pall, in the place where it ought to be paramount—the sanctuary—through the altar frontal, the tabernacle conopaeum, a textile dorsal and the carpet.

CHAPTER VII

Lighting and Heating of a Church

THE general plan of a church must take into account the questions of lighting, heating and seating.

LIGHTING

Daylight lighting is a matter for the architect to plan. The high altar must be well lighted, preferably by windows set deeply in the walls at either side;[1] and it should be possible for people present at a function to read their books without difficulty in any part of the church set aside for them. It is well to avoid a window (unless it be of dark stained glass) at the east end of the church—if the high altar is there—unless it be placed very high above the floor, to avoid the glare of the morning sun shining into the eyes of the priest at the altar or of the people, while leaving the altar in comparative darkness. It is also almost impossible to prevent a civory or tester crossing an east window and partly hiding it. As a church is a place of quietude and recollection, windows are normally placed fairly high up in the walls to prevent worshippers looking out and to lessen noise and distraction from without.

About artificial lighting; this is used for (1) necessity, (2) ornamentation,[2] (3) cultual purposes and mystical reasons.[3]

---

[1] Light from such a source will illumine the altar without shining directly into the eyes of the congregation.
[2] When skilfully used it can display, and even emphasize, the beauty of the architecture, painting and sculpture of a church.
[3] Cf. C.E. I, xii, 17.

History

From at least the 4th century, artificial light has been used in churches not only for practical needs, but also as an ornament (for splendour, solemnity, festivity), for symbolical reasons (light is a symbol of joy, of faith, glory, etc., and also of Christ) and for cultual purposes (to give honour and express reverence, and to excite devotion). Because of their symbolism liturgical tradition has always required two substances as the source of light for cultual use, i.e., beeswax and olive oil, and in the early Church these were amongst the offerings made at Mass by the people, or money for their purchase. In addition to the use of lights for cultual and symbolical reasons at the *Lucernarium* and at the Sunday vigil offices, Easter, Pentecost, Candlemas and *dies natalis* of a martyr were great feasts of light from the 4th and 5th centuries. Lamps, not only of earthenware but of gold, silver, or bronze, richly ornamented, were used in churches in great numbers. There were chandeliers and huge standard candlesticks to hold wax candles, and massive *coronae*[4]—of wonderful and intricate designs of great beauty, adorned with Christian emblems (the cross, the Christus monogram, the fish, anchor, dove, lamb, etc.) hung from chains around the sanctuary or from the roof of the civory. Other types of lamps and candlesticks—some of them with hundreds of lights—were the *pharus,* the *cantharus, gabatha, cicendala.* The emperor Constantine gave to the Church of St. John Lateran in Rome 162 gold chandeliers containing 8,000 lights, while Pope Adrian I (772-795) gave the same church a *corona* holding 1,365 candles. Lights were burned before altars from the 4th century, and before images from the 7th; while from the 3rd century they were carried in funeral processions and from the 4th burned around tombs, especially those of the martyrs.

Law

The law about lights in church contained in the rubrics is, naturally, the traditional law about the use of oil and candles. Modern methods of illumination call for new rules, which have been given by

[4] A *corona,* or crown of lights, was a circlet—single, double or even treble, connected with ornate chains—with prickets for candles or holders for oil lamps (p. 216).

decisions of S.R.C. These have been based on three chief principles:
(1) that electric (or gas) light may not—apart from real necessity—
be used for cultual purposes; (2) that the lighting used for ornament
and greater splendour must have nothing of the puerile or theatrical
about it; (3) that any system of lighting a church must respect the
sanctity and gravity of the sacred place and the dignity of Catholic
worship.[5]

The Church admits the use of electricity or gas in church —"according to the prudent judgment of the Ordinary"[6]—for necessary
lighting; and even for ornamentation, and for greater splendour, on
occasion, provided that there is no suggestion of the theatrical or the
puerile in its use.[7] Hence all theatrical "effects" (spot lights, coloured
lamps, etc.) must be studiously avoided. The scheme of lighting is a
question for the architect and a consulting electrical engineer who is
a specialist in church lighting. The utility lighting must provide for
reading at the altar, in the pulpit and confessional, and by the people
in their places (shaded pendant lamps, hung rather low, are, possibly,
the best for this). The lighting for splendour should be concentrated
on the high altar, the focal point of the church, and may, perhaps, be
effected by light from hidden sources.[8] "And the same method may
be used with due caution to light up pictures or statues with a soft and
sufficient light."[9] Excessive lighting or flat, even lighting of the entire
building, and spots of light or glare, should be eschewed.

For practical purposes (cleaning, repair, etc.), it is important to
have the lights within easy reach, when feasible.

For ornamental lighting it might be possible to use fittings that
recall the traditional *coronae* of lights that lent splendour to the sanctuary on great occasions from the 4th century onwards. Church
fittings should be dignified and simple (so that they may be kept clean
without undue difficulty). The types of fittings used for secular purposes (street lighting, theatres, hotels and the rest) should be avoided.
The scheme of lighting will, naturally, vary with the church for

[5] Cf. S.R.C. 4322.
[6] S.R.C. 4206.
[7] Ibid., and 3859, 4275, 4322.
[8] Cf. Instruction of the Cardinal Vicar for Rome (1932), § 9.
[9] Ibid. Coloured lights around niches of the images of saints, over altars, are forbidden. (S.R.C. 4322.)

which it is planned, and it ought to be possible to design for dignified beauty, combined with utility and economy in maintenance and running cost.

For cultural purposes—i.e., lights on the altar during a function, or before the Most Holy Sacrament, or in front of relics or sacred images —the Church allows only pure wax or natural (olive) oil.[10] Accordingly, gas or electric lighting in any form (e.g., imitation candles) may not be used for cultural purposes; nor for splendour *on* the altar—in addition to the liturgical lighting (candles)—or in its immediate ambit (e.g., on the altar gradine, if there is one).[11] It is expressly forbidden to illuminate with electricity the interior of the tabernacle or throne, or put a light behind the monstrance, when the Blessed Sacrament is exposed, that the Sacred Host may be more clearly seen.[12]

HEATING

There are no liturgical laws about heating a church. It is a matter for the architect and a consulting engineer, who has had practical experience of the problems connected with the heating of a church. Not only has provision to be made for the comfort of the congregation attending a function, but also for the continual maintenance of a certain degree of heat all through the seasons of damp and cold, to preserve the fabric of the church and its contents from damage.

[10] Only under pressure of grave necessity, and with special leave of the Ordinary, is electricity to replace oil; and adulterated materials, such as candles not purely wax, or vegetable oils, are permitted only because of shortage or high cost of the real thing.
[11] S.R.C. 4086, 4097, 4206, 4210, 4322. A small portable electric lamp would not be excluded, if necessary for reading at the altar, since its purpose is utilitarian, not cultual.
[12] S.R.C. 4275. Cf. 2613[5]; I.C. § VI.

Chapter VIII

Church Seating

I n planning a church, apart from the seating for a bishop (his throne or faldstool[1]), or for the sacred ministers and their assistants, there is the question of seating for the clergy (in choir) and for the congregation.

I. The Sedilia

For the sacred ministers (celebrant, deacon and subdeacon, and sometimes an assistant priest), apart from bishops and certain higher prelates who have special pontifical privileges and use a faldstool, the only seat appointed by the rubrics is a movable bench, long enough to seat three persons comfortably, with no divisions (making any distinction between its three occupants), without arms and uncanopied (*sedile* or *scamnum*[2]). This bench must be placed on the floor, not on a platform so that it is approached by steps.[3] It may have a low back, over which the vestments of the ministers can hang, when they sit, to avoid crushing them.

By a series of decrees[4] S.R.C. has forbidden the use of armchairs, or separate chairs of a domestic pattern, by the sacred ministers, since

---

[1] See pp. 93, 243.
[2] C.E. I, vii, 4; ix, 1; xii, 22: II, ii, 6; iii, 4; viii, 36; xviii, 3; xxvii, 13. I.C. § xxv.
[3] S.R.C. 2135[2]; cf. 2027[2].
[4] S.R.C. 320, 743, 2153[3], 2621[6], 3104[4], 3804[11], and 4214, which confirms previous decisions. Cf. I.C. § xxv.

the former are reserved for higher prelates, and the latter are unsuitable for liturgical use.

This bench is, normally, *paratum* (*ornatum*),[5] i.e., covered with a cloth.[6] This should not be of silk (which is reserved for prelates). Its colour may be of the Office of the day, or green (violet for penitential days). For Tenebrae and on Good Friday, and for Requiem functions, the bench is uncovered.[7] Cushions are not permitted on the bench (except for a prelate, or for the canon Hebdomadary in the absence of the Bishop).[8]

The bench is placed, normally, on the Epistle side of the chancel,[9] facing the side steps of the high altar (usually the sacred ministers come down to it from the footpace by the shorter way). For a pontifical service at the faldstool it is usually more forward in the chancel (so that the sacred ministers are not behind the prelate-celebrant).

The rubrics make no mention of fixed sedilia in stone attached to the wall of the chancel on the Epistle side (which were in common use abroad, and fairly general in England by the 13th century), but tradition allows their use. These seats must not, however, be on different levels (so that the celebrant is higher than the deacon and the subdeacon); nor may they be canopied. While such sedilia are often a pleasing architectural feature in the chancel, they are not very comfortable in a cold and damp climate.

II. STOOLS

Undraped wooden stools (*scabella*) are used during liturgical functions, not only for the lesser ministers (e.g., the acolytes and other servers),[10] but for high dignitaries. They are used, at the Bishop's throne, for his assistant priest and canon deacons;[11] and in the sanctuary by the assistants in copes at solemn Vespers[12] (or these may use small benches covered in green). They are even used by bishops and

---

[5] C.E. I, ix, 1; II, ii, 6.
[6] C.E. I, xii, 22; II, iii, 4; xviii, 3.
[7] C.E. II, xxv, 1. Cf. II, xi, 1. For Requiem functions it may be covered in black or violet. (S.R.C. 4172[1].)
[8] S.R.C. 20797, 4172[2].
[9] R.G. xvii, 6; C.E. I, xii, 22, etc.; S.R.C. 1118.
[10] These may also sit on uncovered small backless benches.
[11] C.E., I, vii, 2, 4; viii, 2. S.R.C. 541, 2621[2].
[12] C.E. II, ii, 6; iii, 6.

other high prelates at the five solemn pontifical absolutions of the dead,[13] and other functions. The celebrant at Vespers, or at a sung Mass, may use a stool, instead of the *sedile;* or to preach from the Gospel corner of the footpace, e.g., to explain the ceremonial of Holy Week.[14] A stool is also mentioned in the rubrics as a stand for the celebrant's book at Matins[15] and at the Litanies on Holy Saturday, if there are no cantors.[16]

III. Seating for the Clergy

As the clergy sit at certain parts of the Liturgy, in greater churches (cathedrals, collegiate and conventual churches) sitting accommodation is provided for them by permanent stalls—in rows facing one another—on each side of the chancel. These are first mentioned in the 11th century and became common from the 12th. In time they were raised on a dais, with a dorsal, and became very elaborate in design, with rich carving and raised ornamentation, so that they are a notable feature of some of the great churches. Their use is reserved to the canons[17] and beneficiaries in cathedrals and collegiate churches; to the monks or friars in conventual ones. They are constructed in rows, each row higher than the one in front of it. The highest row, at the back, is that of greatest dignity and, in a cathedral, must not be higher than the Bishop's throne.[18] In lesser churches movable benches, with a back and kneeler (*subsellia*), are used for the clergy.[19]

While stalls are never covered—except the stall of the prelate or canon celebrant at certain functions[20]—these benches, being less ornate, may be covered in green cloth (not silk), or in violet for penitential or Requiem functions.

IV. Seating for the Congregation

History

In the early centuries there were no seats in church, except some

---

[13] C.E. II, xi, 16.
[14] M.R. IV, i, etc.
[15] C.E. II, vi, 5.
[16] M.R. VI, ii, § III, 5.
[17] Cf. S.R.C. 175, 2220[6], 2448[2].
[18] S.R.C. 2049[25].
[19] Cf. C.E. I, xii, 7; xviii, 7.
[20] E.g., C.E. II, iv.

stone benches (which were draped during a function) around the Bishop's throne, in the apse, for some of the higher clergy. The clergy in general stood during ceremonies up to about the 11th century. In some places there were a few benches, along the wall or around the piers, that were used by the aged or the sick, or by some of the women worshippers.

While benches for the entire congregation came into use in some places about the 13th century, they were not common until the 15th and not general until the 16th. These benches were mere forms, without a back and without kneelers, and so were movable. The use of chairs is quite modern. Gradually, the benches became bigger and more comfortable, and sometimes were even elaborately ornamented, with carved ends, etc. They also ceased to be easily movable. In early centuries the sexes were separated in church by a curtain, and while this gradually fell out of use, the separation of men and women has lasted, in some parts, even to this day. Indeed Canon Law (1262, § 1) states that "it is desirable that, in keeping with the discipline of old, women should be separated from men in church." However this separation is not enforced.[21]

Law

The Canon Law[22] and the rubrics[23] permit of special seats in church for persons of high rank, public officials, patrons and the founders of a church, chapel or benefice, but in accordance with liturgical law, and never within the chancel.[24]

Usually the seating in a church is an ugly and conspicuous feature. It is a necessary evil, and the only thing to do is to strive to make it as little unlovely as possible, and best fitted to its purpose, by being at least moderately comfortable. This should be tested by actual trial. Chairs—though noisy, and disorderly unless battened together—are certainly better in small churches or in oratories. Their mobility is

[21] Cf. C.E. I, v. 7.
[22] C.J.C. 1263, § 1; 1455, § 3 (cf. 1448).
[23] C.E. I, xi, 12; xiii, 13.
[24] S.R.C. has insisted over and over again, that, while lay persons may be admitted momentarily into the chancel, they may not (apart from Apostolic privilege) have a place within it during a function. Cf. S.R.C. 159, 175, 275, 959, 1258[2], 1288, 3388[3].

very useful, e.g., to increase the width of passages or provide extra chancel space on the occasion of a special function; and they make cleaning much easier.

Church chairs need to be very strong and intelligently designed for their special purpose—with a hinged kneeler (deep and wide enough for the comfort of a full-sized man), upholstered in leather, rubber or some other suitable material. The top of the back of the chair should be flat (so that the person kneeling behind may comfortably rest his arms on it) and slightly hollowed out. There should be a ledge for a prayerbook; and, lower down, the cross rails arranged so high that a man's hat can be placed on them and not be injured by the feet of the person in front. Most important of all, the rails that cross a chair under the seat must be so placed that ample space is left free into which the feet of the person kneeling in front can fit without difficulty. With chairs neither hassocks nor kneeling-pads are desirable —they are untidy and get very dirty in use.

Benches are ugly in appearance, as a rule, but are a necessary evil in a large church.[25] They are best plain in design, for practical reasons, and the back should have a flat top. A place should be provided underneath the seat for a book, a man's hat, gloves, etc. A good-sized seat is about 18 inches off the ground; some 14 inches deep, with a slope in the back of not more than an inch between the seat and the top, and allowing a space of some 20 inches at least for each person. Benches should be open at the ends, with no doors; and an umbrella rack, with a drip pan, at each end is very useful. The kneelers—some 6 inches or 7 inches off the floor—should be hinged (to permit cleaning under the seats), and upholstered in leather, rubber or some other easily cleaned material. The spacing between benches is very important to allow good room for the feet of the persons kneeling in front; the rows should not be less than 3 feet back to back.

The floor underneath the seats should not be damp or cold. In planning the seating the centre passage down the nave should never

[25] "Liturgically speaking, fixed pews are a nuisance; they turn the church into a lecture hall or auditorium. They not only immobilize the congregation physically to a high degree, but they bring in a psychological element of immobilization and regimentation. The congregation becomes an audience, spectators. The celebrating throngs are gone . . ." (H. A. Reinhold, *Speaking of Liturgical Architecture,* p. 18).

be narrower than 5 feet—so much the better if it can be wider[26]—
and side aisle passages never less than 3 feet wide. Seats should be so
placed that none of the congregation will have his back to the high
altar, or the altar of the Blessed Sacrament. The front row of seating
should be well away from the Communion rail, leaving a wide gap;
and some rows of benches, nearest the chancel, should be movable (or
shorter), in case more sanctuary space is needed for a special occasion,
or room for a coffin or catafalque.[27] Benches are usually yellow-brown
in colour. Why need they always be so dull? There is no reason why,
when they are not made of select wood (e.g., mahogany), they might
not be painted, or, better still, stained (so that the grain of the wood
is visible) in a colour suitable to the church.[28] It is unwise to overseat
a church; there are great advantages in having as many open spaces
as possible.

[26] It would need to be much wider to permit the free passage of three persons
(the celebrant and his two assistants) abreast.
[27] This, however (when not in a mortuary chapel), is better placed some distance
down the church (*in medio ecclesiae*), not in front of all the worshippers.
[28] A green *stain* (not paint), of a suitable tint, can be very beautiful and restful.

CHAPTER IX

Confessionals

U p to the 16th century the confessor used a seat in the open church, and the penitent knelt beside him at the beginning and for the absolving, but sat beside him for the confession itself. The confessor at the absolution laid his hand on the penitent. Only in the 17th century was a grille introduced. It was probably due to St. Charles Borromeo, who, at the first Council of Milan, 1565, ordered a partition (*tabella*) between the confessor and the penitent.

Law

The present law[1] is that the proper place to hear confessions is a church, or a public or semi-public oratory.[2] The confessional (*sedes confessionalis*) for women's confessions is always to be placed in an open and conspicuous position, and normally (*generatim*) in a church, or in a public or semi-public oratory set aside for the confessions of women. The confessional is to be fitted with a fixed, close-meshed grille between the penitent and the confessor.

The confessionals nowadays are considered part of the edifice and are planned to fit into it, being built in stone or brick (which, however, will be cold and possibly damp) into recesses, or constructed as furniture in a style in keeping with the church.

[1] C.J.C. 908, 909; R.R. IV, i, 7, 8.

While confessionals must be in the open and conspicuous—and not relegated to dark corners (because of the law and because of the importance of the sacrament of Penance)—a certain amount of discreet privacy is desirable for the penitent. The confessionals should, when feasible, be recessed, and not encumber the passages. A good position for them is near the church doors (for the convenience of the penitents, and for traditional, symbolical reasons—penitents in early days remained in the narthex and away from the altar). When there are several confessionals they should not be too close to one another. In a large church they are often suitably placed in side chapels.

In a large church the confessionals are double-sided; sometimes they take the form of small rooms adjoining an ambulatory, or a corridor of the presbytery. Confessionals should be properly ventilated and heated, and provision made for light for the confessor. For him a comfortable seat should be provided (not too wide, so that he can hear at each side without having to lean over), with arm-rests, and ample room for his feet, under which the floor should be wooden, and covered with a mat to prevent undue cold.

The best form of door for the confessor's part of the confessional (if it opens out into the church) seems to be a half door for the lower part and two wooden shutters[3] for the upper part, enabling him, if necessary, to open them to speak to anyone, or to control waiting penitents, such as children. There may be an orifice in the grille so that the penitent may pass a note to the confessor (as deaf or dumb penitents sometimes do), or that he may pass a leaflet or picture to his penitent. A veil over the grille is not prescribed by general law; it does add to the privacy of the penitent, but after a time it becomes dirty and very insanitary.

On the penitent's side of the confessional there should be no step, a self-closing door,[4] a wide kneeler with an arm-rest at a convenient height. There should be room for a full-grown person to kneel in comfort, and not be obliged to protrude his feet through the door. The penitent's part of the confessional should be duly ventilated and slightly

[2] Normally, confessions are not heard in a private oratory.
[3] Curtains become soiled and torn after a time.
[4] Curtains suffice, but they get into bad condition, and they give the penitent less privacy. Obviously, it is better that the confessional be soundproof.

lighted (so that he can see where to kneel, etc.). Beside or above the grille it is becoming to hang a crucifix. It is usual nowadays to furnish a confessional with a bell, connected with the presbytery or vestry, to summon the confessor.

In a large church a special confessional—either behind a glass partition or in the sacristy—is provided for the confession of deaf persons.

CHAPTER X

The Pulpit and Ambo

T HERE are only passing references in the rubrics—in C.E. alone (I, vii, 4; xii, 18; xxii, 3. II, viii, 51; xi, 10)—to the pulpit (*pulpitum*[1] *sive ambo*), but much that is said about the ambo[2] is applicable to it. C.J.C. 1184, § 4, speaks of it as "cathedra sive suggestus." (Cf. C.E. I, xxii, 4.)

THE PULPIT

History

At first the Bishop preached from his throne (*cathedra*) in the apse, or from a faldstool placed on the footpace, as he still may do (C.E. II, viii, 48). Sometimes, if the throne or footpace were too distant or the civory impeded the view, the preacher went to the ambo. The priest preached from the altar steps or the ambo. Then in the 12th or 13th century—when the Gospel was no longer chanted in the ambo and sermons were preached apart from the Liturgy—a separate pulpit came into use.[3] Often it was placed well down the nave, because of a crowded congregation. At first the pulpit was a simple structure—sometimes it took the form of a tribune corbelled out on the pier of the sanctuary arch and entered by a stairway through the pier—but gradually it grew in size and became elaborately ornamented (especially from the 16th century).

---

[1] *Pulpitum* = platform, stage. It is used in C.E. (II, v, 5; viii, 45; xxi, 15) also for a lectern.
[2] See p. 79.
[3] Not commonly in England until the 14th century. The pulpit was used earlier in the monastic refectory than in the church.

In the 15th and 16th centuries appeared the canopy or sounding board (which was not in general use, however, until later) and that, too, in time became very elaborate and ornate. In the 17th and 18th centuries many pulpits were very high, possibly because of the use of galleries in churches, and of high-backed pews, which hid the audience unless the preacher were well elevated.

Law

Although from the liturgical point of view the pulpit is an important item of church furniture,[4] there is no liturgical law governing either its construction, permanent ornamentation or position. It is a question of practical convenience and good taste. The pulpit should be designed on a scale proportionate to the size of the church and in harmony with the style of its architecture. Very large and very elaborate pulpits are now frowned upon—the pulpit should not attract attention away from the high altar, the focal point of the edifice. It should be simple and dignified.

The pulpit may be made of any becoming material (stone, metal, wood, even brick), suitably ornamented, e.g., with symbols connected with its purpose (symbols of the evangelists, scenes from the O.T. or N.T. concerned with the giving of God's law and Christ's preaching and teaching) and apposite inscriptions.

The traditional shape of a pulpit is round or polygonal (hexagonal or octagonal). It should not be too high, but should be roomy enough for the comfort of the preacher, with sufficient space for kneeling. For this a kneeler or hassock should be provided; and a folding (hinged) seat is convenient.

The balustrade should be solid (not open, it is distracting to view the feet of a preacher), some 3 feet 2 inches to 3 feet 6 inches high, with a flat top (5 or 6 inches wide) to enable the preacher to place on it his biretta, spectacles, etc.

Attached to the pulpit—but removable—it is convenient to have an adjustable reading desk, with a shaded light over it, the switch within the preacher's reach.

If there is a sounding board—its value is challenged, and nowadays

[4] Our Divine Lord is silent in the tabernacle but speaks from the pulpit.

there are microphones, loud-speakers, etc., in large churches—it should be constructed for use and not ornament (a tester is not a mark of honour over a pulpit as it is over an altar, a baptismal font, or a throne), and so should be not unduly big or over-ornate.

A safe and comfortable stairs—usually out of sight—should lead to the pulpit, and it should have a door capable of being firmly fastened, lest an orator might fall out, if he stepped backwards.

Position of the Pulpit

There is no law about this, but the traditional and correct position is on the Gospel side of the church, for the pulpit is the successor of the ambo and from it the Gospel is proclaimed; and on the Gospel side the preacher can face the Sacred Ministers at High Mass, and will have at his right hand the greater part of the congregation. It is from the Gospel side that the Bishop now preaches from his throne, or the celebrant on the footpace addresses the people. The pulpit should, when possible, be within or close to the chancel—the sermon is part of the Sacred Liturgy, and should be linked up with the chancel and the altar whence proceeds the teaching of the Church. It must not, however, be so placed as to impede a clear view of the high altar.

In a cathedral or abbatial church, however—unless the throne be in the apse—the pulpit is usually on the Epistle side, so that the preacher may face the Bishop or Abbot.

The exact spot on which a pulpit is best placed is where it does not impede a full view of the high altar or sanctuary, and in which the preacher can be seen by as many as possible of his audience and be heard by all. This spot should be located by actual experiment, using a temporary movable pulpit.

In a very small church a pulpit is not really needed; the preacher speaks from the footpace, or from inside the altar rail, and if he needs support a movable lectern can be placed there for him.

Adornment of the Pulpit

On great feasts the pulpit (not its canopy, if there be one) may be adorned with silk hangings of the colour of the day.[5] At a Requiem

[5] C.E. I, xii, 18.

function the pulpit may be draped in black cloth.[6] For a sermon on the Passion, on Maundy Thursday evening or on Good Friday, the pulpit is to be undraped.[7] Sometimes a cushion (green is the most correct colour), with tassels at its corners, is laid on the ledge of the pulpit. It is becoming to hang a crucifix behind the preacher, if this be feasible.

THE AMBO

The ambo or ambon (*pulpitum, suggestus, tribunal, analogium*) is a kind of pulpit or elevated reading desk used in many of the early Christian churches, and still to be seen in some of the very old churches of Rome, e.g., St. Clement's, St. Mary's in Cosmedin, St. Lawrence's, Ara Caeli. It is referred to in several parts of C.E. (e.g., I, xii, 18; II, viii, 40, 45, 51).

History

There are references to the ambo in liturgical history as early as the 3rd and 4th centuries; and the chanting of the Gospel from the ambo is often spoken of in the 8th, 9th and 10th centuries, when the ambo was in fairly general use.

Gradually it dropped out of use (except in Spain), when the practice of singing the Gospel *in plano* prevailed,[8] and the pulpit became the ordinary place for preaching; and it seems to have fallen into general disuse after about the 13th century. The use of the ambo may have been inspired by Old Testament use (cf. II Esdras 8.4; III Esdras 9.42) for Scripture readings, but, in any case, it was natural that an elevated place should be used for public reading and speaking.

The ambo was used for: (1) the chanting of the Scriptural parts of the Mass (the Epistle and Gospel—and on its steps, the Gradual, Alleluia, or Tract); (2) the lessons of the Divine Office; (3) announcements[9] and preaching;[10] (4) the *Praeconium Paschale* (and so the candlestick for the Paschal candle was sometimes permanently attached to the ambo).

[6] C.E. II, xi, 10.   [7] S.R.C. 2891[3].
[8] There is no reference to the ambo in the rubrics of the Missal.
[9] Cf. C.E. I, vii, 4, regarding the announcement of indulgences.
[10] Cf. p. 76.

Ambos were constructed in stone or wood, elaborately and beautifully decorated (with marbles, mosaic, precious metals, etc.). Sometimes there was only one ambo, in the middle of the church, with
double stairs leading to it, and divided into two parts (the Epistle
being sung facing the altar or east end of the church; the Gospel,
facing the people at the west end). More often there were two
ambos, one on the north side[11]—higher and more ornate—for the
singing of the Gospel; the other on the south side for the chanting of
the Epistle. This smaller and less ornate ambo was sometimes divided
into two parts, and the lower part was used by a lector or cantor.

Law

Ambos, placed at the north and south corners of the chancel, may
still be used for the singing of the Epistle and Gospel[12] in a solemn
non-Requiem Mass,[13] and for the Exsultet on Holy Saturday.[14] They
may be built of any becoming material (even brick) and ornamented
by sculptured images or symbols, or with mosaic, etc.; and are generally furnished with a reading stand (the spread eagle is a traditional
design). The ambo on the Gospel side will be bigger[15] (during the
singing of the Gospel the subdeacon stands at the deacon's right) and
more ornate than the other one. C.E. supposes the ambos, on great
feasts, to be decorated with silk hangings of the colour of the day.[16]
The restoration of the use of ambos in greater churches, where High
Mass is often celebrated, and where Latin is understood (e.g., in conventual churches, in the oratories of seminaries) is much to be desired.
Their use helps to unite the congregation more closely with the
Sacred Liturgy.

[11] Sometimes on the south side, when the celebrant at the altar faced the congregation.
[12] C.E. I, xii, 18; II, viii, 40, 45. Cf. S.R.C. 19², 3151, 3160.
[13] C.E. II, xi, 5.
[14] S.R.C. 4057³. In the new rite it is sung at a lectern placed before the Paschal
candle.
[15] If there is only one ambo it will be on the Gospel side (St. Charles Borromeo).
[16] C.E. I, xii, 18.

Chapter XI

The Rood

O N E of the notable features of medieval churches was the Rood or Triumphal Cross, a large crucifix—generally of wood—ornamented at the ends of the arms with the symbols of the four evangelists (a man, a lion, a calf and an eagle), and with the figure of Christ flanked by an image of our Lady and of St. John the Apostle (sometimes also by the images of other Apostles, of doctors of the Church, etc.). Often on the back of the cross were painted, at the extremities, the images of the four great doctors, and an image of the Blessed Virgin in the centre. This great cross was erected on a beam, or on a screen or loft, that ran between the nave and chancel, beneath the chancel arch, or was hung in this position. Sometimes the rood was suspended in the middle of the church. The antiquity of the rood is uncertain. Possibly is was derived from the representation of the cross—painted or in mosaic, but without the figure of the Crucified until about the 12th or 13th century—on the apse or main arch of churches, which was common from the 4th century. Lights used sometimes to be burned in a *corona* before the rood. There are references to this cross in the lives of the Popes of the 8th and subsequent centuries. The rood was common in the 13th and 14th centuries and widespread in the 15th. Most of these great crosses were destroyed at the Reformation in the 16th century,[1] and the practice of having a rood fell largely into desuetude. It is now being revived (e.g., the magnificent rood at Westminster Cathedral).

Law

There is no liturgical law about the rood. It was an object of popular veneration, but is not mentioned in the liturgical books and has no liturgical function.[2] It can be a very decorative and impressive feature, especially in a large church.

[1] Not one English example of the rood remains *in situ* (Cox, *English Church Furniture*, p. 94).
[2] In some places the procession on Palm Sunday used to halt before the rood, and salute the Crucified: *Ave rex noster.*

CHAPTER XII

Lustral Water Containers

T HERE are two kinds of lustral (or blessed) water containers, the fixed one (called stoup, or font), and the portable one. No reference to the former occurs, apparently, in the liturgical books.[1] The portable container—called *vas aquae benedictae,* with its sprinkler (*asperso-rium*)[2]—is referred to for the presentation of lustral water to a greater prelate at his entrance into a church (C.E. I, ii, 5; xv, 3, 4), for the Asperges ceremony on Sundays (C.E. I, xv, 4; II, xxx, 1; xxxi, 3. R.R. IX, ii and iii), and for the use of blessed water at many rites in the Pontifical and Roman Ritual.

History

The use of blessed water for exorcism, for the solace of the sick, etc., can be traced back to the 3rd century in the East and at least to the 5th or 6th in the West, and forms of blessing the water are found in sacramentaries of the 7th or 8th century. In the 8th and 9th centuries, at latest, arose the practice in monasteries and homes of sprinkling lustral water, and from this grew the use of blessed water in the rite of various blessings. The blessing and sprinkling of water in churches on Sundays goes back to at least the 9th century; possibly to the 7th or 8th century. The use by the faithful of lustral water on entering a

[1] R.R. IX, ii, 5, does refer to blessed water being taken away by the people to use in their homes, to sprinkle the sick, the fields, etc.
[2] In English "aspersorium" is used for the vessel of blessed water, and "aspergill (um)" for the sprinkler.

83

church may have arisen from the early practice of washing face and hands at the fountain (*cantharus, phiala*) that stood in the atrium of churches—and which contained unblessed water—before going into the sacred edifice;[3] or, more probably, it arose after the introduction of the Asperges ceremony in monasteries and churches.

At first only the portable aspersorium, often pail-shaped, was in use —made in stone, metal, ivory, terra-cotta and even glass or wood. Then, from about the 9th century, when the use of an ample atrium or vestibule began to die out, it became customary to put a portable aspersorium at the door of the church. It is not possible to say when fixed stoups succeeded portable ones at the door of churches in the West, perhaps not until the 11th or 12th century. Their form varied according to the style of the period. Often they were made like a baptismal font (a bowl sustained by a column or columns), sometimes they were excavated in the walls or pillars of the church, or rested on a console. Some were made in metal, from the 15th or 16th century.

The use of a brush sprinkler, with a metal handle, is late (14th or 15th century); of a metal ball, with a sponge within, is later still.

The traditional sprinkler is a sprig of hyssop,[4] palm, box or some similar plant. Hyssop is still prescribed in the rubrics for certain aspersions (e.g., at the blessing or consecration of a church; at the consecration of an altar).[5]

Law

There is no liturgical law about stoups or about the portable aspersorium. It is a question of what is traditional, practical, becoming.

For the fixed stoup the baptismal font form (without a cover), standing isolated, is very appropriate in large churches.[6] In smaller churches the niche form is suitable and saves space. The stoup should not be over-ornate, nor of a form that easily gathers dirt (hence the shell form is not suitable). To secure that the blessed water will always

[3] From the 4th and 5th centuries, when the faithful became numerous, they merely dipped a finger into the water.
[4] Cf. Numbers 19.18.
[5] Roman Pontifical. Cf. S.R.C. 3364[4].
[6] The use of lustral water is a reminder of baptism.

be absolutely clean—and this is of the highest importance—it is often useful to have in the font a movable container (say of earthenware or of a non-corroding metal) that can be easily emptied and cleaned. The use of a sponge in the font is most unhygienic. A stoup is placed at each entrance to the church and is more convenient when placed at the left side of the door as one enters. One is also put at the sacristy door.

The large font in a big church is a permanent feature, part of the structure, and should be so designed. When of stone this must be of a non-porous kind; if of metal this must be non-corroding.

For the portable aspersorium the usual form is a round container with a base on which to stand it and a handle by which to carry it. It is best made in silver, or in some metal silver-plated; but it may be in brass (bronze is preferable). The interior must be of a material not affected by salt water. The aspersorium should be simple in design and not unduly heavy. The best form of sprinkler is the sprig of a plant, but the usual brush form (if kept clean) is convenient, and much preferable to the ball form (with sponge) which cannot be kept properly clean and resembles a rattle.

CHAPTER XIII

The Holy Oils' Container[1]

THREE kinds of containers are in use for the Holy Oils: Chrism, the Oil of Catechumens, the Oil of the Sick, which are consecrated yearly by the Bishop of the diocese in his cathedral on Maundy Thursday: (1) the large *ampullae* in which the oils are consecrated, and in which the supply for each diocese is kept at the cathedral; (2) smaller containers in which the supply for each parish or church[2] for the year, is kept; (3) the oil "stocks," in which a small supply of each oil is kept by priests for the administration of the sacraments of Baptism, Extreme Unction and, possibly, Confirmation. These various containers should be made of silver, or at least of tin or pewter (not of any easily oxidizable metal, nor of glass), with firm, screw-on lids. Each container must be *clearly* marked in capital letters inscribed on it, C, B (=oleum baptismatis)[3] and I; or better CHR., BAPT. (or CAT.) and INF.[4]

The small oil stocks must each be large enough to allow the priest to put his thumb without difficulty into the stock, which contains cotton-wool saturated with the oil. It is convenient to have a single stock for the Oil of the Sick, and a combined, double stock for the other two

---

[1] Cf. C.E. I, vi, 2; *Pontificale Rom.* (Pars. III); R.R. II, i, 50-53; VI, i, 3.
[2] Some of the Oil of Catechumens and some Chrism will be needed for the hallowing of the baptismal water.
[3] This oil is also called "oleum sanctum" (OS).
[4] It is also useful to mark the name on the lid of each container.

86

oils. Each stock must be clearly marked with the name of the oil it contains.

It is not of obligation to bless the holy oil containers, but there is a special blessing provided for the purpose in R.R. IX, ix, 9.

THE AMBRY FOR THE HOLY OILS

The yearly supply of holy oil is to be kept in an ambry hung on, or built into, the wall in the chancel of the church, on either the Gospel or Epistle side.[5] This ambry made in either stone, metal or wood, is to be lined with silk; violet for Oil of the Sick alone, but white for the other Oils. The ambry is to be lockable, and may becomingly have a veil hung in front of it (not around it like the conopaeum of the tabernacle); violet in colour if only the Oil of the Sick is there, white and violet if the other oils are there also. On the wall, or on the door of the ambry, should be marked OLEA SACRA.

[5] S.R.C. 1260. The ambry might be in another part of the church, but it must be *in the church* (R.R. II, i, 53) ; some rubricians think this might include the sacristy.

Chapter XIV

The Sacrarium

T H E *sacrarium* or *piscina*[1] is a basin with a pipe running directly into the earth (or into some place where things other than sacred are not thrown) intended for the becoming disposal of sacred things such as water that has been used for ritual purposes (e.g., for the ceremonial washing of sacred linens; the water from the bowl in which the priest washes his first finger and thumb, after the distribution of Holy Communion), or the ashes of sacred or blessed objects which have been destroyed in a becoming manner by burning (e.g., cottonwool used to wipe away the holy oil after an anointing). The sacrarium is spoken of in *De Defectibus* of the Missal (X, 5, 6, 7, 12, 14, 15) and in R.R. V, ii, 8; VI, ii, 9.[2]

History

The sacrarium is mentioned from about the 9th century for the disposal of the water which the celebrant of Mass has used to cleanse the chalice and his hands (Leo IV, about 850, directed that a sacrarium should be built near the altar). It was Innocent III (1216) who first ordered that two piscinae be used, one for the wine and water with which the chalice was cleansed, the other for the water the celebrant used to wash his hands. Later he ruled that the priest should

---

[1] Both words have several other meanings also.
[2] The sacrarium of the baptistery is referred to in R.R. II, i, 5, 11; viii, 9.

drink the ablutions, but only gradually did this practice obtain, and it was not widespread until the 14th century.

Law

The sacrarium is normally of pedestal form (like a baptismal font) or is excavated in the wall (often with a shelf above the basin, which —when the sacrarium is in the chancel—can be used as a small credence).[3] In some of the medieval churches it was quite an architectural feature—encased with elaborate mouldings, sometimes surmounted by a canopy, etc. Normally, it should be a stone basin some 9 inches or more in diameter, and about 4 inches deep, with a *good sized* opening[4] (say 3 inches in diameter and covered with a wide-meshed little grille) leading into a pipe[5] which will conduct liquids or small solids directly into the earth (not into a drain used for other purposes), where a hole is made, filled with broken fragments of stone or brick, so that the water may soak into the ground. The sacrarium itself (the basin) should have a lockable cover, and be labelled "Sacrarium" or "Piscina" to prevent it being used for profane purposes.

By liturgical tradition the sacrarium is placed on the south side of the sanctuary (the Epistle side), close to the high altar, and in that position—if it is not too high—its shelf can be used as a (small) credence. It may also be placed in the sacristy.

[3] It is referred to in R.G. xx as "fenestella" (a small window-like niche). Such a shelf would be, say, 12 inches or 15 inches long by 6 inches to 9 inches deep.
[4] Sometimes solids (e.g., ashes, breadcrumbs used to cleanse the hands after the use of the Holy Oils) have to be disposed of into the sacrarium.
[5] The pipe may be of lead or copper or earthenware.

CHAPTER XV

The Organ and Choir

THE ORGAN

THE organ—at first a portable instrument—seems to have been used in churches since the 8th or 9th century. From about the 10th century its use to accompany vocal music in church was admitted, and the organ was in universal use by the 13th century. At that time, too, the large organ made its appearance. From the second half of the 15th century began improvements in the art of organ building, which have continued to the present day. From the 16th century the organ, in some churches, began to be a prominent feature of the edifice, ever growing in size, and becoming more powerful and more magnificent, and was installed in a special tribune.

Law

By liturgical law and tradition, the organ[1]—a noble and dignified instrument—is the only instrument really permitted in the Liturgy.[2] The special permission of the Ordinary—to be obtained on each occasion—is needed for the use of any other musical instrument in church.[3] In large churches there is often a grand organ (which is rather a concert instrument than a liturgical one, and may be used only with

---

[1] With its substitute, the harmonium, for small churches.
[2] C.E. I, xxviii; cf. *Motu Proprio (Inter Pastoralis)* of St. Pius X (1903), § 18; *Divini Cultus Sanctitatem* of Pius XI (1928), § VIII.
[3] M.P. §§ 15, 20; S.R.C. 4156, 4226.

caution, avoiding the theatrical) and a small choir organ, of a simple kind, for accompanying the singing.[4]

Liturgical Use of the Organ

In general the playing of the organ is a sign of joy and solemnity, and so there are laws forbiddingg its use at certain seasons, or at certain functions.[5] The organ is allowed to: (1) accompany the singing (strictly speaking liturgical chant is unaccompanied); (2) supply the liturgical text in certain cases;[6] (3) play interlude music.[7]

Place for the Organ

There is no law about the place for the organ in a church, but there is a tradition based on practical considerations; the choir organ —which has a liturgical function—should, obviously, be near the choir and the congregation, and so near the sanctuary (on the floor or in a tribune); the grand organ—used for interlude music, and sometimes to accompany a large congregation—may be in any suitable place. Often it is at the west end of the church, over the main door, but this place is not always desirable: it interferes with the lighting and obscures the west window, it is too detached if it is to accompany singing, it is a source of distraction (tempting people to look around).[8] The proper position for the grand organ, in any particular church, should be chosen by the architect and organist having regard to acoustics (including nearness to the choir, if there is not a small chancel organ), architectural fitness, accessibility (for doing repairs) and safety (so that it suffers no injury). The organist should be able to see the altar and the choir master—either directly or through a mirror—from the console.

[4] In private replies to different queries (1938, 1939, 1943, 1949) about the use of modern substitutes for the organ (the auto-organ, the electrophonic or electrotone pipeless organ) S.R.C. withheld its approval, but on July 13, 1949, the Congregation declared that, while the reed organ is the more suitable for liturgical use, the Ordinary—having heard the views of diocesan musical council—may, in individual cases, when a pipe organ cannot be easily got, permit the use of an electrophonic organ, with such improvements as the council may suggest.
[5] C.E. I, xxviii, 2; cf. M.P. n. 17.
[6] C.E. I, xxviii, 6, 7, 8, 9; M.P. n. 8.
[7] C.E. I, xxviii, 3, 4, 7, 9; M.P. n. 17. Cf. O'Connell, *Celebration of Mass*, p. 548.
[8] If there is an organ gallery it should have a press for music; and if it is used by the choir, there should usually be accommodation for the choristers' dress.

There is a special blessing for an organ in R.R. IX, viii, 2.

THE CHOIR

The Choir

In a large church the singers comprise the clergy (in their places in the chancel), the schola (with its special chanters) and the congregation. In early days the *schola cantorum* (subdeacons in chasuble, minor clerics and boys in alb) occupied a special place railed off in front of the high altar,[9] especially when the *presbyterium* was behind the altar. The schola has a special liturgical function[10]—to lead the congregation in the responses, and alternate with it in the common chants, and to execute the more difficult musical pieces (whether plainsong or polyphony). The schola is part of the liturgical assembly and so should be in close contact with the sanctuary (not cut away from the altar) and with the congregation. Hence the schola should be placed before the altar—the singers may even be admitted into the chancel when dressed in cassock and surplice—or to one side, but near the chancel (if in a special tribune, they should be screened off from sight).[11] This is its logical, liturgical and traditional position. The schola is sometimes placed behind the altar, but this is possible only when the altar has no dorsal, and it rather detaches the schola too much from the congregation.

[9] This is still to be seen in certain churches, e.g., St. Clemente, or St. Maria in Cosmedin in Rome.

[10] M.P. § 13.

[11] M.P. § 14. Such a tribune is sometimes built over the sanctuary at the side.

CHAPTER XVI

The Bishop's and Abbot's Throne

THE BISHOP'S THRONE

THE bishop's chair (*cathedra, sedes episcopi*) was in use from the earliest centuries. At first it often took the form of a simple faldstool (p. 243), but soon developed into a high-backed arm-chair, made in wood or stone (sometimes cut into the rock in the catacombs). At first it was simple in form, but gradually—even from the 5th century —it grew more and more elaborate. Often it was made of precious metals, or of ivory, richly ornamented, jewelled, carved, etc. The use of a dais or canopy over the chair is referred to as early as the 5th century (by St. Augustine); and there is mention of a footstool from the 11th or 12th century. From early centuries the *cathedra* was elevated — at first a little; later on, more — and draped, as a mark of distinction.

The *cathedra* became a symbol of the bishop's power to rule and duty to teach, and from the 4th century there has been a liturgical feast of St. Peter's Chair.[1] At first the bishop's throne was placed in the semicircular apse, and on each side of it around the apse were the seats of the higher clergy. The *cathedra* was moved from the

---

[1] The feast on Feb. 22 (St. Peter's Chair at Antioch) is the original one.

apse to the Gospel side of the chancel as early as the 9th or 10th century in some places (in England not later than the 12th), when the form of the altar changed, and the celebration of Mass facing the people had declined.

Law[2]

A bishop's throne consists of a high-backed[3] arm-chair, set on a height, and surmounted by a dais. The chair (which should be some six inches higher than an ordinary chair) may be made of any becoming material, stone, wood, etc., suitably ornamented (carved, inlaid, etc.). The chair is to be on a platform approached by three steps—so that it is higher than the canon's stalls in the chancel, but not higher than the footpace of the high altar[4]—and there may be a footstool at the foot of the chair. The platform must be spacious, as on it are placed stools for the assistant priest and deacons. The chair is surmounted by a dais[5] (a back, and a canopy large enough to cover the Bishop and his three assistants), square-shaped, with flounces hanging to the ground. For a pontifical function the throne is covered with a silk[6] cover of the colour of the vestments, and on the chair is a cushion covered in silk of the same colour. The covers may be adorned in gold for a cardinal only. For a Requiem function, a non-silk fabric, violet in colour, is used;[7] for Tenebrae,[8] and Good Friday, and during the vacancy of the see, the chair is undraped.

Outside the time of pontifical functions, the throne is draped in red for a cardinal (and may be ornamented in gold for him),[9] green for a bishop; for penitential days or at Requiem functions, violet for both prelates.

A bishop's throne may be surmounted by a canopy (which is a mark of jurisdiction and of special honour,[10] not allowed over the seats of lesser prelates, or of the laity, even of high rank) only if the

[2] C.E. I, xiii, 1, 2, 3; xiv, 1.
[3] "Praealta [so that it overtops the bishop's mitred head] et sublimis" (C.E. I, xiii, 3).
[4] Ibid.; S.R.C.. 2049[25], 2231[7].   [5] C.E. I, xiii, 3; xiv, 1; S.R.C. 2471[5].
[6] Velvet is reserved to the Pope.   [7] C.E. II, xii, 1.
[8] C.E. II, xxii, 17.   [9] Cf. S.R.C. 2289[5].
[10] And so C.J.C. (canon 239, § 1.15; 240, §3) speaks of the right of a cardinal to use "a throne and canopy in all churches outside Rome, in his titular church in Rome."

high altar is surmounted by a similar or more beautiful canopy[11] (civory, tester or baldachin). By Roman usage the canopy of the throne (at the corners) and the dorsal are adorned with the arms of the cardinal or bishop who uses it.

The steps of the throne are carpeted—preferably in green, but red may be used for a cardinal—provided that the steps of the high altar are also carpeted.[12]

The throne in a cathedral is a fixed one, placed either in the apse or on the Gospel side of the chancel;[13] elsewhere it is a temporary structure, to be removed after use. The throne should be placed well away from the altar steps to allow the maximum space for ceremonial movement.

While the Ordinary's own throne is used for a cardinal if present at a function, or may be granted to any bishop (with a few exceptions)[14] to preside on occasion, a special (temporary) throne is erected, on the Epistle side of the chancel, for the Archbishop of the province, or for a Nuncio or Apostolic Delegate in the place of his jurisdiction.[15]

AN ABBOT'S THRONE

The throne of a ruling abbot[16] must be a temporary one only, erected for a pontifical function, with two steps.[17] It may be adorned with plain silk drapery, and its dais must be simpler than that over the high altar, and not ornamented in gold.[18] The abbot uses a throne only in his own abbatial church.

[11] C.E. I, xiii, 3.
[12] S.R.C. 569, 574.
[13] C.E. I, xiii, 1, 2; S.R.C. 2212, 2471[5].
[14] Cf. S.R.C. 4023, 4355[v,3].
[15] C.E. I, xiii, 9, 10.
[16] An abbot *nullius* has the rights of a bishop in his own territory (C.J.C. 325).
[17] S.R.C. 156[3], 1131[3].
[18] S.R.C. 1131[2,3], 2183.

CHAPTER XVII

Images

1. HISTORY OF IMAGES

IMAGES were in use (e.g., in the catacombs) from the 2nd and 3rd centuries for adornment and instruction. They were quite general after the 4th century. Sometimes they covered the entire walls (e.g., the Pantocrator,[1] or the Lamb of God on the apse). At first there were drawings and paintings depicting our Lord[2] or our Lady, but more generally the images were symbolical and allegorical (the vine, symbols of the sacraments, the parables). Biblical scenes were portrayed in churches from the 4th and 5th centuries; and scenes from the life of a saint, or of some historical event, appear shortly after the 4th century. Once paganism was dying out and there was no longer danger of idolatry, mosaics and statues (generally in precious metals) began to come into use. Rome itself was not, at first, very favourable to statues, but there were images in gold and silver in the Roman basilicas in the 8th century.

From the 5th or 6th century began *the veneration of images,* and this became widespread (especially in the East) in the 6th and 7th centuries. The cross was the first image to receive (relative) veneration. In the 8th and 9th centuries there was a reaction against the veneration of images, and (in the East) arose the heresy of Icono-

[1] Christ ruling from heaven.
[2] At first there was some hesitation about depicting a divine person, yet in the West there was a symbolic image of the Blessed Trinity from the 4th century; an image of God the Father as a hand pointing from heaven, and as an old man from the 5th century.

96

clasm, involving the destruction of images and the persecution of their defenders. The veneration of images was vindicated by the Second Council of Nicea (the seventh general council) in 787, the Councils of Constantinople (869) and of Florence (1438); and by the Council of Trent (1563) against the western Iconoclasts, the Reformers.

In England, in medieval times, a feature of most churches was the image of our Lady, on its bracket on the north side of the east-end wall, and that of the Titular on its south end.

Images were not placed *on* altars until about the 10th century, and this practice was not general until the 15th century. Even the cross was not, as a rule, *on* the altar until the 12th century.

From the 5th century it was forbidden, out of respect, to have any image of our Lord on the floor.

From the end of the 12th century to the 14th century, sculpture was at its best. Decadence began to set in from the 15th century. In the Middle Ages, images seem to have been used more for ornament and instruction than for veneration, and were chiefly used on the outside of churches.

II. Nature of Sacred Images

Images are part of sacred art, i.e., art which is not merely Christian, not merely religious, but art which is directly and in due manner employed in the service of God's House and in divine worship.

These images—which may be paintings on canvas or on stone, mosaics and similar works of art (such as *opus sectile*), statues, or images that constitute the ornamentation of the fabric of a church—are regulated by laws[3] based on the nature of the Sacred Liturgy, on tradition, and on the directives of ecclesiastical authority. Images are used in churches for (1) ornament, (2) the instruction,[4] inspiration and edification of the faithful,[5] and (3) sacred images—which should

---

[3] E.g., C.J.C. 1255, § 2; 1276; Instruction of the Holy Office on Sacred Art, June 30, 1952 (§§ 3, 4, 5, 7, 15 *sqq.*). The only references in the liturgical books to images (apart from the Passiontide veiling of them) are in C.E. I, xii, 12, 13. But many decisions of S.R.C. deal with images.

[4] St. Gregory the Great calls them "the book of those who cannot read," and Urban VIII "the catechism of the unlettered." (Cf. S.R.C. 810.)

[5] "In order that our senses may be stimulated to salutary purposes the Church desired images of the Saints to be exposed in our churches, always to the end that we may imitate the virtues of those whose images we revere" (Pius XII, M.D., § 167).

be blessed—are exposed for veneration to the glory of God, our Lady, the Angels and Saints. Accordingly, images placed in churches should be distinguished from images in general by "a holiness that shuns the profane, truly artistic correctness . . . and a universality which, while respecting legitimate local customs, manifests the unity of the Church."[6]

The artist has a vast field of subjects from which to choose. He can seek his inspiration in the Old Testament and in the New, in the history of the Church and the lives of the Saints, in theology (depicting the mysteries of the faith, the Christian virtues, etc.), in the Liturgy itself—the Mass, the sacraments—in every aspect of Christian activity. But the image he creates should be worthy of its purpose and of a place in an edifice consecrated to God and sacred things. His work must be in accordance with the requirements of the Catholic faith, of Christian piety and the prescriptions of liturgical law. "What we have said of music," writes Pius XII in *Mediator Dei*,[7] "is to be said proportionately of the other fine arts, especially of architecture, sculpture and painting. Modern pictures and statues, whose style is more adapted to the materials in use at the present day, are not to be condemned out of hand.[8] On condition that these modern arts steer a middle course between an excessive realism on the one hand and an exaggerated symbolism on the other, and take into account more the needs of the Christian community than the personal taste and judgment of the artist, they should be allowed full scope if, with due reverence and honour, they put themselves at the service of our churches and sacred rites. Thus modern art may lend its voice to the magnificent chorus of praise which men of high talent throughout the ages have sung to the Catholic faith. We feel bound at the same time, however, to deplore and condemn certain modern pictures and statues which are a disfigurement and degradation of genuine art, and are sometimes inconsistent with Christian decorum, modesty and piety, and offensive to true religious sentiment; these must be barred from our churches, and likewise, in general, anything that ill-beseems the sacred character of the church."

[6] Pius XII, M.D., § 188.
[7] § 195.   [8] Cf. § *Ibid.*

In a recent Instruction (June 30, 1952) on Sacred Art the Holy Office recapitulates the traditional teaching of the Church and recalls the provisions of Canon Law (C.J.C. 485; 1161; 1164, § 1; 1178; 1261, § 1; 1268; 1269, § 1; 1279; 1280; 1385; 1399) on this subject. It refers to the laws concerning Christian iconography issued by the Council of Trent (Session 25) and cites its exhortation to the bishops: "Let bishops exercise such diligence and care concerning these matters that nothing disordered may meet the eye, nothing distorted and confused in execution, since sanctity belongs to the House of God." It adds (§ 5) the words of Urban VIII: "Let those objects which are exposed to the gaze of the faithful be neither disordered nor unusual in appearance, and let them engender devotion and piety."

III. CANON LAW AND IMAGES

The code of Canon Law points out that veneration and worship is due to sacred images, a worship that is referred to the persons whom they represent;[9] and that it is good and profitable to honour the images of the Saints and especially of our Lady.[10] And Pius XII censures those who wish to exclude pictures and statues from churches.[11] The Code of Canon Law makes the following laws about images: (1) No unusual[12] image, sacred or not, may be placed in churches or other sacred places[13] without the consent of the Ordinary of the place.[14] (2) The Ordinary may not approve of sacred images

[9] Cf. C.J.C. 1255, § 2.
[10] Cf. C.J.C. 1276.
[11] M.D., § 62.
[12] Unusual in form or symbolism, i.e., one that represents persons or events in a manner that has no justification in Sacred Scripture, or in Catholic tradition. For example, (1) it is forbidden to depict the Holy Spirit in human form, (2) in 1916 the Holy Office condemned an image of our Lady wearing priestly vestments. The "unusual" seems to refer chiefly to the subject of the representation and to details of the composition rather than to the style of painting or carving, or to the medium used by the craftsman. The law does not completely forbid the "unusual" as it does rule out an image which is not in harmony with the approved usage of the Church (canon 1279, § 2)—but it does require the approval of the Ordinary before an "unusual" image is exposed in a church or other sacred place. What is "unusual" must be determined by decisions of authority (e.g., of S.R.C.), by a knowledge of Christian tradition, and by a correct religious and liturgical "sense" or "tact." What is "unusual" sometimes depends on the community for which the image is intended. Hence judgment on the suitability of an image for public veneration is left to the Ordinary. He will know what would shock or disturb the faithful of his diocese.
[13] Cf. C.J.C. 1154.
[14] C.J.C. 1279, § 1.

to be exposed for the veneration of the faithful that are not in keeping with the approved usage of the Church.[15] (3) The Ordinary may not allow the display, in churches or other sacred places, of any image which might suggest any false doctrine, or is unbecoming, or offends against propriety, or is capable of leading the ignorant into perilous error. (4) Should images (exposed for the veneration of the faithful in churches or public oratories) that are of great value—because of their age, or artistic value, or because of the veneration given them—need repair, the consent of the Ordinary in writing must be obtained before they are restored; and the Ordinary, before giving his consent, should seek advice from prudent and competent experts.[16] (5) Images of great value or which are much honoured by the people in any church may not be validly disposed of nor moved permanently to another church without the permission of the Holy See.[17]

IV. Image of the Titular

Apart from the image of the Crucified required at every altar where Mass is celebrated, no image is prescribed by the Church, but she desires that an image of the Titular[18] of any church, or of any consecrated altar be exposed for veneration,[19] to mark the close connection between that person or mystery and the church or altar dedicated in his (its) honour.[20] Accordingly, if there is an image of a saint over any "fixed" altar, it must be that of the Titular.[21] An image in stained glass behind an altar is not regarded as connected with the altar. It is permitted to *add* the image of another saint to that of the Titular, but the latter's image may not be removed, except by Apostolic indult.[22] The image of the Titular of a movable altar,[23] however, may be changed with leave of the Ordinary.

---

[15] C.J.C. 1279, § 2. Thus the Holy Office, in March 1921, condemned the artistic productions of a certain school of painting in Belgium. (Cf. *Questions Liturgiques,* May 1921, p. 159.)
[16] C.J.C. 1280.
[17] Cf. C.J.C. 1281.
[18] Cf. pp. 19, 169.
[19] S.R.C. 4191[4].
[20] A church or altar is always dedicated *to* God, but often *in honour* of some saint.
[21] Cf. p. 140.
[22] Cf. S.R.C. 2752[5,7], 2762, 4191[3].
[23] Cf. pp. 169, 140.

V. FORBIDDEN IMAGES

1. *Some General Rules*

(*a*) Images of canonized saints only may, generally speaking, be exposed for public veneration, not those of the beatified, for the public veneration of these is limited to the place, and in the manner, determind by the Pope.[24] When the veneration of a beatified person is allowed in any place, his image may adorn the walls (only); where his office and Mass are allowed his image may be placed over an altar.[25]

(*b*) Images of persons who died with a reputation for sanctity, but are not canonized or beatified, may not be put on altars; nor depicted away from altars with an aureole or other marks of sanctity. But their image, or incidents in their lives, may be portrayed on the walls or in stained glass, provided such images do not suggest any cult or display any special signs of sanctity, and have nothing profane about them or out of keeping with the usage of the Church.[26]

(*c*) In the same church—*a fortiori* at the same altar—it is forbidden to have two images of the same person.[27] In the case of our Lord or our Lady, it is permissible to expose for veneration images whose titles are different. Accordingly, S.R.C. has decided that in the same church there may be an image of the Immaculate Conception and also of our Lady of Lourdes, provided that the latter shows all the details that characterized the apparitions[28] (the dress and posture of the Blessed Virgin, the figure of St. Bernadette, etc.). On the other hand S.R.C. ruled that there may not be an image of our Lady of the Rosary and one of our Lady of Pompeii in the same church, as the latter really represents the former.[29]

(*d*) A Brief of Urban VIII in 1642[30] forbade images to be shown in the habit of any religious Order, or the dress of any special nation. The toleration of the practice of clothing images of our Lady in gar-

---

[24] Cf. C.J.C. 1277, § 2; S.R.C. 1097, 1130[1,2].
[25] S.R.C. 1130[2], 1156[1], 4330. To dedicate an altar to a *Beatus* requires an Apostolic indult (C.J.C. 1201, § 4).
[26] S.R.C. 3715, 3785, 3835.
[27] S.R.C. 3732. This does not apply to the crucifix.
[28] S.R.C. 3791[1] (cf. 3419[1]).
[29] S.R.C. 3723, 3732.
[30] S.R.C. 810. Cf. 824, 879.

ments of different colours for different feasts or seasons is referred to the Ordinary[31] (with a proviso).

2. *Particular Images that are Forbidden*

The following particular images may not be exposed for public veneration: (*a*) the Blessed Trinity depicted under the form of a man with three heads, or a man with two heads and a dove; (*b*) the Holy Spirit in human form[32] (for which there is no warrant in Sacred Scripture); (*c*) the Heart of Christ apart from his body exposed for public veneration[33] on an altar; (*d*) emblems of the Eucharistic Heart;[34] (*e*) the Head of Our Lord,[35] (*f*) our Lady of Sorrows (permanently) clothed in black with a crucifix in her left hand,[36] but it is allowed to expose, on the evening of Maundy Thursday, a statue of our Lady (temporarily) clothed in black with the dead Christ in her lap;[37] (*g*) the Heart of Mary depicted apart from her body;[38] (*h*) our Lady in priestly vesture;[39] (*i*) the heart of St. Joseph (the cult of which is forbidden).[40]

VI. THE TRADITIONAL FORM OF SACRED IMAGES

The approved usage of the Church—tradition—is a guide to the correct form of sacred images.[41]

(1) *The Blessed Trinity:* The Church has never given positive approval to any pictorial representation of the Most Holy Trinity, but has tolerated an image of three persons all alike (an ancient image) because of the vision of Abraham at Mambre (Genesis 18), in which some commentators see a theophany of the Blessed Trinity. *Emblems*[42]

---

[31] S.R.C. 3690.　　　　　　　　　　[32] Holy Office, March 16, 1928.
[33] Holy Office, Aug. 26, 1891; S.R.C. 3492. The Heart by itself may be used as an ornament, e.g., in stained glass (though this is scarcely becoming), or for veneration by private devotion (as, e.g., in Sacred Heart badges).
[34] Holy Office, March 3, 1891; April 3, 1915.
[35] A special devotion to our Lord's head is forbidden. (Holy Office, June 18, 1938).
[36] S.R.C. 824, 3818[2].
[37] S.R.C. 2375[4], cf. 2682[52].
[38] This is permissible for private devotion (S.R.C. 3492). (This Heart, with our Lady's body, may be depicted in the form approved by the S. Inquisition—S.R.C. 3470.)
[39] Holy Office, April 8, 1916.
[40] S.R.C. 3304.
[41] Cf. C.J.C. 1279, § 2.
[42] For decoration and instruction. The Church has never permitted public, official veneration of *symbols,* not even those of God or Christ.

of the Trinity traditionally used are the equilateral triangle, interlaced circles (from the 13th century), the trefoil.

(2) *God the Father:* There has never been positive approval of an image of the First Person as a man, but tradition allows[43] him to be represented as a bearded old man,[44] crowned (sometimes with a triple crown) and haloed, enthroned, with a globe in one hand, a sceptre in the other (or sometimes with a crucifix in his arms). Beside him is often shown a younger man (the Second Person) with an aureole, enthroned, with a cross in his hand, and sometimes with a globe at his feet. Between, or above, these two figures the Holy Ghost is depicted as a dove, with a triple aureole. The *emblems* of the First Person are the first and last letters of the Greek alphabet (alpha and omega),[45] an all-seeing eye, a hand emerging from a cloud.

(3) *God the Son,* the Second Divine Person, is depicted as the Lamb of God;[46] as a man, he is portrayed with long hair and bearded,[47] robed in tunic and cloak (*himation, pallium*). A very early image of him (from the 2nd century) is in the guise of the Good Shepherd. He is also depicted according to his attributes, e.g., as a king of suffering. *The Sacred Heart* usually shows the full figure of Christ (or at least his head and shoulders), showing his heart. This is often portrayed as seen by St. Margaret Mary in vision,[48] i.e., in flames, wounded, girded with thorns and surmounted by a cross. While direct devotion to *the Holy Face* is not permitted[49] (it must be regarded as one aspect of devotion to the Passion) veneration of *the image* is permissible. This is generally a copy of the Face as it appeared on the Veil of Veronica, or the image as venerated at Tours, or that taken from the Holy Shroud (Turin).

(4) *God the Holy Spirit:* May be depicted under the form of a dove, as he appeared at Christ's baptism; or, in symbolical form, as a tongue of fire, as he showed himself at Pentecost.[50]

---

[43] Cf. Benedict XIV, Constitution *Sollicitudini* of Oct. 1, 1745.
[44] Inspired by Isaias 6.1; Daniel 7.9; cf. Apocalypse 4.2.
[45] Applied to the Father in Apocalypse 1.8, and (probably) 21.6; and to the Son in 22.13.
[46] John 1.36; Apocalypse 5.6.
[47] In the early centuries he was sometimes portrayed unbearded.
[48] And this was permitted by the S. Inquisition, Jan. 3, 1891.
[49] S. Inquisition, May 4, 1892; March 8, 1893.
[50] Matthew 3.16; Luke 3.22; Acts 2.3.

(5) *The Blessed Virgin Mary:* Our Lady is portrayed in a variety
of forms, under innumerable titles. The commonest image (in use
since the 5th century at least) shows her as the mother, carrying the
Divine Child. Some of her images are based on Sacred Scripture, the
Woman of the Apocalypse,[51] or on her apparitions, e.g., the well-
known images of our Lady of Lourdes, our Lady of Fatima. Since
the end of the 14th century the Blessed Virgin has been shown in her
sorrow, holding the dead body of our Lord (Pietà). The emblems
of our Lady are innumerable (e.g., the burning bush, the ark of the
covenant, the lily, the morning star).

(6) *The Angels:* Angels are depicted in human form, because of
their appearance in this form related in Sacred Scripture; but because
of the high dignity of his nature and office an angel is portrayed as a
spiritualized type of man, showing a harmonious combination of the
best characteristics of both sexes of mankind, manly strength and
vigour, combined with beauty, grace, etc. Angels are shown with
wings (because of their agility and because of the references in Sacred
Scripture to the winged Seraphim) and are usually depicted in adoration of God, or chanting his praises, or acting as his messengers. Archangel Gabriel is linked with his mission to Zachary and to our Blessed
Lady;[52] Archangel Michael is portrayed as an armed warrior, tread-
ing the devil under foot,[53] and sometimes holding a balance (weigh-
ing up human values); Archangel Raphael is shown as the traveller
with Tobias, with the fish, etc.

(7) *St. Joseph:* There is no historical warrant for depicting him as
an old man. He is often shown with a lily (symbol of his virginity),
or the flowering rod, or the tools of a carpenter. Sometimes he holds
the Child Jesus, as his foster-father and guardian.

(8) *The Saints:* Modern saints are usually depicted according to
correct portraiture and dress, so that it may be possible to identify
them, and often with emblems connected with events of their lives,
their work, mission, virtues, their death (e.g., the instruments of torture of a martyr).

[51] Apocalypse 12.1.
[52] Luke 1.
[53] Apocalypse 12.7 (cf. Jude 9).

VII. THE CRUCIFIX

(9) *The Crucifix:* The crucifix means the cross with the figure of our Lord on it.[54] At first Christians avoided the use of a cross or crucifix,[55] because of its pagan associations as an instrument of torture of criminals. When it began to make its appearance it was in a symbolical or disguised form (the trident, anchor, monogram). After the conversion of Constantine and the finding of the true Cross in Jerusalem (326), it became a glorious emblem.[56] From the 5th century the cross appears in art, first without any figure, or with only the medallion of Christ, or with him depicted as a lamb, but with his human form from the 6th century. From that period until the 12th or 13th century the Christ represented on the cross was, nearly always, the triumphant Redeemer of the world, reigning from the Cross[57]— alive, with open eyes, clothed in the colobium[58] (long robe) and often wearing a jewelled crown. There were but few examples at that period of the suffering Christ on his gibbet. From the 11th to 13th centuries came the departure from the mystical idea, and the gradual approach to realism in the portrayal of Christ crucified. From the 13th century he is mostly depicted as dead, with eyes closed, head dropped, an anguished face, bleeding wounds, crowned with thorns, and naked (except for a loin cloth). This at first shocked the faithful and even aroused indignation.

Details of a Crucifix

Our Lord is usually shown in Italian art with the crown of thorns,[59] in French art without it; with the title over his head (John 19.20); fastened with four nails (three sometimes, since the 13th century).

---

[54] Sometimes (e.g., in the rubrics of the liturgical books) "cross" is used for crucifix.

[55] A few crosses were found in the catacombs dating from before the 4th century, and one was found near St. Peter's tomb in 1942.

[56] The West was later (7th or 8th century) than the East in its use of the cross.

[57] Cf. the Preface of the Cross (*qui in ligno vincebat*), the commemoration of the cross in Eastertide, the solemn blessing of a cross (in R.R.), the *Vexilla Regis* and *Pange lingua . . . lauream certaminis* (both written by Venantius Fortunatus in the 6th century), the two feasts of the Holy Cross.

[58] Still retained in the East, in the West until the 9th century.

[59] The Holy Shroud of Turin depicts Christ as having been so crowned; and nailed through the wrists, not the palms.

It is more correct, according to tradition, to show the wound made by the spear in the right side. A foot-rest occurs in early specimens of the crucifix, but appears less from the 13th century. To want *exclusively* "crucifixes that do not represent the bitter sufferings of the Divine Redeemer" is censured by Pius XII in *Mediator Dei* (§ 62), but this does not mean that the medieval crucifix, depicting the triumphant Christ, is excluded. A too realistic crucifix is not favoured, as it tends to obscure the divinity of Christ and the victory of the cross ("It is achieved"—John 19.30). The ideal crucifix expresses the resignation, nobility and serenity of the Crucified, inviting sorrow, confidence and love.

VIII. THE MAKING OF IMAGES

Since sacred art attempts to express the spiritual, the ideal, by means of the material, in general, sacred images should show something of the supernatural (of grace, sinlessness, etc.) and should display in appearance, in attitude, in dress, the majesty, dignity, nobility, holiness and beauty that the Catholic mind associates with God, with his mother, his angels and his saints.

Yet the artist "must avoid an exaggerated attention to (*cura*) expression, and an excessive preoccupation with ethnographic or archeological realism."[60] "When an artist is called upon to picture a saint, he must acquaint himself sufficiently with the life of the saint, with the period and environment in which he lived, with the iconographic forms which tradition has associated with him, with the special manifestations of devotion connected with his feast, and the like."[61] "The law of traditional Christian iconography is dignity. This dignity, which is the fruit of inspiration, lifts religious images above all vulgar realism, and confers on them that supernatural light and that mystic beauty which renders them liturgical, i.e., noble instruments of external worship before which it is possible for us to kneel down and pray. In Christian iconography, therefore, what is important is not so much physical realism as liturgical reality, i.e., the character of holiness (*splendor veritatis et caritatis*) which makes

[60] Costantini, *Fede ed Arte*, I, 130.
[61] Ibid., p. 138.

the divine transcend the human."[62] A good painter or sculptor will aim at conveying by his work something of the sanctity and glory of the person whose image he depicts, so as to bring home to the beholder that this person is worthy of veneration.

Usually images for veneration in churches are statues, sometimes a painting.[63] There is no law about their fabrication. By tradition any becoming material may be used, gold, silver, bronze, ivory, alabaster, marble and stone of all kinds, wood, terra-cotta, ceramics. The most undesirable material is plaster. Obviously, the material for an image should be durable, and so such things as oleographs are banned from the church. Evidently original statues are best. If casts are used, it is desirable that they be taken from good classical models, from the best sculptures available.

The Aureole (Nimbus)

In paintings, sometimes in sculpture, in textiles and embroidery, a nimbus—a bright disk surrounding the head—representing a crown of glory,[64] marks an image as that of a divine Person or a saint. It is sometimes termed "aureole," but it seems more correct to reserve this name for a bright oval cloud or halo, investing the entire figure ("vesica" or "glory"). The use of the nimbus or aureole as a mark of majesty, greatness, power is pre-Christian. From the 3rd century onwards it is rare to find an image of Christ without the nimbus (cruciform, or charged with the monogram, or with alpha and omega, or both). From about the 5th century it is found about the head of the Lamb. About the same period began the use of a (round) nimbus for the apostles Peter and Paul, and in the 6th century its use was general for the other apostles also. From the 5th century a nimbus —larger than that used for saints—was used in images of our Lady, especially when she was depicted carrying the Child, and this nimbus was sometimes bordered with stars.[65] From the 6th century the nimbus began to be used for personages of the Old Testament. In

---

[62] Costantini in *Liturgical Arts*, 1935, p. 11; 1939, p. 65.
[63] Images in stained glass are not venerated (cf. S.R.C. 4191[4]), nor are symbols.
[64] "How beautiful that crown which the Lord will bestow on them [the just]" (Wisdom 5. 17).
[65] Cf. Apocalypse 12.1.

the 7th century it was used for portraits of popes and bishops (a square nimbus for the living). The symbols of the Evangelists came into use in the latter part of the 4th century, and in the 6th were sometimes nimbed.

The nimbus is depicted in colour[66] or in gold; sometimes it is rayed, sometimes jewelled, sometimes bearing the name of the saint. The vesica surrounding the entire person, symbol of heavenly glory, is used only for the Divine Persons; occasionally for our Lady. For God the Father and God the Holy Ghost the nimbus has three-pronged rays, or an equilateral triangle; for God the Son the nimbus is round and charged with a cross.[67] Urban VIII (1623-1644) forbade the use of the nimbus for a *beatus,* but allowed the use of rays or a luminous glow (around the head).

IX. THE PLACE OF IMAGES

In planning a new church provision should be made for the proper placing of images (over altars, in side chapels, in niches, on consoles, etc.) so as to have harmony, unity of design, etc. Where there are a number of real altars (not mere stands or pedestals), a place for an image of the Titular[68] of the altar should be provided behind and above the altar. It should be placed well above it, to be clearly visible and not mingled indistinguishably with the lines, colour, etc., of the altar or its furniture. Its size is of importance, not too big to dwarf or draw attention away from the altar (which is the more important), not too small so as to be insignificant. Statues should not be placed *on* an altar on which Mass is celebrated (this is forbidden, by implication, in the General Rubrics of the Missal, XX; and an altar must not seem to be a mere stand for other objects). Images other than those of the Titular are best placed in niches or on consoles[69]—thus saving space, and providing best for order and cleanliness—or, failing these, on pedestals.

[66] In the Middle Ages the colour sometimes varied according to the category of the saint.
[67] As a rule, restricted, since the 6th century, to the Second Person, but occasionally used for the other Persons.
[68] P. 100.
[69] This also prevents injudicious sacristans from piling up candlesticks, flower-vases, etc., around statues.

Though there is no formal prohibition, it is better to avoid placing images which are objects of veneration within the sanctuary (except the image of the Titular of the high altar). They distract attention from the High Altar—the focal point of every church—and from the Blessed Sacrament.[70]

The rubrics of the *Caeremoniale*[71] do make provision, in greater churches, where the high altar is spacious, for placing temporarily on the altar—as an ornament on great feasts—images in silver or other precious materials. Generally these images take the form of busts of saints, which are used as reliquaries. They are placed between the candlsticks, and the rubrics[72] give directions about incensing them when the altar is incensed. An image may *not* be placed: (1) before the tabernacle, e.g., on a feast day,[73] nor (2) on it[74] (this would make the tabernacle a mere stand and would prevent its being properly veiled), not even at the back;[75] nor (3) *a fortiori*, in the Exposition throne,[76] if there is a fixed one behind the altar. Neither may an image replace the tabernacle on the high altar,[77] nor occupy the place where the cross should be, or interfere with its correct position. During Exposition of the Blessed Sacrament, which is not of short duration (e.g., not merely for Benediction), an image permanently placed over the altar must be removed or veiled (preferably in white).

There is a certain order to be observed in the placing of sacred images: (1) if they are in different chapels or on different altars, the place of greatest dignity is the Gospel side of the church, nearest the high altar; the second place on the Epistle side nearest the high altar, and so on; (2) if they are in the same chapel or at the same chapel or at the same altar, the image of the person of highest rank should be in the place of greatest honour[78]—in the middle.

[70] In Rome, in the great basilicas, images are not placed in the Blessed Sacrament chapel.
[71] C.E. I, xii, 12.
[72] *Ritus celebrandi*, IV, 5. This use of reliquaries on the altar dates from the 8th or 9th century. They are not allowed on the altar in Passiontide (C.E. II, xx, 3).
[73] S.R.C. 2906.
[74] S.R.C. 2613[6], cf. 2740[1,5] and S. Consistorial Congregation, Oct. 8, 1932.
[75] Cf. S.R.C. 3673[2].
[76] S.R.C. 3589.
[77] Cf. S.R.C. 3241[4], 3320. I.C. § III.
[78] An accidental liturgical rank is that of Titular (p. 19), and so, e.g., if there were (separate) images of our Lord, our Lady and St. Joseph behind an altar of which St. Joseph was the Titular, his image should be in the middle.

X. VEILING IMAGES

At Passiontide (since at least the 12th century), images which are objects of veneration[79]—and not mere ornaments—are to be entirely veiled by violet, unadorned, opaque veils, from before First Vespers of Passion Sunday until: (1) the veneration of the Cross on Good Friday for all crosses; (2) for all other images, until the intonation of the *Gloria in excelsis* of the first Easter Mass.[80] Stations of the Cross need not be veiled.[81]

XI. BLESSING IMAGES

While it is not of strict obligation to bless images exposed for veneration, this is, obviously, very desirable and has been the practice from early times. A blessing is provided in R.R. IX, ix, 15. If it is solemnly carried out, it is reserved to the Ordinary, who may delegate any priest to do it.[82] There is a special solemn blessing for a cross, R.R. IX, ix, 13, 14 (also reserved, if carried out in solemn form); and *Pontificale Romanum* (Part II) has a special solemn blessing for an image of our Lady reserved to a bishop.

XII. IMAGES IN A CHURCH

A church is not a picture gallery or museum, and so the number of images exposed for veneration should be kept within reasonable limits. "We consider it our duty," writes Pius XII in *Mediator Dei* (§ 189), "to reprove the ill-educated piety which, in churches intended for the worship of God, and even on the altars, displays for veneration an unreasonable multiplicity[83] of pictures and statues . . . " And the Holy Office, in its recent Instruction on Sacred Art (June 30, 1952), says:[84] "Let Ordinaries severely forbid second rate, and for the most part stereotyped statues and pictures, to be multiplied and improperly and absurdly exposed to the veneration of the faithful on altars themselves,

[79] Including the processional cross (M.R. III, IV).
[80] C.E. II, xx, 3, and rubric of missal. S.R.C. 1158, 1275[2], 2682[34], 2965[2], 3293.
[81] S.R.C. 3638[2].
[82] C.J.C. 1279, § 4.
[83] To avoid this it might be a good idea to keep images (the smaller ones, at all events) stored away, and bring each one out for veneration only on the feast of the person it represents.
[84] § 19.

or on the neighbouring walls of chapels." Good taste and some education in matters of art are essential for the choice of suitable images for a church. Let them be few, of the highest craftsmanship,[85] suited to their setting and properly placed; worthy of their purpose—not only to instruct and delight—but to be objects of pious veneration. Let them be worthy, too, of their subjects, mirroring even in a faint way the supernatural—the majesty of Christ, the beauty, dignity and serenity of his Mother and his saints. Images in church must not lack "that sacred and liturgical stamp which all art should bear when it enters the House of God,"[86] but be such as to do honour to God, to our Lady, to the angels and saints, and uplift, delight and sanctify those who behold them.

[85] Cf. Exodus 35, *sqq.*
[86] Cardinal Schuster, *The Sacramentary* (I, 171).

CHAPTER XVIII

Stations of the Cross

"THERE are certain other pious practices," wrote Pius XII in his Encyclical *Mediator Dei* (1947),[1] "which, though not belonging strictly to the Liturgy, nevertheless enjoy a special importance and dignity, such that they are regarded as raised to liturgical rank, and have received repeated approval from this Apostolic See and the Episcopate. Among these are . . . the Stations of the Cross."

History

The Stations are a diminutive *via dolorosa* of Flemish origin. In their present form they were not known in northern Europe before the end of the 16th century. The devotion of the Way of the Cross spread in the 17th and 18th centuries, especially through the influence of the Franciscans, to whose care the devotion is committed. The Stations did not appear commonly in churches before the 17th century. The present number of fourteen Stations was fixed by Clement XII in 1731.[2]

Law

The Stations now form a permanent feature of nearly all churches

[1] M.D., § 182.
[2] S.C.I. 100.

and oratories, and account must be taken of them in planning a church. They should be in keeping with the size and style of the church, and the architect and competent artists should be consulted about them. In reference to the liturgical features of the church (e.g., the consecration crosses) the Stations, however, are a subordinate feature; and they should not be too prominent,[3] as they tend to be because of their number. As the wooden crosses *are* the Stations and images of any kind, though desirable to help in "making the Stations," are not essential, it is much better to be content with crosses alone (accompanied by the title of each Station) unless it is possible to have worthy images.

Erection of Stations[4]

Stations may be erected only by those who have the faculty to do so. By common law this faculty is given to cardinals (who may erect Stations by using one only[5] of the three prayers given in R.R. for the blessing of the crosses); to residential and titular bishops (who must use the form of erection set forth in R.R.); and to priests of the Order of Friars Minor. The blessing of the crosses is essential for a valid erection, of the images for a lawful one. The crosses must be blessed, by the person duly authorized, in the place where the Stations are to be erected. They may be blessed before or after they are put in place;[6] and they may be fixed in place by anyone,[7] at any time.

The erection of the Stations attaches *to the place* where they are erected, and so once it is validly done *no* new erection is necessitated in the following cases: (1) if a new church replaces the old one on more or less the same spot and retaining the old Title;[8] (2) if the pictures, or other images, are entirely changed or removed[9] (provided the crosses remain); (3) if the crosses are removed temporarily[10] (e.g., for the cleaning or painting of the walls), or their position is

---

[3] Hence there is more scope for the artist or craftsman in planning Stations to be erected outside a church.
[4] R.R. IX, xi.
[5] Cf. De Angelis, *De Indulgentiis* (1950), pp. 27, 347.
[6] S.C.I. 447.
[7] R.R. and S.C.I. 311. In a convent of enclosed nuns the crosses are blessed at the grille and may be fixed in place by the nuns (S.C.I. 100, § 8).
[8] S.C.I. June 6, 1905.
[9] S.C.I. 258, 264[4], 332.
[10] S.C.I. 257[1], 264[4], 270[5], 275[1].

changed within the same building,[11] (4) if one or more of the crosses are renewed, provided that a majority of the original crosses remain.[12]

Material of the Stations

The crosses must be plain wood (without a figure), and must appear as such;[13] they may not be made of any other material. They may be of any colour. They may be attached to the images, or, better, detached from them, and placed over (preferably) or under the images. As the images are not essential—their purpose is to help those who make the Stations to recreate in their imagination the scenes of the Passion[14]—they may take any suitable form: paintings (on canvas or on the walls), sculptures (in stone, wood, etc.), bas reliefs, terracotta figures (coloured), mosaic or opus sectile, even stained glass. Plaster is undesirable. If paintings are used they are best in very simple, plain frames which will set off, not distract from, the image.

"The representation of the drama of the Way of the Cross should be clear, vivid, appealing, becoming and dignified."[15]

Place of the Stations

Stations may be erected in any becoming place, not only in a church or oratory but in an ambulatory, along a corridor or cloister, or even in the open air.[16] More than one set of Stations may be erected in the same place. Stations are to be placed in a continuous line (beginning, in a church, on either the Gospel or Epistle side),[17] all around the church, or on one side only. Normally they are fixed to the main walls, but they may be attached to pillars.[18] They should not be so placed as to break the line of vision in the church, or distract attention from its focal point, the high altar. Accordingly, suitable places must be planned out for them in designing a church, so as to fit them in

[11] S.C.I. 311[4], 328 (cf. 275[3]).   [12] S.C.I. 223[1], 258, 270[5], 311[3], 328.
[13] S.C.I. 261, 442[2], and March 27, 1901.
[14] Hence unusual, or startling images should be avoided.
[15] Cardinal Costantini, Commentary on the Instruction of the Holy Office, 1952, p. 66.
[16] Then they must be suitably protected against disrespect (e.g., railed off). When Stations are erected outside a church or oratory, they should begin at the church, or end near it (S.C.I. 100[3]).
[17] This is sometimes determined by the direction in which the figures—if images are used—face.
[18] This is not a good plan as the Stations break the lines of the edifice.

after spaces have been arranged for side chapels, windows, confessionals, consecration crosses, etc. The Stations (at least the crosses) must be firmly fixed,[19] and at a certain distance—not determined by any law—from one another,[20] so that a person "making the Stations," shall move around and trace the miniature *via dolorosa.*

For a large church the figures of the Stations, in a painting or sculpture, need to be of sufficient size to be seen at a distance—when a whole congregation is "making the Stations"—and, normally, it is better to avoid a large number of persons in the representations, so as not to distract attention from the central figures in each incident that is depicted.

[19] Cf. S.C.I. August 14, 1904.
[20] S.C.I. 119, 1941.

CHAPTER XIX

The Sacristy[1]

THE sacristy is an integral part of the church and a very important part, but it is not a "sacred place" (cf. C.J.C. 1154), as it is not consecrated or blessed with the church. Because it is part of the church and usually closely attached to the chancel, the chief sacristy is a place that demands a certain reverence and quietude. In greater churches —cathedrals,[2] collegiate and conventual churches, and large parish churches—the sacristy is a very important and imposing edifice. It is important for the clergy and for the due service of the church, and in the general plan must be fitted in harmoniously by the architect. In such large churches it is better that it should not immediately adjoin the sanctuary, but be separated from it by a corridor. Even in the smallest churches or oratories two sacristies, however limited in size, are really necessary, one the clergy sacristy (which shall here be called "the vestry"), the other a working sacristy (which may be called "the second sacristy").

History

In the early centuries the clergy vested in public and the requisites for the Sacred Liturgy were stored around the church—though there

---

[1] The word *sacristia* occurs in the liturgical books, as do also the words *sacrarium* and *secretarium*, which have the meaning sometimes of sacristy, but have also other meanings.
[2] In a cathedral the sacristan is a priest, and C.E. devotes a chapter to his duties (I, vi).

116

was sometimes a special room off the church called *sacrarium* or *diaconicum*. The sacristy as we know it now is of quite late appearance in liturgical history (16th century), except in great churches.

The vestry is the place of assembly and vesting of the clergy taking part in liturgical functions, and usually houses the more valuable requisites of divine worship (church plate, vestments, etc.). The second sacristy is often the place of assembly and robing of the servers, choristers and other assistants (if there is not a special room for them), is the storeroom of the less valuable equipment of the church and, especially, is the workroom of the sacristan and his assistants. It is useful to have an electric bell or buzzer connecting the two sacristies.

Law

There are no liturgical laws about a sacristy. The rules that direct the construction and furnishing of sacristies are based on practical experience of what is needed, and have become, in large part, enshrined in tradition. The sacristies should be properly lighted, heated and ventilated rooms—as large as possible. It is well to have the vestry on the south side, if possible, as it will thus be brighter and drier. There should, when possible, be access to the sacristies not only from the chancel but also directly from the body of the church, so that no one is obliged to pass through the sanctuary in order to gain the sacristy. There should also be access to the sacristies (or to a vestibule or corridor adjoining them) from outside the church. It is convenient if the vestry be connected with the presbytery. While the vestry—generally placed at the southeast corner—may be at the west end, so that a ceremonial procession from it to the chancel passes right through the church, it is much more convenient that the vestry adjoin the sanctuary. The second sacristy certainly must do so.

The vestry should be on the same level as the sanctuary, without steps. Its doors should be wide, to allow—if possible—the passage of three persons abreast; and high, to permit a mitred prelate, or the processional cross, to pass without difficulty. Because of the valuables it houses it needs well-protected windows and a strong exterior door with a good-quality lock. Generally sacristies are much too small. They can scarcely be too large—though, naturally, their size will be in proportion to the size and importance of the church they serve—or have too many presses and drawers to secure order and cleanliness. The vestry should have a lavatory close by. A small window opening into the chancel from each sacristy (or a small grille—a "judas"—in the door) is useful for the sacristan and the assistants at ceremonies to see what is taking place at the altar.

I. Furniture of the Vestry

The chief article of furniture in a vestry is the table on which vestments are prepared for any function. Nowadays it takes the form of a large press, containing many drawers and perhaps cupboards. Shallow flat drawers, lined with cedar, are used for sets of vestments (unless these are hung up, which is the better plan); deep large drawers serve for albs and surplices, humeral veils, preaching stoles; smaller drawers for the burses of vestment sets, conopaea, veils for missal-stands, for monstrances and for ciboria, etc., and the small linens.[3] The vesting table should be covered with a (green) cloth to prevent vestments slipping off it, or gathering dust when laid out—a good plan is to have the cloth on a roller to keep it in place. Over the vesting table there should be a crucifix or some sacred image.[4] The other furniture of the vestry comprises: (1) a deep press (at least 2 feet 6 inches deep), with a bar running from end to end, to hold sets of vestments on hangers; these are specially made to take a chasuble, and have an arm (under the cross-piece) on which the stole, maniple and chalice veil of each set may be hung. Wider hangers are used for copes.[5] Vestments not often in use are covered with calico covers; (2) a press or chest for altar frontals; (3) a wardrobe for cassocks; (4) an iron safe for church plate and registers; (5) a hat and coat rack, with an umbrella stand; (6) a lavabo, with towel rail and possibly a rail for drying linens; (7) prie-dieus (at least two will be needed for the use of priests and for weddings, etc.) with a card (framed or covered in mica) before them containing the prayers of preparation for, and thanksgiving after, Mass; (8) chairs and stools

---

[3] A good plan is to have a long nest of small drawers at the back of the vesting table, and in the middle of it a press (with a glass front) to take the books kept in the sacristy. [4] R, II, 1.
[5] A wooden hoop, covered over with cloth, makes an excellent hanger.

(e.g., for Vespers); (9) a pier glass is a useful thing, that sacred ministers may see that they are properly vested; (10) a reliable clock.

Near the door of the sacristy leading into the church it is proper to have a lustral water stoup, and a bell that will announce to the congregation the beginning of a function.

Hanging up in suitable places in the sacristy should be: (1) a chart showing the name of the Titular of the church, of the reigning Pope and of the Bishop of the place, with an indication of any *oratio imperata;* (2) a list of the days on which Benediction may be given; (3) certificates of the erection of the Stations of the Cross, of the authenticity of relics, etc.; (4) a list of foundation Masses (if any); (5) the vesting prayers (hung somewhere convenient at the back of the vesting press).

The books needed in the vestry include missals, *Missale Defunctorum,* Epistolary and Evangeliarium (usually in one volume), *Ritus Servandus* or 'Benedictionale,' *Ordo Administrandi Sacramenta* (or the Roman Ritual), the Manual of Prayers, book of the Epistles and Gospels, a Bible, *Memoriale Rituum* (in small churches), *Liber Usualis* (for singing), a register for the names of visiting priests who celebrate Mass, cards (covered in mica, or protected in some other way) with vernacular prayers after private Mass, the responses for Mass servers, and the prayers at the incensation of the altar (if these are not given on the altar cards). In cathedrals and other greater churches there will be a copy of *Caeremoniale Episcoporum,* of *Pontificale Romanum,* the *Canon Pontificalis,* a card with the music of the *Confiteor* and with the form of the indulgence at episcopal functions, and the music of the Passion for Holy Week. The registers needed in a parish church[6] comprise those of baptisms, of confirmations, of marriages (with a special secret register, in addition), of the dead, and of the *status animarum.* There may be also a register of foundation Masses.

II. Furniture of the Working Sacristy

A working sacristy needs much accommodation for the material equipment of a church, and it is of great advantage to have a store-

[6] R.R. Appendix IV.

room, if possible, attached to it. A tall press will be needed for such things as the processional canopy and umbella, the catafalque and mortuary candlesticks,[7] the Tenebrae candlestick (hearse), the candlestick for the Paschal candle,[8] banners and poles, a lectern, standard candlesticks (if used). Presses are also needed for: (1) acolytes' candlesticks, thuribles (hanging up) and incense boats, bells and clappers (if used in Holy Week), the lustral water vat, etc.; (2) the Exposition throne, missal-stands, the stand for the processional cross; (3) candlesticks and flower-vases; (4) the Christmas crib and the requisites for Holy Week (including a temporary tabernacle and the casket for the Altar of Repose); (5) a ewer and basin, small salvers, collecting plates, carpets, cushions, etc.; (6) for cleaning things (brushes, pails, etc.); (7) for music (unless provision is made for this near the organ). Special lockable presses will be needed for altar wine and candles; and a place for storage of oil, charcoal[9] and tongs, with a receptacle for candle ends. Stands (with slots lined with rubber or felt) are necessary for the processional cross (and the special wooden cross for Stations of the Cross, if this be used), torches (six usually), lanterns (if used in outdoor processions), candle extinguishers. A wardrobe is essential for servers' cassocks, cottas and slippers. If the sacrarium is not in the sanctuary, it must be provided in one of the sacristies. A very important thing in a working sacristy is a washing-trough, and beside it a draining-board. Nearby a small press, or at least a shelf, for altar cruets, with a rack to dry finger-towels, etc. The sacristy furniture should include a working-table, chairs, a small table for occasional use in the sanctuary (for the blessing of candles, ashes, palms, etc.), and portable steps.

In a cathedral there must be provision for storing faldstools; extra portable stools, credences and lecterns; the bishop's hand-candlesticks (*bugia*), ewer and basin (*bacile*); extra small salvers; a stand for a crozier and, possibly, for an archbishop's cross.

In a large vestry there is often an altar; and, adjoining the sacristy,

---

[7] Unless these can be stored suitably in the mortuary chapel.
[8] And a special stand to hold the candle before the altar, if the new rite of Easter Eve is followed.
[9] Some provision must be made in this sacristy for lighting charcoal when needed, with a wire basket to hold it over a flame (gas or electric).

a confessional (for occasional use, e.g., for the deaf), a priest's office (with registers locked up in a cupboard, a desk, with parish archives, forms, etc.), a room for meetings (with table and chairs, reference books, a map of the parish, etc.).

Near the exterior door of the sacristy, outside, there should be a large vat—with a tap—containing a supply of lustral water for the use of the people. It should be marked "LUSTRAL WATER" or "HOLY WATER."

CHAPTER XX

The Baptistery and Baptismal Font

THE BAPTISTERY

Aᴏᴛᴇʀ the high altar, the baptistery is the most important part of a parish church—it is the second focal point. Liturgical law has not much to say about the baptistery, but tradition has a great deal. Hence the rules about its construction and furnishings are derived from the rubrics, tradition and practical convenience. By its position, construction and ornamentation the importance of the baptistery should be emphasized.

History

In the early centuries baptism was mainly of adults, sometimes in great numbers, and done by immersion,[1] and so it was carried out wherever convenient near water (a fountain, a river, sometimes the sea). Yet even in the catacombs there is some evidence of the use of a baptistery. The early form of a baptismal font was a vat or tank. From the 4th century a separate building—spacious and highly ornate —came into use for the baptistery near great churches,[2] usually at the north or west corner of the church. Such baptisteries often had two distinct parts, a portico for the preparatory rites, and the baptistery itself. The larger ones had adjoining rooms (as dressing-rooms for the candidates, for the anointing by the priest, and the *consignatio* by the bishop), and sometimes there was also a chapel with an altar for the celebration of Mass.

---

[1] By infusion in case of necessity, even in the 2nd century.
[2] E.g., the baptistery of St. John Lateran's built by Constantine; the great baptisteries of Florence, Pisa, Ravenna.

At first the blessing of the baptismal water and the baptism of candidates was (apart from cases of necessity) limited to cathedrals; and took place on the great baptismal days, Easter and Pentecost eve (and, in a few places, at Epiphany, as in the Eastern Church). By the 6th century a baptistery was permitted in rural churches, in basilicas and in monasteries. Gradually all parish churches had a baptismal font (by about the 11th century), and the power to bless the baptismal water, baptize and anoint with chrism was extended to priests. From the 7th century there was a gradual decline in adult baptism, and in baptism by immersion. Infant baptism became the established practice (it was general about the 8th century). Baptism by immersion began to disappear from the 9th century, although it lasted on, in some places, until the 13th or 14th century,[3] and was common in England in the 16th century. Baptism by infusion was general by the 13th century, and almost exclusively used by the 15th (not, however, in England). Gradually the baptistery grew smaller, became attached to the church building, and eventually part of it (from about the 9th century). The baptistery as a separate edifice began to cease from about that date, though the practice lasted on in Italy until the 13th or 14th century.

The font itself had three forms: a vat beneath the floor level (*piscina*), for immersion; or a standing font on floor level, or (from about the 9th century) above floor level. Gradually the font form succeeded the bath form, and—as baptism by immersion died out—became smaller in size. Local legislation in the 13th century ordered the font to be covered, and, by degrees, this cover became bigger and more ornate—often dome-shaped or pyramidal in form (from the 14th and 15th centuries)—and sometimes surmounted by a civory or canopy.

Law

Every parish church is to have a baptismal font,[4] and the proper place for the administration of baptism is the baptistery in a church or public oratory.[5]

[3] It may still be used, if customary (R.R. II, i, 10; ii, 20).
[4] The word "baptisterium" has many meanings in liturgical language. Two of these are the baptistery and the baptismal font itself. (e.g., R.R. II, i, 42, 46).
[5] C.J.C. 773; 774, § 1. It must not, normally, be administered in the sacristy (S.R.C. 3104[9]).

The traditional place for the baptistery is at the north-west[6] corner of the church and, normally, near the main entrance, for symbolical reasons (the north is associated with the darkness of paganism, and entry into the Church is by baptism) and for practical reasons, since the preliminary rites of baptism are begun in the narthex or porch of the church, and so the baptistery should be near the main door.

The baptistery should, if possible, be a quite separate chapel—closed off by a grille—and it is becoming and traditional that it be *below* floor level, so that the candidate for baptism descends to the font (baptism means burial with Christ, followed by resurrection with him).[7] If a separate chapel is not feasible, a corner of the main edifice must be railed off and used as a baptistery.[8] Entrance to the baptistery should not be directly from the narthex or porch, but from the church, since the rite of baptism is begun in the narthex, continued in the church outside the entrance to the baptistery and finished at the font within it.[9] The baptistery may be of any shape (octagonal or round was the most usual form when it was a separate building), and its size will depend on the size of the church, but it should be spacious enough to accommodate comfortably those who take part in the solemn blessing of the baptismal water (on Holy Saturday[10] and the eve of Pentecost), or the persons present at the administration of baptism. It should be open to view from the church (so that the people may see the ceremony that takes place there—the initiation of a new member of the Church concerns the local spiritual community, the parish), and the entrance should be closed by a gate that can be locked.[11]

The baptisteries of former days were richly decorated—roof, walls, floor—with symbols connected with baptism and the hallowing of baptismal water. The traditional symbols are the Good Shepherd, the monogram of Christ, A & Ω, the lamb; the four rivers of Paradise, the palm tree, the hart (cf. Psalm 41), the phoenix, the peacock. It was

---

[6] In a church that has not got a great west door, the baptistery may take the form of a chapel at the west end, in the middle of that end wall.
[7] Cf. Romans 6.4; Colossians 2.12. Three steps are suitable for symbolical reasons.
[8] Cf. R.R. II, i, 46; ii, 12: M.R. VI, ii, § IV, n. 6.
[9] R.R. II, ii, 1, 12, 17.
[10] This, however, may now take place at the high altar.
[11] Unless the font itself is locked, as R.R. I, ii, 46, directs. Even then it is better to keep the baptistery locked to preserve this hallowed place from any irreverence.

also customary to depict scenes from the Old Testament, and from the New (e.g., the Samaritan woman at the well, the marriage feast of Cana, the curing of the paralytic at the Probatica Pool, the resurrection of our Lord). The rubric[12] now orders that, where it can be done without difficulty, the baptistery be adorned with an image (statue, painting, sculpture, stained-glass window) of St. John the Baptist baptizing our Lord. There is nowadays[13] no special blessing of the baptistery. It shares in the consecration or blessing of the church of which now it forms a part.

THE BAPTISMAL FONT

The font has two parts: the basin that holds the water (the font itself) and the base. While the latter may be made of any suitable material, the former should be made of a non-porous material, preferably stone—favoured by tradition and because of its symbolism[14]—or a non-rusting metal, or of wood lined with metal (lead, bronze or any silver-plated metal). The base may be a solid structure, or a column, or several columns. A good height for the font is about three feet (the child has to be held over it at the moment of baptism). The font itself—which may be any shape (round or elliptical, without corners, is best)—is divided into two unequal parts;[15] the larger one to contain the baptismal water, the smaller to receive the water that is used at any particular baptism;[16] each should have a pipe leading to the sacrarium[17] of the baptistery. The top of the font should be flat and some inches wide, so that things used at baptism may, if necessary, be laid on it. The font itself must be fitted with a tight-fitting cover that can be locked,[18] that the baptismal water may be preserved from dirt, or from any profane or superstitious use. This cover should be

---

[12] R.R. II, i, 46.
[13] There was one once, e.g., there is a form of blessing in the 12th century Roman Pontifical, and in the Pontifical of Durandus of Mende (13th century).
[14] Moses drew saving water from a rock; "the rock that was Christ" (I Corinthians 10.4).
[15] Cf. M.R. VI, ii, § v. 9.
[16] Unless this is received into some separate vessel and afterwards thrown into the sacrarium.
[17] See p. 88. If the font itself is not fitted with a pipe, the container of the water must be movable so that it may be emptied from time to time for the renewal of the water. This movable container is very convenient when (as in the new rite for Holy Saturday) the baptismal water is solemnly blessed in the chancel, and then carried in procession to the baptistery.   [18] R.R. II, i. 46.

easily movable, and if very heavy should be suspended by a pulley or worked by some similar device. As the font is to be *decenter ornatum,*[19] the base is often carved or otherwise decorated—with symbols of Baptism, or the Resurrection, etc.—and the font is sometimes (in a larger baptistery) surmounted by a civory or canopy. The font may be veiled in white silk or other becoming fabric. Sometimes a dove, representative of the Holy Spirit, is suspended overhead.[20]

The font is best placed in the middle of the baptistery for convenience in carrying out the rite of baptism and should not be raised over steps.

The baptistery should be properly lighted and heated. It ought to have a small table to hold the requisites for baptism and there should be a lockable ambry permanently fixed there[21] to hold the sacred Oils, marked OLEA SACRA or OLEA BAPT. This ambry is lined with white silk and a white veil may be hung before its door. Another ambry is convenient in which to keep cotton-wool, salt in a damp-proof vessel, the candle and white robe, and the ladle or shell used at baptism, the stoles—or one double one—and the ritual, with, perhaps, the baptismal register (which, however, should be kept under lock and key, and so a standing desk, with a lockable compartment, is very useful in a baptistery).

In medieval times the baptistery was blessed,[22] especially from the 11th century. The blessing was common from the 13th. No rubric today prescribes the blessings of the baptistery, nor is any form of blessing provided in the liturgical books; but after the altar and tabernacle, the baptistery is the most sacred spot in any church. It houses the consecrated water and is the scene of the Christian regeneration and of incorporation into the mystical Body of Christ. It is becoming and traditional to ornament it with flowers, especially on Holy Saturday and the eve of Pentecost.

[19] R.R. II, i, 46.
[20] In the Middle Ages it sometimes contained the Holy Oils.
[21] Cf. R.R. II, i, 53.
[22] There is a form of blessing in the Gelasian Sacramentary. Many of the forms of blessing found in medieval texts were, however, probably for the font itself, not the baptistery.

CHAPTER XXI

Church Bells

O U R present Liturgy[1] mentions two kinds of bells, the large church bell (*campana*) erected in the tower or in a special belfry, and the little bell (*tintinnabulum, parva campanula*), called "the sacring bell," rung at the altar during a sacred function.[2]

In the Middle Ages there was also a medium-sized bell, often erected in a little bellcote on the roof of the church, and rung from the chancel, at the Sanctus, to warn those in the vicinity of the church that the Consecration of a Mass was about to take place. It was called the "Sanctus Bell."

History

The first references to the use of a bell for church purposes date from the 5th and 6th centuries (later, about 800, in England). It seems to have been first used in monasteries to call the monks to the divine offices. There were bells in some basilicas as early as the 5th century, and in some parish churches in the 6th. At first the bells were small, but from the 8th century larger bells came into use; and their size grew ever greater until it reached its maximum in the 14th, 15th and 16th centuries. The special belfry made its appearance in the 8th century, and from the 12th big bells received a name (were "baptized"). They were often decorated with religious motifs and symbols,

---

[1] In C.E., Missal, M.R., R.R. and P.R.   [2] See p. 230.

with a coat of arms, etc. The ringing of the church bells at the Elevation began in the 13th century; and for the Angelus at eventide in the 13th century, in the morning in the 14th, and at midday in the 15th or later.

There was a simple rite of blessing a church bell from the 7th century. In the succeeding centuries (8th and 9th) arose the present elaborate rite of the consecration of a church bell, when the Franks and Celts added lustration with specially blessed water, anointings with Chrism and Oil of the Sick, and fumigation with perfumes.

Law

Canon Law (canon 1169) lays down that it is becoming that churches should have bells to call the faithful to worship, that these bells should be consecrated or blessed,[3] and that their use is entirely under ecclesiastical control. There are no rubrics regarding the form or number of bells, nor concerning belfries.

Two tones are used in bell-ringing, the joyous and the mournful. Generally the sound of church bells is joyous, and so they may not be rung during the last three days of Holy Week. Nowadays, bells can be rung by electricity.[4] It is a prudent precaution, however, to see that they can also be rung by hand in case of the failure of electric power. In theory the bell-ringer should be a cleric, have received the minor order of *ostiarius* or door-keeper, among whose duties is named, at his ordination, the duty of ringing the bell. The Ceremonial (I, vi, 3) gives bell-ringing as one of the duties of the sacristan.

USE OF THE CHURCH BELL

The church bell is used: (1) as a signal, to call the faithful[5] to all services, or announce them beforehand[6] and for the "Angelus,"[5] (2) as a signal and a mark of honour at the Elevation of the Mass,[5] at Benediction, at the Communion of the sick,[7] during a procession of the

---

[3] P.R. (Part II) has the rite of the consecration of a bell; R.R. (IX, ix, 11) has a form of blessing for a church bell.
[4] It is for the Ordinary to determine if an electrophonic bell may be used (S.R.C., Feb. 3, 1951).
[5] C.E., I, vi, 3.
[6] E.g., the Forty Hours' Prayer (I.C. § XI).
[7] C.E. I, vi, 3; R.R. V, iv, 13.

Blessed Sacrament,[8] and to announce the arrival of the Bishop or other "greater prelate" on great occasions;[9] (3) as a sign of joy at *Gloria in excelsis* on Maundy Thursday,[10] Easter Eve or Day,[11] and the Vigil of Pentecost;[12] (4) as a mark of sorrow and of appeal for prayer, when someone in the parish is dying (if this be the custom),[13] to announce a death,[14] and at a funeral.[15]

[8] Cf. S.R.C. 2530.
[9] C.E. I, xv, 4; S.R.C. 3888[1].
[10] Missal and M.R.
[11] C.E. II, xxvii, 23; Missal and M.R.
[12] Missal.
[13] R.R. VI, viii, 2.
[14] Ibid., 4.
[15] R.R. VII, iii, 1. Not, however, on great feasts (from first Vespers) when the Exequial Mass is forbidden (S.R.C. 3570[1], 3946, 4130, 4105[7], Oct. 21, 1927). For the funeral of a child, if the bell is rung, the joyful tone is used (R.R. VII, vi, 2).

PART II

THE ALTAR

CHAPTER I

The History of the Altar[1]

$\mathbf{T}$HE history of the altar in the Roman Rite may, for convenience in a brief treatment, be divided into five periods: (1) the period up to the 9th century; (2) from the 9th to the 14th century (the Relic Age); (3) from the 14th to the beginning of the 19th century (the great reredos period); (4) the 19th century (the Exposition age); (5) the 20th century (the reformation period).

1. To the Ninth Century

Until after the 2nd century Mass was normally celebrated in private houses, while being celebrated, occasionally, also in catacombs and in overground cemeteries. From the 3rd century Christian churches began to make their appearance despite persecution. At first the altar used for the celebration of Mass was a very simple one—a small table; or a small[2] portable altar, square in shape, in wood or stone, laid on a table. It was unconsecrated,[3] unadorned, covered usually with a linen cloth,[4] and with nothing whatever on it except the bread and wine (later on, the book of the Gospels and, sometimes, the pyx containing the Blessed Sacrament for the Communion of the sick). Only from

---

[1] The history of the altar is long and complicated. Only a very simple and brief outline of it can be given here. For a more detailed study readers are referred to the Bibliography (p. 255).
[2] Up to the 11th century the altar, generally speaking, was not bigger than three feet square.
[3] There was no formal consecration of an altar before the 6th century. In the early centuries the celebration of Mass on an altar was considered sufficient to hallow it.

about the 11th century were the cross and lights placed *on* the altar. While the early altar usually had the form of a table, it sometimes was made like a tomb (derived from the celebration of Mass over the tombs of the martyrs in the catacombs or cemeteries). Gradually stone began to supersede wood as the material for the altar[5] (this began to be of obligation, at first by local law, from about the 6th century), the altar became fixed, and relics of the martyrs[6] began to be associated with it.

The practice of covering the altar with a canopy (the civory[7]) began in the 4th century and was a great feature of the high altar especially from the 7th to 9th century. After the Constantinian peace (4th century) great altars were erected in the chief churches of Rome and elsewhere. While these were often made of precious materials (gold, silver, marble, porphyry, etc.) and surmounted by elaborate civories, the essential character of the altar—the simple, unencumbered stone of sacrifice—was kept. All ornament was above or around the altar, not on it. Not until the 9th century was it permitted to place *on* the altar anything that was not abvolutely essential for the celebration of Mass. In the Western Church in the early centuries, Mass was celebrated in close association with the congregation, taking an active part in it—the altar prominent and visible, the celebrating priest often facing the congregation.

2. *Ninth to Fourteenth Century* (*the Relic Age*)

The 9th century was especially the century of widespread popular devotion to relics of the saints. It was in this century that many relics

---

[4] There is mention of this from the 3rd and 4th centuries.
[5] P. 142.
[6] The cult of the martyrs dates from the 2nd century. By their "relics" then—and for several centuries later in the West—was meant the entire body of the saint, honoured at the place of its burial by a *tropaeum* or *martyrium* constructed over it. Only in the 7th or 8th century did the Popes consent to the *translation* of bodies from the place of their burial (a common practice earlier in the East), and to the dismemberment of bodies to make smaller relics. At first the relics of martyrs were under altars (in a crypt or *confessio*); then came—in the 6th and 7th centuries— the practice of sometimes putting relics, in a casket, *into* the altar, which was then a kind of tomb. The 8th and 9th centuries saw the beginning of our modern usage of inserting small relics *into the table* of the altar; and at the same period it was allowed to place reliquaries *on* the altar during the celebration of Mass (p. 135). Finally came the practice (from the 9th century) of putting relics for veneration *over and behind altars* (p. 135).
[7] P. 188.

were enshrined for the first time and "elevated" (placed over altars for public veneration). Up to this time the high altar stood out in the church as the prominent feature, the table—the stone of sacrifice—being kept unencumbered and treated with special respect. Now it began to be invaded by reliquaries, placed either on the table,[8] or, the larger ones, enshrined behind and above the altar. This relic invasion was destined to change, little by little, the character, disposition and even the situation of the high altar. It became necessary to combine the altar with the relic shrine, and so the table, from being square and small, became oblong and larger. The reliquary behind and above the table became bigger and bigger, ever more ornate, and more and more the centre of attraction, so that it ended up by becoming a far more prominent feature of the sanctuary than the altar itself. The accessory usurped the place of the principal.[9] The ever-growing relic shrine led to the abandonment of the *confessio* and to the gradual disappearance of the civory. This, in turn, led, about the 11th century, to the placing on the altar table—at first only during Mass—of the lights which had hitherto generally hung from the roof of the civory, and of the cross, which previously often surmounted the canopy, or had hung from it, or had stood on the floor.

In the 11th and 12th centuries an elementary fixed retable made its appearance, first often as a support for one end of the reliquary over the altar. This grew ever bigger and more ornate until it grew into the huge reredos that was the dominant feature of the altars of the third period (the 14th to the 18th centuries). The position of the altar, too, was changed. Instead of being fully detached and standing out clearly in the middle of the sanctuary, it was moved back against the east wall and became more and more merged into its background, the actual altar itself (the table) becoming ever more insignificant. All these changes in the altar, in the second period of its history, came about not by the legislation of the Church, but through the increasing pressure of popular piety, ever exalting the accessory at the expense

[8] The famous *Admonitio Synodalis*—a Gallican document of uncertain authorship, of the late 8th or early 9th century, possibly dating, in substance, from St. Caesarius of Arles (543)—first recognized and sanctioned the practice of placing reliquaries on the altar. This practice became general in the 10th century.
[9] The same phenomenon occurred in the 19th century, when the Exposition throne became the dominant element of the altar.

of the principal. The building of monasteries on the grand scale in the 11th and 12th centuries, also led to a departure from the simpler altar of the early centuries in favour of the huge, elaborate constructions of the later period.

3. *From the Fourteenth to the Eighteenth Centuries (the Great Reredos Age)*

By the end of the 14th century the retable—which was at first of such modest proportions—had become a great towering structure, the happy hunting-ground for the sculptor and painter. Each decade it grew bigger, and in design ever more complicated and flamboyant. Some retables were even divided into storeys; sometimes there were two altars, one above the other (as in the Sainte Chapelle in Paris). These immense reredoses sometimes stood on their own foundations, sometimes rested on the altar itself—but always they gave the impression that the table of the altar was just "a serviceable base for a superincumbent mass of ornamentation."[10] The dominant features of the high altars of this period were size and over-ornamentation, and these features were in keeping with Renaissance ideas, and with Baroque and Rococo styles of architecture. Not only was the permanent adornment of the altar overdone, but on great feasts temporary adornment (extra candlesticks, reliquaries, church plate, etc.) was piled on to the table of the altar. To add to the complications gradines made their appearance at the end of the 15th century and the beginning of the 16th; while from this century also the tabernacle became an ordinary feature of the high altar. Sometimes it was an elaborate structure—in keeping with the altar itself over-sized and over-ornate; at other times it was a mere cubby hole, lost in the great structure in which it was embedded. The result of this mania for immense, elaborate superstructures was that the altar itself—the table of sacrifice—lost all its significance, was dwarfed out of all recognition and ceased to be the focal point of the church. In a few places, however, the simple, dignified altar of earlier times was preserved; and in the 17th and 18th centuries came a certain reaction which led to the restoration in some churches of the Roman type of altar (that had always

[10] E. Bishop, *Liturgica Historica,* p. 30.

been kept in the great basilicas of Rome), i.e., the simple table with six great metal candlesticks and, in the centre, a great metal crucifix, the whole surmounted by a civory. Just as the "Masses" of Mozart or Beethoven were great musical masterpieces suitable for the concert hall, but not for the church, so many of the "great" altars of the period from the 15th to the early 19th centuries were, possibly, masterpieces of sculpture and painting suitable for exhibition in art galleries and museums, but not conformable to the Church's idea of another Calvary.

4. *The Nineteenth Century (the Exposition Period)*

From the 14th and 15th centuries arose the external worship of the reserved Sacrament by expositions and processions, and from the 16th century was added Benediction with the Sacred Host. All through the 17th, 18th and 19th centuries expositions and Benedictions grew ever more frequent. The true character of the high altar as the place of sacrifice became obscured, the medieval devotion to the altar disappeared, and the altar came to be regarded as the "home of the Blessed Sacrament"—its table, ever more loaded with candles and flowers, the stand for these manifestations of popular piety to the reserved Host. The tabernacles were big and ornate—with crockets, finials, statuettes and all the rest—set into a reredos or into gradines and difficult if not impossible to veil, as the law of the Church prescribes. The idea was current that even for a simple Benediction—lasting but a brief time—it was necessary to enthrone the Sacred Host over the altar, and so arose the practice of having a permanent throne for exposition over every high altar,[11] making it still more impossible to veil the tabernacle, and often (sometimes necessarily) causing the altar cross to be placed in this throne, which is forbidden.[12] Side by side with these manifestations of popular piety to the Blessed Eucharist, there existed an almost universal disregard of what the Church *orders* as permanent and essential marks of respect for It: a canopy (civory, tester, baldachin) overshadowing the entire altar, a veil covering the entire tabernacle.

[11] The altar was built for Reservation and Exposition rather than for Mass.
[12] S.R.C. 3576[3], 4136[2].

To sum up: at different periods in the Church's history, since the 9th century, various usages—largely the result of the impact of popular piety—arose that tended to obscure the real nature of an altar (especially the high altar) and to diminish the respect due to it as the consecrated stone of sacrifice, the focal point of the entire edifice: (1) relic shrines on and above the altar (from the 9th century); (2) retables (from the 11th); (3) immense tabernacles (from the 16th); (4) exposition thrones (especially in the 18th and 19th centuries); and (5) gradines (from the 16th century) piled with candlesticks, flower-vases, reliquaries, etc.

5. *The Twentieth Century*

Our own century has seen the inauguration and development of a movement to restore the real character of the high altar. First of all by having, when possible, a *real* high altar, i.e., a "fixed," consecrated altar (p. 140), not a portable altar—which is not intended for permanent use—set in an elaborate and often costly framework of stone or wood (which is regarded and called "the altar," when in reality it is merely a support for an altar stone). Secondly, by treating that altar as the Church desires — indeed formally orders — that it should be treated, i.e., by having it fully clothed, not only with altar cloths but with a frontal (p. 192), and surmounted by a canopy (p. 188). Thirdly, by respecting the sacred character of the altar *table,* by not making it a mere pedestal for the support of candlesticks (other than those prescribed), flower-vases and other "ornaments." The aim to-day—and may it be crowned with success—is to restore the *dignity* of the altar and the realization of its sacred character, by observing the prescriptions of the Church in its regard; by due attention to the essential elements of an altar, not merely to its temporary decoration.

CHAPTER II

Definition of An Altar

1. WHAT AN ALTAR IS

An altar is an elevated structure on which sacrifice is offered. In the early centuries of Christianity it was known as *altare*,[1] *trapeza*, *altarium, mensa Domini,* and the earliest ideas of it were derived from the table of the Last Supper and from the Cross, not from Jewish or pagan ideas. The Christian altar is a consecrated table of natural stone in which relics of the saints are enshrined, and on which the Christian sacrifice—the Mass—is offered. It is the altar that designates a gift as victim,[2] that signifies its offering to God and its acceptance by him. It is a *table*—because gifts to God are laid on it and the first Christian altars were tables—and so of a certain shape and size. It is made of *natural stone* because this is durable and strong, and for a mystical reason, because the altar represents Christ,[3] the rock, the corner-stone.[4] It *enshrines relics* of martyrs, because from the earliest Christian times the Mass was associated with the martyrs (*Christus inter membra*[5]), and in the earlier centuries the placing of relics in the altar was the chief element in its consecration. The altar is hallowed by a solemn rite, becomes a sacred thing, that it may more perfectly

[1] The term *ara* was avoided, because of its pagan associations, but later it was sometimes used for a portable altar (e.g., R.G. XX).
[2] Cf. Matthew 23.19.
[3] See pp. 167, 193.
[4] I Corinthians 10.4; Ephesians 2.20; I Peter 2.4.
[5] Cf. Apocalypse 6.9. See p. 134.

symbolize Christ; it acquires a certain spiritual power for the more perfect fulfilment of the chief act of the Sacred Liturgy—the offering of Mass—and for the sanctification of those who take part in this. The altar is reserved for the celebration of Mass and for some other liturgical acts closely connected with it; and, while Mass may be celebrated in almost any place, it may never be celebrated except on a consecrated altar.[6]

II. Kinds of Altars

In law there are two kinds of altars, in practice there are three. A *fixed* altar consists of a table (*mensa*) with its supports (*stipites*) consecrated as one whole.[7] A portable altar is a stone—generally small—which is consecrated by itself (i.e., without a base or supports, and so is movable), or the same stone with a base which, however, is not consecrated with it[8] (the stone is merely laid on this base or inserted into it). A fixed altar in a wide sense[9]—which is a very common form in our churches—is a large structure[10] (and so, in practice, immovable) of a permanent character, made in stone or wood, attached to the floor, or to a wall or column of a church or oratory, on the table of which is laid a portable altar (an altar stone). Such a structure—however permanent or immovable—is, liturgically speaking, a "portable" altar.[11] Yet, in ceremonial it is treated as if it were "fixed," e.g., it is incensed.

The distinction between the two kinds of altars arose when the consecration of an altar became a general law. A "fixed" altar is a symbol of the perpetual sacrament-sacrifice; its symbolism is more complete, and so there must be at least one "fixed" altar in every consecrated church (normally the high altar). In a church which is not consecrated, but only blessed, all the altars may be portable—though one or more of them may be consecrated.[12]

---

[6] Apart from very exceptional circumstances such as persecution, when the Holy See may dispense from this.

[7] C.J.C. 1197, § 1. It is "fixed" in relation to its supports, so that if the table were separated from these the altar would lose its consecration. (C.J.C. 1200.)

[8] C.J.C. 1197.   [9] S.R.C. 3162[1], calls it "ad modum fixi."

[10] See p. 152.

[11] It is better to call such an altar a "stable" one, reserving the term "fixed" for the altar consecrated with its supports.

[12] C.J.C. 1197, § 2. S.R.C. 303, 1321[2], 3162[1], 3978[6].

III. Forms of an Altar

History

The earliest Christian altar was a table (generally wooden, round or square or oblong, four-legged, or three-legged, or even one-legged), or the *acrosolium* of the early tombs, and so most forms of altar are derived from these two. The relic cult[13] of the 6th and following centuries gave rise to the tomb form of altar.[14] For many centuries the table was mostly square and small (generally some three feet square). The cult of relics—placed in the altar itself (not merely within the table, as the later practice was) at first, and, later, on or over it—tended to increase the size of the table of the altar, and by the end of the 15th century there were altars with a table as much as twelve feet or more in length.

Law

The present law of the Church allows great freedom in the choice of the form of an altar provided its essential features (*mensa* and *stipites*) are preserved. It may be one solid block of stone, with miniature supports;[15] or a stone table supported on columns (four, five or six),[16] or on slabs of stone at the ends and/or at the back—the space between the columns or slabs being open or filled in (with cement, brickwork, etc.). Or the altar may have the form of a sarcophagus (like a chest or urn), empty or solid.[17] According to the present rubrics the table should be rectangular, not round or oval, because of the four anointings made at its corners—to weld indissolubly table and supports—at the consecration of the altar, and also because the altar is to be clothed in its frontal.[18]

[13] See p. 134.
[14] There were some tomb altars from the second half of the 4th century.
[15] See p. 144. A few such altars existed from the 5th or 6th century; they were fairly general from the 12th.
[16] In early centuries—even up to the 13th—sometimes only one column was used. Since the publication of the *Pontificale Romanum* (1596) there must be stone supports at least at four corners of the table.
[17] See illustrations pp. 150, 151.
[18] See p. 192.

CHAPTER III

The Construction of An Altar

1. THE MATERIAL OF AN ALTAR

At first altars were of wood, an ordinary table being used, or even when a special altar was built; but stone was also used, even from the earliest Christian times, for both movable and immovable altars, in the catacombs or cemeteries. After the Constantinian Peace (4th century) altars in great churches were sometimes made of precious metals (gold, silver, etc.), though often these only covered an altar of wood or stone. But quite soon stone began to oust wood as the material of an altar, because it was durable and strong and easily obtainable; because of its symbolism (natural stone, anointed with sacred oil, more fully symbolized Christ[1]); and because of the early association between altars and the tombs of the martyrs. Stone altars were pretty general from the 6th century—there were some in England then, and even earlier in Ireland. Yet side by side with altars of stone were wooden altars as late as the 11th century, or even later. As early as the 6th century there was local legislation[2] requiring altars to be made of stone. In 769 and 806 the Capitularies of Charlemagne forbade wooden altars. In England and Spain, in the 11th century, there was synodal legislation requiring altars to be of stone. This material was universally used by the 12th and 13th centuries. Finally, the General Rubrics of the

[1] A symbolism in use from the 4th century.
[2] E.g., the Council of Epaon (France) in 517 laid down that only stone altars may be anointed with chrism.

142

Missal[3] (xx) and the rubrics of the Roman Pontifical (1596) prescribed stone for all altars.

Law

Only natural stone may be used for the table and the essential supports of a "fixed" altar; and a portable altar must be one piece of
natural stone.[4]

II. THE CONSTRUCTION OF A "FIXED" ALTAR

A "fixed" altar has three essential parts: (*a*) the table (*mensa,
tabula*), (*b*) the supports (*stipites, tituli*), (*c*) the sepulchre containing relics buried in the table.

1. *The Table of an Altar*

This must consist of one single natural stone, whole and not easily
breakable.[5]

A natural stone is one that corresponds to the mineralogical definition of a stone and is not a composition. Hence synthetic or artificial
stone, concrete and the like may not be used. Any hard stone—common or precious, of any colour—not easily breakable is permitted;
e.g., granite, sand stone, travertine, marble, porphyry and even slate
or schist.[6] Pumice stone, cement, plaster are, obviously, excluded.[7]

The altar table must consist of one single stone slab, unbroken,
without parts, fractures or crevices[8]—symbolizing the personal unity
of Christ—its surface normally being smooth and polished. The slab
must extend at four corners to the supports[9] (on to which it is anointed
at its consecration). The altar table should be thick (say 4 or 4½
inches) for solidity and because the sepulchre must be cut into it. To
mark the place where the stone is signed with blessed water and
anointed at its consecration, it is usual—though not prescribed[10]—to

[3] Beginning of the 17th century.
[4] See p. 140.
[5] R.G. XX; C.J.C. 1198, § 1.
[6] S.R.C. 3674².
[7] S.R.C. 2862¹, 3674³, 4032², 4145¹. A porous stone is undesirable because of the
use of oil on the table at its consecration.
[8] C.J.C. 1198, § 1; S.R.C. 2862¹, 3725, 3750, 3907³, 4191¹.
[9] C.J.C. 1198, § 2.
[10] Cf. S.R.C. 3771.

incise five crosses on the table,[11] one at each corner (some distance from both edges and directly above the supports), and one in the middle.[12] Metal studs may be inserted at the back of the table for fixing altar cloths in position.

2. *The Supports*

The support or base for the table must be of natural stone.[13] It may consist of two stone slabs (one at each end) or of columns (four, five, six).[14] These need not be of one piece (monoliths). The table must be laid *immediately* on the stone supports—with only the cement used for fixing it intervening—and is joined permanently to these by the anointings towards the end of the consecration ceremony.[15]

Regarding the supports: (*a*) only the top of the supports that is joined to the table by the anointing need be of natural stone; the lower part may be of some other material. The supports may be cased in metal, but this should not be done until after the consecration of the altar, so that for this ceremony the supports may plainly be seen to be of stone,[16] (*b*) the stone supports need not (it would seem) necessarily extend to the floor or be fastened to the floor, but of course the entire altar must not be easily movable,[17] because a "fixed" altar is supposed to be stable and there must be no danger of separating the table from the supports, when the altar would be desecrated;[18] (*c*) it would seem that the table should not merely be laid on the supports, but should be cemented firmly to them (*apte cum stipite cohaerere*)[19] because of the danger, otherwise, of separation of table and supports;[20] (*d*) the supports should be close to the table edge, at the

[11] These crosses made their appearance very early—even as early as the 6th or 7th century—though most altars were without them up to the 12th century. They are normally (but not infallibly) a permanent mark of the consecration of the altar.
[12] This cross is distinct from that on the cover of the sepulchre (pp. 150-151).
[13] C.J.C. 1198, § 2. S.R.C. 3282, 3364[2], 3698[1].
[14] It would seem that one (central) pillar would not do. C.J.C. 1197, § 1. speaks of *stipites,* and the table must be joined to them by anointings at the consecration of the altar.
[15] S.R.C. 3364[2], 4073[1], 4075, 4225.   [16] S.R.C. 3698, 4073.
[17] Cf. S.R.C. 4225[1].   [18] C.J.C. 1200[1].
[19] C.J.C. 1198, § 2. Cf. rubric of P.R. at anointing of table and supports (*quasi illa conjungens*). In the case where the table itself forms the cover of the sepulchre (p. 151), it must be cemented on with the cement blessed at the consecration.
[20] A "fixed" altar does not lose its consecration if moved, provided the table is not separated—even momentarily—from the supports.

sides, since at the consecration of the altar, the bishop anoints the table to the support, and also across the line where they meet (e) it is doubtful if one solid block of stone would be apt for consecration,[21] it does not fulfil the requirements of an altar (*mensa* and *stipites*); it must have stone supports, however shallow they may be. In any case, in the rite of consecration the table must be joined permanently to the supports by an anointing with chrism.

If the table be supported on stone slabs, one at each end, or on columns, the intervening space may be left open, or may be filled in[22] with any material (e.g., stone, brick, cement), but the actual supports immediately adjoining the table must be of natural stone. If there is a space under the table, opening from the back, it may not be used as a cupboard,[23] even for sacred vessels.

At its consecration the altar is anointed on its front face—either in the middle of the support (solid[24] or column), or, if there is no support in the middle, on the front of the table itself (in its thickness) in the centre.[25]

It has been the practice—since the early centuries (6th or 7th) in some places—to mark the spot where this anointing is made with a cross, engraved on the stone. Sometimes this cross is painted on the stone or is made of metal affixed to the stone. In these two cases it should be added after the consecration of the altar.

It is desirable to inscribe on the base, or on the edge of the table, of the altar the names of the saints whose relics are enshrined in it at its consecration.

At the end of the rite of the consecration of a "fixed" altar, a rubric directs that its table be covered with a *chrismale,* i.e., a waxed linen cloth. This cloth is to prevent the linen altar cloths from being stained by the holy oils with which the table had been anointed. It may be discarded as soon as all trace of these oils has disappeared.

[21] Bliley (p. 64) allows it; so does Nabuco (II, p. 36), and then considers the floor (*basis super qua petra reponitur*) as a stipes for the anointing!
[22] In the sarcophagus type of altar the base, while solid in appearance, may be hollow (S.R.C. 3282).
[23] Cf. S.R.C. 3741.
[24] If the front is solidly built of a material other than stone, a natural stone is inserted into the centre of this to take the anointing.
[25] Cf. S.R.C. 4225².

A.   Plan of a large altar, with no gradine, surmounted
by a civory

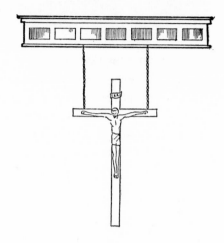

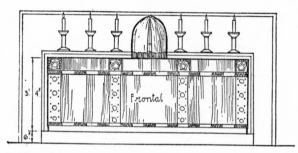

B. Plan and elevation of a smaller altar, showing a gradine and a base for a
monstrance stand or throne, with a tester and a hanging cross.

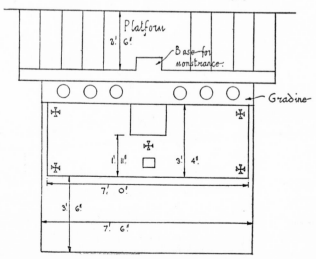

3. *The Relic Sepulchre*

The third essential part of an altar that is to be consecrated is the "sepulchre": a small, square or oblong cavity cut in the table, or (in the case of a "fixed" altar), if preferred, cut or built into the base of the altar. It is so called because the relics which it is made to contain represent the bodies of saints buried under the altar, as they sometimes were in the *confessio* constructed under the high altar in some of the

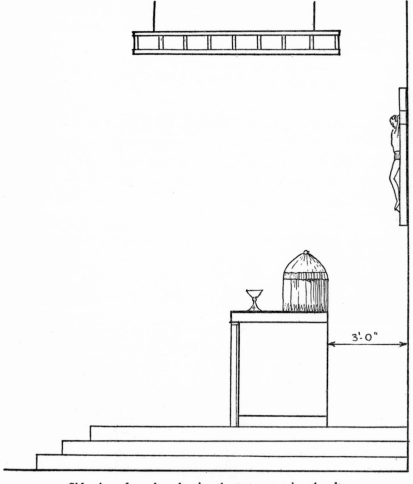

Side view of an altar showing the tester covering the altar
and the celebrant.

old churches.[26] The sepulchre is generally placed in the middle of the altar table towards the front edge, but—in a "fixed" altar—it may also be placed midway[27] between the table and the floor, either in the front or back of the altar;[28] or it may be located in the middle on the top of the support, under the table (which, in this case, may be used as the cover of the sepulchre).[29]

The sepulchre must be made of *natural stone,* of any kind, and so must be either cut into the table (the usual and most convenient way of constructing it) or into the support, if this is stone; or must be built, in stone, into the support, if this be made of some other material.[30] It must be closed by a lid—sufficiently solid—of natural stone.[31] This cover should fit easily into a rebate made to receive it (allowance being made for the cement used to fix it), and should, when fixed, be flush with the table of the altar.

At the consecration this lid is anointed with chrism on its lower face before being fixed on; and on its upper face, after it has been cemented in place. It is the practice—but is not prescribed—to incise a small cross on each face of the lid to mark the place of these anointings. The lid is permanently fastened down, in the course of the ceremony of consecration, with cement mixed with the "Gregorian water"[32] and specially blessed.[33] If, by accident, in chiselling out the sepulchre the altar table should be perforated, it suffices to place a fresh piece of stone over the perforation, at the bottom of the cavity, to close it up before the relics are enclosed.[34]

Into the sepulchre in the course of the consecration ceremony are placed a reliquary,[35] three grains of incense and a parchment—which

[26] The rubrics of P.R. call the sepulchre *confessio.*
[27] When the front is solid. The sepulchre is cut into it if the front is of natural stone; built into it (in stone) if the front be of other material. See illustrations pp. 150, 151.
[28] It may be necessary to adopt this method if the relics are too bulky for burial in the table itself.
[29] Obviously, this form of sepulchre is the least convenient.
[30] C.J.C. 1198, § 4. S.R.C. 3162², 3567¹, 3585¹, 4082¹, 4227¹.
[31] For valid consecration a metal lid is *tolerated,* but not cement or wax (S.R.C. 3567, 3585, 4082¹).
[32] Water into which salt, ashes and wine have been mixed. Its blessing forms the first part of the rite of consecration of an altar.
[33] The prayer of blessing speaks of cement composed of lime and sand; other materials may be used. If they are, the prayer is to be altered to name them (S.R.C. 4165¹). [34] Cf. S.R.C. 3884, 4204.
[35] In a portable altar the relics are placed directly in the sepulchre.

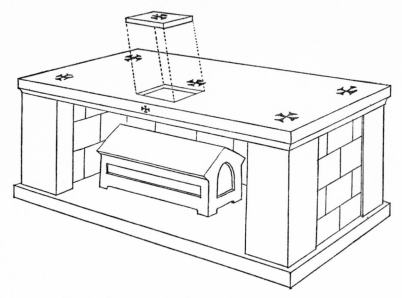

Fig. 1. Open altar showing sepulchre set in the table,
stipes at each corner.

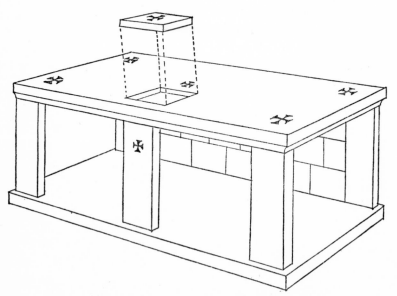

Fig. 2. Another type of open altar with five or six stipites

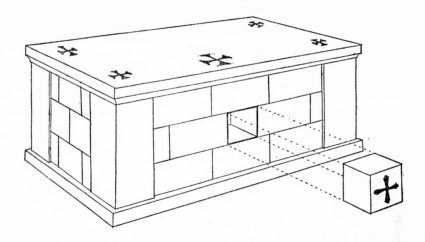

Fig. 3.   Closed altar with sepulchre set into the front

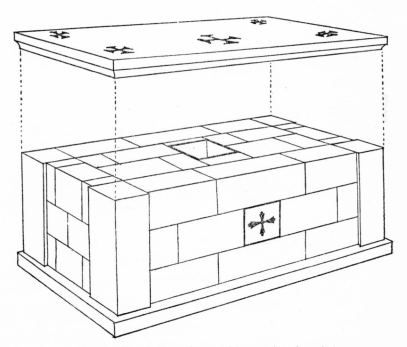

Fig. 4.   Closed altar with sepulchre set into it and the
table used as its cover

may be enclosed in a glass or metal vial to preserve it—containing the attestation of the consecration.[36]   The reliquary—which may be made of any "becoming and clean material" (P.R.), preferably of a non-corroding metal, gold, silver or lead—should contain the authenticated and primary[37] (or direct) relics of two canonized martyrs.[38] For validity the relics of one saint suffice, provided they are those of a martyr;[39] but the rubrics and prayers of the rite of consecration suppose the relics of martyrs.   Other relics may be added; and it is very becoming to add a relic of the Titular of the church or altar, if available.   Relics of a beatified person will not do.   Relics must be enclosed in the sepulchre at the consecration, even though a body of a saint is entombed beneath the altar.[40]   In the centre of the cover of the reliquary a slight circular sinking is formed and a cross engraved on it. When the relics, etc., have been placed in the reliquary this is tied with a ribbon, and sealed at the knot (usually with the seal of the consecrating prelate), the seal being placed in the sinking.

The sepulchre must be big enough to permit the bishop to anoint its four interior corners—he signs each corner twice with chrism—and to contain the reliquary, incense and attestation.   A suggested size is 4¾ inches long by 3¾ inches wide by 1¼ inches deep.

III. The Stable Altar

An altar that is not "fixed," nor yet "portable" and which S.R.C. speaks of as "ad modum fixi"—may, for clearness' sake, be called "stable."   It is a very common type of altar and may have two forms: (1) a large wooden or metal base (called popularly and liturgically treated as "the altar"), having laid on it, or embedded in it, a portable altar (an altar stone);[41] (2) a full-sized stone altar, which has not been consecrated as a "fixed" altar, and so, to be used for Mass, must have an altar stone laid on it or inserted into its table,[41] when an

---

[36] The form is given in P.R.   It mentions the Titular of the altar and the names of the saints whose relics are enshrined.   The relics of an unknown saint may be used, if authentic (S.R.C. 542).
[37] Part or parts of their bodies.   Probably primary relics (p. 199) are necessary for validity.
[38] S.R.C. 2991³, 4082¹.
[39] S.R.C. 4180³; cf. 2777, 3155.
[40] Cf. S.R.C. 3330.
[41] This, then, is the real altar and not the large structure on which it lies.

altar stone is thus laid on the table, and so protrudes above it, it is dangerous since it makes it easy to overturn the chalice. This danger can be eliminated by: (a) laying a wooden table over the altar table with the stone set in this, almost flush with its surface; or (b) sinking the altar stone into the altar table.

If this is done with a stone table, will the cavity made to take the altar stone prevent the table being apt for consecration at some future date? It would seem not, for such a cavity would not, normally, be an "enormous fracture"[42] in the table; and indeed it might possibly be used for the sepulchre when the altar is to become a "fixed" one.

It suffices to have a "stable" altar in a church which is only blessed and not consecrated.[43] Such an altar receives liturgical honour (e.g., is incensed at solemn Mass or Vespers), may have a Titular[44] and may become a "privileged altar"[45] (a portable altar may not).[46]

IV. THE PORTABLE ALTAR

History

The portable altar (*ara, altare viaticum*) at first was just a movable piece of wood or stone unconsecrated, but held sacred because of the celebration of Mass on it. From about the 7th century, apparently, there were some portable altars as we know them now, first wooden and then, more and more, of stone—sometimes of precious stone (e.g., of jasper). Many of these small stone altars were encased in wood or in precious metals,[47] and some had relics *under* them[48] (from the 13th century). Some took the form of caskets, set on short legs.

The earliest legislation about portable altars dates from the 8th century. The first permanent, non-portable altars were erected over the tombs of martyrs—often in a *martyrium* or memorial chapel—pos-

[42] Cf. C.J.C. 1200².
[43] S.R.C. 303, 3162¹.
[44] Cf. C.J.C. 1201, § 1.
[45] S.C.I. 334², and July 18, 1902. It would seem that a certain permanency, immobility, is demanded of a "stable altar" to enjoy these privileges (cf. S.R.C. 2510, 3162¹, 4220²).
[46] Cf. O'Connell, *Celebration of Mass,* p. 163.
[47] Such an altar was called *superaltare.*
[48] Relics *in* them, as we have now, is quite a modern requirement. Though prescribed by P.R. (since its first official edition, 1596), they were not considered necessary for validity until decisions of S.R.C. of 1837, 1844, 1846, 1847. Even after that time—up to the promulgation of C.J.C.—a faculty to use an altar stone not containing relics was freely given.

sibly as early as the 3rd century, and certainly after the Constantinian Peace (4th century).

Law

A portable altar (altar stone) is a single slab of natural stone, unbroken and not easily breakable.[49] It is usually square in shape—perhaps oblong is better—and of sufficient thickness to permit of the evacuation of a sepulchre in it. In general, the same rules apply to it regarding material, the sepulchre, etc., as to a "fixed" altar. The sepulchre must be cut into the upper flat surface of the altar stone, not into its thickness in front, though this is not necessary for the validity of its consecration.[50] The relics are put directly—without any reliquary but in an envelope—into the sepulchre, but they must be put *into* the sepulchre, and the lid cemented on with blessed cement.[51] An attestation of the consecration enclosed in the sepulchre is not prescribed for a portable altar. Nor is the special sealing of the relics with the episcopal seal done, as they are not in a case.[52] It is laudable to inscribe on the stone the names of the saints whose relics are enclosed in it at its sacring.

An altar stone, after its consecration, is usually covered over with strong linen or calico, waxed on the inside (because of the remains of the holy oil on the stone) to protect it.

There is a special rite for the consecration of a portable altar in P.R. If an altar was consecrated with the rite for the consecration of a "fixed" altar, because it was believed apt for this, and later it was discovered that the consecration was invalid because of some defect *in the supports* (e.g., the supports were not of natural stone, or were not adhering directly to the table),[53] the altar may be considered a duly consecrated *portable* altar.[54]

[49] C.J.C., 1198, § 1. Cf. S.R.C. 4032[2].
[50] S.R.C. 3671, 4032[2]. S.R.C. in this latter reply ordered that relics must not in future be inserted in the thickness in front; for existing altars of this kind (it said) they were, when it could be conveniently done, to be consecrated with the shorter form.
[51] S.R.C. 3567[2], 3726[1].
[52] S.R.C. 3726[3].
[53] Cf. p. 144.
[54] *Dictionnaire de Droit Canonique,* fasc. XIX, 253.

V. The Dimensions of an Altar

1. Dimensions of a "fixed" altar

No complete dimensions can be given for a "fixed" altar; when it is the high altar, it will vary in size with the dimensions and importance of the church, and the table may be anything from 6 to 12 feet or more in length; 2, 3, 4, or more, feet in depth.[55] Certain dimensions are fairly constant, i.e. (a) the height, 3 feet 4 inches or 3 feet 5 inches, (b) the depth 1 foot 9 inches to 2 feet from the edge of the table to the tabernacle; or to the gradine (if there is one) or back of the table, if there is no tabernacle. The suggested measurement for this depth of the table is based on two considerations: (a) a priest of average height should be able to reach *into* the tabernacle without strain; (b) it should be possible to read without difficulty the centre altar card, which is, normally, placed against the tabernacle or against the cross. If, therefore, there is no tabernacle, and the card is supported by a strut, the table may be of any depth.

The table should: (a) protrude well outside its supports in front, so that the frontal may be fixed well back from the edge of the table to avoid contact with anyone standing at the altar; and (if the support be solid) to avoid hitting the altar with the left knee when genuflecting there; (b) be at least the length of the base,[56] but not too much beyond the supports, at each end, since, at its consecration, the table is joined permanently to these by an anointing with chrism. The table would need to be some 4 inches, or more, thick for solidity, and in order that the sepulchre may be suitably excavated from it. The very minimum an altar suitable for Mass could be is 3 feet by 10 inches.

If a "fixed" altar is found too short or narrow after consecration, it may be added to at either or both ends of the table, or at the back,[57] provided that in doing this the original table is not separated from the supports to which it was fixed at the consecration.

The sepulchre must be capable of containing the reliquary (and this will, of course, vary in size), three grains of incense and the at-

---

[55] Four feet at least will be needed if there is a tabernacle and the altar cross behind it. Room may be needed also for the base of a temporary exposition throne (p. 185).
[56] C.J.C. 1198, § 2.
[57] The added bits are *not*, of course, consecrated.

testation of the consecration. A good average size is 4¾ by 3¾ by 1¼ or 1½ inches deep.

The *footpace* should extend at least some 6 inches beyond the base of the altar (so that when the priest stands at the corner of the table, he will not be at the extreme edge of the footpace) and it is usually carried around it on its two (N. and S.) sides. Its depth will depend on the size of the altar and the importance of the church—a much deeper footpace is necessary in, say, a cathedral, where the Bishop (sometimes with several assistants beside him, seated also) often sits to perform some function. Obviously, the footpace should normally be some 4 feet deep; and the very minimum depth is 3 feet 6 inches to allow the priest at the altar to genuflect without extending his right foot beyond the platform.[58]

2. *Dimensions of a Portable Altar*

A really portable altar—intended to be carried about—should be small and not too heavy; if intended to remain enclosed in the table of a stable altar, it should, for greater convenience, be larger. The very minimum measurement for a portable altar—which must be able to hold the host (on the paten) and the greater part of the base of the chalice,[59] and, in practice, a ciborium also—is some 10 inches square. It must be at least 2 inches thick to enshrine the relics. In a stable altar it is placed in the centre of the table about an inch from the front edge. Instead of setting it exactly flush with the table, it is convenient to have it the *slightest bit* either raised or sunk, so that its position may be easily perceptible to touch.

While a portable altar is, normally, a small square altar stone, it may be the entire stone table of a stable altar.[60]

---

[58] *Re* altar steps, see p. 162.
[59] Cf. C.J.C. 1198, § 3; R.G. XX.
[60] S.R.C. Aug. 21, 1951. This is not desirable, however, as the entire altar (which is really only a portable altar) may then be regarded as a "fixed" altar.

CHAPTER IV

Position of the High Altar

EARLY altars were completely detached and plain — without retables, gradines, etc. In greater churches the high altar stood between the apse (with its choir) and the nave. It was placed on the axis of the apse under the central arch or, less commonly, under a central dome. Often it was built over a *confessio* (a crypt in which the relics of a saint or saints were enshrined). At the back of the apse —with the altar facing towards it and not towards the nave—was the Bishop's throne, flanked by the seats for the clergy. The disappearance of the *confessio,* the change in the position of the throne from the apse to the Gospel side of the chancel (in some places as early as the 9th or 10th century), the appearance of large reliquaries on or behind the altar, the advent of the retable and gradines (from the 11th century), and the placing of the tabernacle on the altar (from the end of the 13th century), all tended to drive the altar from its forward position to the back of the apse, and not infrequently it was embedded in the very structure of the apse (especially in the 16th and 17th centuries).

The position of the altar was also affected by the question of orientation,[1] and the change in the relative position of priest and people for the celebration of Mass.[2] By A.D. 1000 nearly all high altars were turned towards the nave, with their back to the apse.

[1] See p. 16.
[2] See p. 17.

157

Law

There is no general law about the position of the high altar—it may be placed in the apse, either set back or well forward,[3] or situated more towards the centre of the church under a dome.   But it must not be set into the apse—the altar is a separate entity, not part of the structure of the church—and, if it is to be consecrated (and for other practical reasons), it must have a clear passage between it and the wall of *at least* 2 feet 6 inches or 3 feet.

As the high altar is the focal point of the church,[4] it should be raised, well lighted and not set too far back—that it may be clearly visible to all,[5] and may, by its very position,[6] suggest the close link between the priest and the people, and encourage the congregation to take an active part in the Sacred Liturgy.

The height of the position of the altar will depend on the size and shape of the church; it should not be set too low, and so not clearly visible to some of those present in church; nor yet too high, unduly detaching the sacred ministers in the sanctuary from the people.   The high altar usually has three steps[7]—it must have at least one (a foot-pace)—it may have more, and sometimes has in greater churches. The steps by tradition, not law, are uneven in number.   Lesser altars often have only one step (the footpace itself); and these may be, and often are, placed against the wall (they are seldom "fixed" altars).

A window at the east end, behind the altar—though often found and favoured by some architects and artists—is undesirable, unless it be set very high above the altar, because of the morning sun shining into the eyes of priest and people, leaving the altar in comparative obscurity.   But the high altar should be well lighted from the sides of the sanctuary, or from the roof, and from the west end of the church also.

The high altar may be set in the centre of the church, so that the congregation may assemble all around it.[8]   But this position, while

[3] Cf. C.E. I, xii, 11, 13; xiii, 1.
[4] See p. 23.
[5] And the church should be so constructed that this is possible.
[6] Ideally, the people gather around the altar rather than before it.
[7] See p. 162.
[8] See p. 160.

perhaps encouraging the people to take a more active part in the liturgy, has some serious inconveniences: it splits the congregation into sectors, some facing one another, and makes preaching difficult; it cuts off the sanctuary from the sacristy and, in a crowded church, may make the arrival and departure of the sacred ministers and their attendants difficult, or even impossible; and the congregation is not sufficiently barred off from the sanctuary to emphasize its sacred character and to ensure due reverence and prevent disrespect. It suffices —in a large church—to have the people on three sides of the altar, but not on the fourth.

"It seems important," writes Geoffrey Webb,[9] "that the balance between prominence and reverent seclusion should not be hastily upset. There is all the difference between the excess of mystery resulting from the withdrawal of the altar behind the impenetrable screen of the Eastern Orthodox rite, and the opposite extreme of defenceless proximity of an altar to a congregation pressing all around it."

FORBIDDEN POSITION FOR AN ALTAR

(1) An altar on which Mass is celebrated, or at which the Blessed Sacrament is reserved, may not be built under an apartment used as a bedroom.[10]

(2) An altar may not be placed over a tomb.[11] No burial—whatever the rank of the dead person—is permitted nowadays[12] under an altar. A dead body may not be buried nearer to an altar than one metre (3 feet 3 inches)—measured not merely in depth, but in every direction, and from the angle of the table of the altar.[13] An altar may be constructed over a crypt in which bodies are buried, the crypt being by its roof cut off from the altar.[14]

[9] *Post-War Church Building*, p. 113.
[10] Cf. S.R.C. 756, 3525[2], 4213[3].
[11] C.J.C. 1202, § 2. S.R.C. 3944[2], 4220[1], and cf. 3339.
[12] In the early centuries it was customary to bury a bishop or even a priest, under the altar. But even from the 7th century there was local legislation prohibiting this and general legislation from the 17th century.
[13] S.R.C. Oct. 25, 1942.
[14] S.R.C. 3460[2], 4100[5].

Memorial Tablets

It is forbidden to place in churches or their crypts, when these are intended for divine worship, memorial tablets—*a fortiori* monuments—to those who are not buried there and may not, in accordance with Canon Law (canon 1205[2]),

History

MASS FACING THE PEOPLE

From the 4th to the 6th century it was the practice in all greater churches to celebrate Mass facing the congregation. The choir (the clergy) was at the east end; the subdeacon stood behind the altar facing the celebrant. Even in private houses, or in chapels, or even in the catacombs, the celebrant faced the people, when this was physically possible (sometimes, e.g., in the catacombs the celebrant necessarily faced the arcosolium). It is certain that Mass was celebrated facing the people in a church where the Bishop's throne was in the apse, or where there was a *confessio* (the approach of this was from the nave, at the back of the altar),[15] or where the people were at the east end of the church,[16] facing West. The practice of celebrating with the celebrant's back turned to the congregation gradually arose with the change in the position of the people, desiring to face East at prayer, with the growth of the number of priests for missions and in monasteries,[17] and with the multiplication of Masses "for a private intention" and private Masses for the dead (these Masses were said in small chapels, not at the high altar). The practice of saying Mass back to the people, at side altars, gradually spread to the high altar. Yet both systems of orientation[18] and both ways of facing at Mass existed together from the 6th to the 9th or 10th century; and then the eastern apse, and the celebrant facing it, became the prevailing usage. But the practice of celebrating Mass at the high altar facing the congregation has continued to this day (e.g., in the great Roman basilicas and in some of the catacomb chapels) and is now being restored in certain great churches (e.g., in the cathedral of Lisbon).

Law

There is no written law forbidding the celebration of Mass facing the congregation,[19] in fact provision is made for it in the rubrics[20]—

be buried there (S.R.C. 4376). Some authorities opine that this decision does not apply to war memorials since they are not erected to the glory of individuals (*L'Ami du Clergé*, 1922, p. 759).

[15] As now, e.g., in St. Peter's, Rome.   [16] See orientation, p. 16.

[17] Only about A.D. 1000 were the majority of choir monks priests. [18] See p. 17.

[19] This was recognized by the 5th Council of Malines in 1937 (and its Acts were approved by the Holy See) and by the bishops of France in 1945.

[20] R., V, 3; XII, 2.

but in many places there is a legal custom to the contrary, and so permission of the Ordinary must first be obtained before it may be done, and before building an altar for this purpose. To celebrate Mass in this way, turned to the people, is more logical (especially in regard to the parts directly addressed to them),[21] and as it makes it easier to see and hear the celebration it renders active participation by the people more feasible. A further advantage is that it would keep the high altar clear of retables, gradines, etc., and "ornaments." There are, however, practical difficulties about the structure of an altar fitted for this celebration because of the obstruction to the view of the people caused by the essential altar furnishings (cross and candlesticks) and by the tabernacle, which is, normally, on the high altar. Occasionally, too, the altar may be needed for Exposition. These difficulties can, in fact, be overcome: the cross and candlesticks[22] can be slight in design, and the cross may be hung above the altar (and a double-faced cross can, and indeed should be used); the tabernacle may be quite low,[23] and yet ample in size in its interior; the column type missal-stand[24] does not obstruct the view much. In large churches—especially where there is a reto-choir—there is a growing practice of having a double high altar, so that, on occasion, Mass may be celebrated facing the congregation. Another arrangement, in a large church, is to have two altars, one above the other, the higher allowing the celebration of Mass facing the people, the lower (with the tabernacle) for Low Mass with the celebrant not facing the congregation.[25]

[21] Such as the Epistle and Gospel.
[22] For private Mass where only two are needed they can be placed one at each end of the table of the altar.
[23] The Blessed Sacrament need not always be reserved at the high altar (p. 172).
[24] P. 227.
[25] See, e.g., *Liturgical Arts*, Nov. 1950, p. 20 and illustration.

CHAPTER V

The Altar Steps

AT first the altar stood on the ground, but quite early—from the 4th century perhaps—it was placed on a platform (the footpace or predella) that it might be better seen and attention more securely focused on it. Later the use of steps arose, the number varying in different places and at different periods. By the 15th century the usual number was three.[1] In the early centuries the bishop's throne in the apse was higher than the altar—he dominated the assembly and he "descended" to the altar.

Law

According to the rubrics only two structures in the church have *a right* to steps; the high altar and the bishop's throne (which now must not be placed higher than the altar).[2] Steps to the altar are supposed by C.E., e.g., I, xii, 10, 11, 16, and by *Ritus,* e.g., II, 2, 4; III, 1, XII, 6 (it speaks of the celebrant ascending and descending). C.E. I, ix, 5, speaks of the deacon "in gradu altaris infra suppedaneum," and R., IV, 7, directs the deacon and subdeacon to stand behind the celebrant "unus post alium" and afterwards to "ascend." The steps may be of any suitable material; it is best, however, to have a wooden footpace (because of the cold in winter). By tradition the number of steps is uneven (so that one arrives on the footpace on the

[1] Possibly because of the position of the deacon and subdeacon at Mass, standing behind the celebrant at different levels, because of the difference in rank of all three.
[2] See p. 94.

same foot that one began the ascent with), and will vary according to
the size and position of the altar.[3]   It is desirable that the footpace
and steps should have rounded corners, to avoid possible nasty knocks
against them when moving about during a ceremony. The steps of
an altar should be easy—low and deep, for safety and comfort—say
at least 12 or 13 inches deep,[4] 5 or 6 inches high. The steps are normally carried around the altar on its north and south sides, but they
should not be carried across the sanctuary (the inferior ministers at a
ceremony should, when at rest, be on the ground level, lower than
the sacred ministers).

[3] Often a cathedral high altar has five steps; this ensures that its footpace will be
higher than that of the throne. To have more than five steps to an altar would be
inconvenient for ceremonial (cf. S.R.C. 1265[4]).
[4] Some authorities prescribe as much as 24 inches, especially in a large church
where there is ample space.

CHAPTER VI

Side Altars[1]

In the early centuries the principle of one altar in one church was observed. As there was one Christian community under one head, with one liturgy with its single sacrifice, concelebrated, one altar must be the external sign of this. Unity was demanded also by the symbolism that saw in the altar the representation of Christ. In the great basilicas the high altar was reserved for the Pope; in cathedral or monastic churches the high altar was often reserved for the Bishop or abbot, or used for the conventual Mass only. By the 6th century, however, the multiplication of altars in a church was fully established. It necessarily arose with the increase in the number of priests and of private Masses[2] and the gradual disappearance of the early practice of concelebration (which almost disappeared in the 9th century). Chapels in a church were also multiplied when the cult of the saints and their relics increased, and when chantries grew more common. From the 13th to the 15th centuries the number of altars became excessive —they were placed not only in side chapels (which preserved the unity of the high altar), but along the walls or against pillars in the church; and this not only in greater churches, where many Masses were celebrated, but also even in parish churches, where many altars were not at all needed. In the more correct churches, however, the tradition about the unity of the altar was maintained, and side altars

[1] See p. 14.
[2] This became an abuse in the 9th and 10th centuries and there was papal legislation to check it in the 11th and 12th centuries. This resulted, for a brief period only, in a reduction in the number of altars.

164

were placed in side chapels, or at least recessed (e.g., at the end of transepts) so as to be scarcely, or not at all, in view from the west end of the church.

Law

There is no law forbidding the multiplication of altars in a church —they are essential in greater churches; and even in a small parochial church one side altar, at least, is necessary for Maundy Thursday and for the second day of the Forty Hours' Prayer—but the traditional practice should be observed of maintaining the unity of the altar, and so side altars should be in side chapels, or, at least, entirely cut off from the high altar, and so recessed that they are not seen from the west end of the church. Side altars should not either by their position or their number distract attention from the high altar.[3] Nor should unnecessary side altars be erected in any church. Statues should be placed on pedestals, or on corbels or brackets; an altar should not be erected merely as a stand for a statue.

Side altars may be, but usually are not, "fixed" altars. No permanent tabernacle should be constructed on them (or, at most, only on one of them)—not more than one extra tabernacle is ever needed in an ordinary church, and that may be a temporary, movable one. A tabernacle should not—even when empty—be used as a base for a statue, reliquaries, flowers, etc. This is definitely forbidden, of course, when the tabernacle contains the Blessed Sacrament.[4]

When possible, side altars should be so placed that the priest when celebrating at them is facing East[5] and will not have his back to the high altar. The more dignified[6] side altars are placed nearer the high altar (the most dignified on the Gospel side).

The length of a side altar will depend on its setting, it should not, if possible, be less than 3 feet; its depth at least 15 to 20 inches.[7] Its height will be the same as for a high altar (some 40 inches). The normal furniture of a side altar is a cross and two candlesticks.

[3] It is quite incorrect to have side altars flanking the high altar, and actually within the chancel. Nor should they be placed against side walls, unless they are recessed.
[4] S.R.C. 2613[6], 2906.
[5] This is traditional, there is no law about it.
[6] If the altar is a "fixed" one it is of greater dignity; if several altars are "fixed" their relative dignity is that of their Titulars.

THE ALTAR OF THE BLESSED SACRAMENT

In cathedral, collegiate and conventual churches, where the choir functions are carried out at the high altar, the Blessed Sacrament is to be reserved, as a rule, not at the high altar but in a distinct chapel.[8] This may happen also even in other churches, for a special reason.[9] The altar in this chapel is to conform to the rules regarding ornamentation, etc., laid down by the rubrics for the high altar at which the Blessed Sacrament is, normally, reserved. The chapel of the Sacrament should be the most beautiful of all the chapels in any church.[10] Its decoration should be Christocentric (inspired, say, by the Apocalypse) and appropriate to the Blessed Eucharist as sacrament-sacrifice. "The classical custom in the great Roman basilicas is to dedicate the Eucharistic altar exclusively to the adoration of the Blessed Sacrament; hence pictures of the Madonna or of the saints are excluded in favour of representations of the most holy Trinity, the angelic choirs, or even those celestial beings who, lost in rapturous adoration, pay homage to the divine Guest in the tabernacle."[11]

[7] Deeper, of course, if there is a tabernacle. The footpace should be at least 3 feet 6 inches deep.
[8] C.J.C. 1268, § 3. C.E. I, xii, 8.
[9] P. 173.
[10] C.J.C. 1268, § 2. C.E. I. xii, 8, 16. "Ornatissimus locus"; "Altare prae ceteris sumptuosius ac nitidius exornandum est."
[11] Cardinal Schuster, *The Sacramentary* (I, 172).

CHAPTER VII

The Sanctity of the Altar

ACCORDING to the mind of the Church an altar is primarily the stone of sacrifice on which the divine Victim is offered; it is also the sacred table from which the people are fed with the Body of Christ, and a tomb in which the relics of his martyrs lie buried. The altar is a holy place by: (1) *its solemn consecration,* by an elaborate rite of lustrations, anointings, incensings, with numerous prayers, etc., whereby it is, as it were, baptized, confirmed and hallowed for its sacred purpose; (2) *its use* as the stone of sacrifice, the place of reservation of the Blessed Sacrament and the table of the Divine Banquet; (3) *its symbolism* as the figure of Christ (the anointed King, Priest and Prophet), of Calvary and of the Table of the Last Supper. Accordingly, the Church honours the high altar as *the* sacred place in the church: the ministers of the sanctuary bow or genuflect to it;[1] the celebrant kisses it no less than eight times in the course of a solemn Mass, and he alone may place his hands on its table when he genuflects there; it is incensed at High Mass, at Lauds and Vespers; lights burn before it;[2] on Maundy Thursday, after Tenebrae, it is washed with wine and water by the Bishop and his clergy in some cathedrals.

Because, then, of the sanctity of the high altar the Church *orders* that it be specially honoured by being surmounted by a canopy and

[1] E.g., R., II, 2; XII, 6. C.E. I, xviii, 2.
[2] C.E. I, xii, 17, directs at least three lamps to burn before the high altar, at all events on great days (even when the Blessed Sacrament is not reserved there).

clothed with a frontal and altar cloths, and permits that it be adorned, on occasion, with reliquaries and flowers. Apart from these appointed ornaments, and what is essential for Mass or other sacred functions (such as the cross and altar lights), the altar is to be unencumbered.[3] Because of its consecration, its symbolism and its use, the altar—in its position, in its setting, in its ornamentation—is to be austere, dignified, majestic and awesome. This sacred character of the altar is emphasized and secured from disrespect when the laws of the Church concerning its structure and ornamentation are observed.

[3] R.G. XX and the episcopal charge of the clergy at a Synod (*Ordo ad Synodum,* in P.R., Part III).

CHAPTER VIII

The Title of An Altar

I n origin the "Title" was a stone embedded in the front of a Roman house having on it the name of the owner. Then "Title" was used for the inscription, on the base of an altar of the name of the saint whose relics were there, and to whom the altar was dedicated.[1] Each "fixed" altar,[2] at least, must have a Title, and the high altar of a church is to have the same primary Title as the church itself.[3] It may have a second Title added to that of the church. If the high altar of a church has a different Title from that of the church itself then: (1) If the altar is to be consecrated, it must then be given, as primary Title, that of the church; (2) if it is already consecrated an indult must be sought from the Holy See to change the Title.

A portable altar may have a Title; and ought to have one if it is "quasi-fixed,"[4] bestowed on it when it is erected as such. The Title of a fixed altar may be changed only by Apostolic indult; that of a portable altar by leave of the Ordinary.[5] While, in the past, the Title of an altar was the saint whose body lay beneath it, now the Title may be different from the saint(s) whose relics are enclosed in the altar. An altar—like a church—may not be dedicated to a *Beatus* without Apostolic indult.[6] Two altars in the same church may not have the

[1] Cf. Genesis 28.17-18. The term "titulus" is also used of the support (*stipes*) of the table of an altar.
[2] P. 140.
[3] C.J.C. 1201, § 2.
[4] P. 152.
[5] C.J.C. 1201, § 3.
[6] C.J.C. 1201, § 4.

same Title, but different titles of our Lord or our Lady may be chosen.[7] The feast of the Title of an altar is not celebrated in any special way;[8] that of the high altar is celebrated with the Title of the church.

Image of a Titular

There is no strict law requiring that an image of the Title of an altar be placed above it, but it is very becoming to do this—especially for the high altar, whose Title is that of the church.[9] No other image may be used over an altar that has a Title, but the image of another person may be added to that of the Title.[10]

[7] S.R.C. 3723[3], 3732, 3791.
[8] S.R.C. 3072.
[9] It is becoming also to have externally an image of the Title of a church over the main door.
[10] S.R.C. 2752[5,7], 2762, 4191[3,4]. An image in stained glass does not count as a cultual image.

CHAPTER IX

Additions to An Altar

I. THE TABERNACLE

1. History of Reservation of the Blessed Sacrament

Reservation of the Blessed Sacrament dates from the earliest centuries of the Church, not for private worship but (a) for the liturgical purpose of the *fermentum* (a sacred Particle sent by the Pope from his Mass to the cardinal priests of Rome, or by a bishop to the priests of his city, to be put into the chalice at the Fraction of their own Masses, in token of the unity of the holy Sacrifice wherever offered, and of the intimate union between a bishop and his flock); (b) for the Communion of the sick; (c) to communicate the faithful in time of persecution, and (d) for Communion in private houses when the Liturgy was not possible, or on days when it was not carried out. The form of Reservation has differed much at different periods and in different places; there was no uniformity until after the 16th century. At first the Blessed Sacrament was reserved in the private house; or even on the person, of a bishop, or priest, and indeed, sometimes of a layman. Then came: (a) Reservation in a cupboard in the *sacrarium* (a room adjoining the sanctuary of the church); this continued in some places in the West until the 12th or 13th century, and was fairly common in North Italy even as late as the 16th. (b) Reservation in an aumbry in a wall of the church; this was the common form in Italy, Germany and Spain until the 16th century. (c) In the West, from about the 11th century or perhaps earlier, the sacred

---

[1] There is no certain evidence of the private worship of the Blessed Sacrament in England, until the 11th or 12th century.

Hosts were suspended in a dove,[2] tower, pyx, cup or basket of precious material (gold, silver, alabaster, ivory, crystal), or, in poor churches, even of tin or wood (but generally lined with gold), covered with a canopy or veil, and hung from the civory of the high altar or from a crozier-like pole. This was the usual form of Reservation in England[3] up to the Reformation, in France until the Revolution;[4] it was not common in Germany or the Low Countries, nor in Italy, and was almost unknown in Spain. (d) Reservation in a "sacrament house" or tower (often a large and elaborate structure) built in the church. Sometimes the Sacred Host was visible, being enshrined in a transparent container. This form of Reservation was much used in Germany and in the Low Countries, from the 14th to the 18th centuries. It was used in some places in France, in Italy, Switzerland and Scotland (at the end of the 15th century). (e) Finally the Blessed Sacrament was sometimes reserved *on* the altar, temporarily, in a pyx, casket or movable tabernacle, but there is no certain evidence of permanent reservation on the altar before the 9th century, or even much later.

Law of Reservation

The present Law of the Church on Reservation is found in C.J.C. 1265-1271[5] and in an Instruction of the S. Congregation of the Sacraments of March 26, 1929, and of Ascension Day 1938. C.J.C. 1268 deals with the *altar of Reservation:* (a) The Blessed Sacrament is to be reserved habitually at only one altar in any church; it may be reserved temporarily[6] (e.g., to give Holy Communion during the Forty Hours' Prayer, to give Benediction in a side chapel) at a second altar. (b) Reservation is to be at the most important and finest altar and so, ordinarily (*regulariter*)[7] but not necessarily always[8]—at the high

---

[2] The use of a hanging dove *as a symbol* (e.g., of the Holy Spirit) is very early; the first certain reference to the suspension of the Blessed Sacrament in a dove is in the 9th century (some say not before 1000).
[3] The pyx or cup was more used in England than the dove.
[4] By special privilege it still obtains in Amiens cathedral and in the Benedictine Abbey of Solesmes.
[5] See also C.E. I, vi, 2; xii, 8, 16; and R.R. V, i, 6.
[6] Cf. S.R.C. 3449[3], 3525[4], 3576[6].
[7] C.J.C. 1268, § 2. In a church where Exposition is continual the Sacred Particles for Holy Communion are kept at a side altar (S.R.C. 3449[3]).
[8] S.R.C. 3449[1], 4071[3].

altar, unless another altar is more convenient and becoming to give the reverence and worship that are due to so great a sacrament. (*c*) In cathedral, collegiate or conventual churches, in which choral functions take place at the high altar, it is proper that the Blessed Sacrament be usually reserved at another altar.[9] and this should, if possible, be out of sight of the choir.[10] (*d*) The altar of Reservation is to be ornamented beyond all others.[11]

2. The Structure of the Tabernacle

History of the Tabernacle

In the Old Testament the "Tabernacle" was the movable, tent-like sanctuary of the Jews.[12] In the liturgical language of the Middle Ages the word "tabernacle" had many meanings: an altar surmounted by a civory, an ostensory or monstrance, a tower-shaped vessel for preserving the Blessed Sacrament or relics, the veil over the casket containing the Sacred Hosts, and finally the safe in which Reservation takes place. Reservation in a locked tabernacle, placed permanently on the altar, was first ordered in France (by the Archbishop of Paris, Eudes de Sully) in 1198. Local legislation tried to enforce this, but suspension of the Blessed Sacrament continued. In England in the 13th century there were some fixed and locked tabernacles, but attempts to extend this usage were resisted in England and Ireland. Cardinal Pole (16th century) ordered the Blessed Sacrament to be reserved in a fixed locker above or near the high altar, but the tabernacle was not common in England until well after the Reformation. In Germany the mural aumbry or the sacrament house continued to be used, and the oldest tabernacle belongs to the first half of the 14th century. In Italy tabernacles became more general in the 16th century; in the North, however, only in the 17th and 18th centuries. Legislation from the Holy See about Reservation is remarkably late. Innocent III (1198-1216) and Honorius III (1216-1227) did order that the Blessed Sacrament must be kept in all churches under lock

[9] C.J.C. 1268, § 3; C.E. I, xii, 8; S.R.C. 3335[1], 4071[3].
[10] Cf. S.R.C. 2903. The ideal place for Reservation is a special chapel where this is possible; in a large church this chapel should be easily discoverable by visitors.
[11] Its chief and essential ornament being a canopy (C.E. I, xii, 13; xiv, 1. S.R.C. 1966, 2912). See p. 188.
[12] Cf. Exodus 26.

and key; C.E. (1600) supposed a tabernacle for the Reservation,[13] and the Roman Ritual (1614) definitely ordered this. Finally a decree of S.R.C. in 1863[14] abolished all other forms of Reservation. The tabernacle way of reserving the Sacred Hosts became essential for safety's sake, and when Communions became frequent; and it was the universal form of Reservation by the middle of the 18th century.[15]

Law Regarding the Tabernacle

The liturgical law regarding the tabernacle is found in C.J.C. 1269, R.R., V, i, and the Instructions of the Congregation of the Sacraments of March 26, 1929, and May 26 (Ascension Day), 1938.

(a) *Place of the Tabernacle.* The tabernacle must be placed "in media parte altaris,"[16] either on the table itself, or on a gradine, if there is one, or between gradines, but *not built into a gradine or reredos,* for: (i) the tabernacle is, and ought to appear as, something distinct from the altar itself, (ii) it should be covered at the back and sides by the conopaeum,[17] (iii) it must not prevent the altar cross being placed in its proper position, i.e., behind the tabernacle in the same line with the candlesticks.[18] If the tabernacle is placed on the table itself, it should be slightly raised so that its door will open out easily over the altar cloths. It must not be too near the front edge of the altar, so that there is no proper space for the corporal when spread for Mass; nor too far in—or too high—so that the priest (especially if small in stature) has difficulty in reaching *into* the tabernacle.[19] If a tabernacle has a deep base (and this may sometimes be a convenience, allowing the middle altar card to lean against it, below the level of the door, so that it is not necessary to move the card whenever the tabernacle is opened) care must be taken to place it nearer to the front edge of the altar, so that the priest may without undue strain reach the ciborium inside it. The permanent

---

[13] C.E. I, xii, 8.
[14] Not in the present collection of decrees.
[15] Only in the 16th century did the tabernacle become part of the structure of an altar.
[16] This marks the link between the Blessed Sacrament and the table of sacrifice.
[17] See p. 177.
[18] See p. 207.
[19] Normally the distance between the edge of the table of the altar and the tabernacle should not be less than 21 inches or more than 24 inches.

tabernacle must be *inamovibile,* and so securely fastened to the table
of the altar, or to a gradine, or to the wall at the back of the altar.[20]
A perfect altar has no gradine, and if it is "fixed" the altar will be
standing well away from the wall,[21] so the normal way to secure a
tabernacle is to fasten it to the table of the altar.   For this purpose
the table may be pierced, but if it is desired to avoid this a way has
been suggested by Canon Mahoney:[22] "to fix the tabernacle to the
lower structure of the altar.   This can be done by means of a rectangular metal plate, a quarter of an inch, or less, in thickness, of the
same width as the tabernacle, and long enough to cover the space
behind and the thickness of the *mensa.* The base of the tabernacle will
be fastened to one arm of this plate resting upon it as on the horizontal of a bracket [and so the tabernacle will be slightly raised, which is
desirable]; the vertical arm of the bracket will be fastened to the back
of the altar, just beneath the *mensa.*"

(*b*) *The Material of the Tabernacle.* The tabernacle must be *un-
dequaque solide clausum* and so should be absolutely strong in construction, so made in stout and solid material as to be burglar-proof
and fire-proof.   No material is prescribed, and only solid and becoming material may be used.   The best form of tabernacle is an iron or
steel safe, with tight-fitting doors to exclude dust and insects, and the
usual precautions in construction against thieves.[23]   This safe should
be covered with stone or wood to give it an artistic appearance and
to make it more becoming for its purpose.

(*c*) *The Form of the Tabernacle.* The tabernacle may have any
form—polygonal, square, round—but it is very desirable that the
upper part be domed or pyramidal: (i) for the *entire* tabernacle
must be covered by the conopaeum, (ii) to prevent the top of the
tabernacle being made a base for relics, statues, flowers, etc., which is
forbidden,[24] or the erection of a permanent Exposition throne above
it, which is also prohibited.[25]

When so shaped the dome may be surmounted by a small movable

[20] Cf. the Instruction of 1938, § 4.
[21] See p. 157.
[22] *Questions and Answers,* II, Q. 660.
[23] The Instruction of 1938 even suggests a burglar alarm.
[24] S.R.C. 2613[6], 2740[1]. S. Consistorial Congregation, Oct. 8, 1932. See p. **165.**
[25] S.R.C. 3576[3], 4136[2], 4268[4] (cf. Vol. IV, p. 203).

emblem[26]—in stone, metal or wood—such as a plain cross, a crown and sceptre, or any emblem of the Blessed Sacrament. This is lifted off when the conopaeum is being changed and then replaced, so keeping the veil in its place. If the door of the tabernacle opens outwards it should be split into two parts, so that when opened it will not strike a chalice or a ciborium that may be standing on the table of the altar. The tabernacle should be damp-proof and frost-proof, and so—unless it is made in wood—should be lined with cedar, poplar, maple or linden. In addition the interior—including the door—out of respect for the sacred Hosts, must be lined either with gold plate or white silk.[27] If the latter be used, a removable veil, hooked up all around inside, is preferable, as it can be cleaned from time to time. Inner curtains hung before the door of the tabernacle are "tolerated,"[28] but are not desirable. On the floor of the tabernacle is placed a well-starched linen corporal,[29] usually a special one shaped to the form and size of the tabernacle floor.

(d) *Dimensions of the Tabernacle.* Usually tabernacles are made too big in height; the correct dimensions will, naturally, depend on the size of the altar and the Communion requirements of the church. Very large tabernacles are undesirable,[30] they are obtrusive and detract from the importance of the altar itself; they are impractical, since it is difficult to veil them fully, as liturgical law requires. Interiorly the tabernacle must be large enough to contain, at least, two ciboriums[31] (small or large, according to the needs of the church) and the custodia containing the Benediction Host, or a pyx containing Hosts for the Communion of the sick.

(e) *Ornamentation of the Tabernacle.* The tabernacle is to be *affabre extructum . . . decenter ornatum ad normam legum liturgi-*

---

[26] Cf. S.R.C. 1270 and Vol. IV, p. 203.

[27] S.R.C. 3150, 3254[7,8], 3709, 4035[4]. Some authorities allow gilded wood for the interior.

[28] S.R.C. 3150. The use of them probably arose as a substitute for lining the door of the tabernacle on the inside.

[29] This is not expressly prescribed but its obligation follows from R.R. V, ii, 1; IV, 15; I.C. § 5, and C.J.C. 1269, § 3.

[30] A tabernacle can be quite spacious inside without being, exteriorly, unduly large. A low tabernacle is best also, because of the altar cross standing behind it.

[31] The tabernacle door must be large enough to admit these ciboriums easily; and also suitable for showing the ciborium in case of private exposition.

carum. The tabernacle itself should be of excellent workmanship, of a design in keeping with its setting, and may be ornamented with symbols of the Blessed Eucharist, etc., but it is impractical to ornament it unduly since it must be *fully covered* by its conopaeum,[32] which is its chief ornament, strictly prescribed by liturgical law. The exterior adornment of the tabernacle must not be such as to prevent the conopaeum being properly fitted and falling gracefully around the tabernacle.[33] Hence projecting corners, crockets, finials and all such ornaments are highly undesirable, in addition to being useless.

(*f*) Nothing may be kept in the tabernacle, except a vessel containing the Sacred Hosts, or—temporarily—an unpurified chalice or ciborium.

(*g*) *The Key of the Tabernacle.* The tabernacle must have a specially good lock for the guardianship of the Blessed Sacrament. The key—which should be in duplicate—is usually gold or silver plated (being part of the tabernacle) and often has a chain or silk tab or tassel attached to it. It ought to be kept in a special case, to preserve it from injury.

The Instruction of 1938[34] and C.J.C. 1269, § 4 prescribe strict rules for its safe custody.

A tabernacle should be blessed,[35] and the form of blessing is given in R.R. Tit. IX, ix, 6, and is a reserved blessing.

NOTE: *A New Form of Tabernacle*

Some years ago a firm in U.S.A. introduced a new form of tabernacle of the usual shape, but constructed with a lining of amianthus or asbestos between metal plates. The door, instead of opening outwards, revolves inside on ball-bearings, so that it cannot be opened without the key. The opinion of S.R.C. about this tabernacle was sought, and it replied "Nihil obstare,[36] de cetero ad Revmum. Episcopum"—leaving the decision to introduce this tabernacle to the Bishop. This new form is in full harmony with liturgical law.

[32] See p. 178.
[33] One advantage of the conopaeum is to prevent tabernacles of a bizarre form.
[34] §§ 6, 7, 8.
[35] S.R.C. 4035⁴.
[36] Mgr. Piacenza (of S.R.C.) highly recommended the new design in *Ephemerides Liturgicae,* 1908 (p. 205).

3. *The Conopaeum*

History

The conopaeum is a tent-like veil[37] covering the tabernacle. The name "conopaeum" seems to be derived from the Greek *konopeion* (*tentorium*), a mosquito net used over a bed as a protection against these insects. The origin of the tabernacle conopaeum is uncertain. It may be derived from the curtains that used to hang around the civory, or, more probably, it is the successor of the veil that—for protection against dust, and as a mark of respect—used to cover the hanging pyx containing the Blessed Sacrament. The first authentic local legislation about the use of the conopaeum dates from St. Charles Borromeo († 1584), but the veil was not new in his day. The first legislation for the entire Latin Church is contained in the Roman Ritual of Paul V (1614); and the earliest reference to the conopaeum in the decrees of S.R.C. is in D.1615 (in 1678). Evidently there could not be express legislation about it until a tabernacle, of modest dimensions, came to be definitely placed on the altar table.

Law

The conopaeum is to cover the *entire* tabernacle[38] (front, back and sides). It is the real ornamentation of the tabernacle and the only certain sign of the presence of the Blessed Sacrament in the tabernacle (lamps are lighted before the high altar even when the Blessed Sacrament is not reserved there; lights should burn before relics that are exposed, and may burn before images), and is removed when the Blessed Sacrament is not there. The use of the conopaeum on any tabernacle containing the Blessed Sacrament is *absolutely obligatory*. It is prescribed directly by the Roman Ritual (V, i, 6) and indirectly by C.J.C. 1269, § 2, and S.R.C. has decided that neither custom,[39] nor the presence of an inner veil,[40] nor the fact that the tabernacle is of precious material or of rich workmanship,[41] dispenses from the observance of this law. It is an abuse to deny to the Blessed Sacra-

[37] To the eye, the tabernacle should look not like a little edifice, but like a tent (cf. John 1.14, where the literal translation of the Greek is, "and [the Word] tabernacled amongst us").
[38] For illustrations see Anson, *Churches*, p. 92, and *infra*—Plates 8, 14, 20, 21, etc.
[39] S.R.C. 3035[10], 3150, 4137.   [40] S.R.C. 3150.   [41] S.R.C. 3520; cf. 4000[1].

ment the chief mark of honour to it ordered by the Church; it is a grave abuse that new tabernacles should be so constructed that to veil them properly, in accordance with liturgical law, is impossible. The conopaeum is ordered not only to preserve the tabernacle from dust, but still more for symbolical reasons, as a mark of respect for the Real Presence, as the ark in the Old Law was veiled,[42] and as sacred vessels are now veiled. Curtains hanging before the doors of the tabernacle are no sufficient substitute for the conopaeum. The tabernacle is to be *fully* covered (*conopaeo decenter opertum,*[43] *tegendum*).[44]

Material of the Conopaeum

Apart from local legislation the conopaeum may be made of any material that is not transparent (lace will not do). As it is the real ornamentation of the tabernacle, it is best made from rich fabrics like brocade, velvet or (real) cloth of gold, or of supple and beautiful materials like silk, or damask, or silk poplin. The shape of the veil will depend, naturally, on the shape of the tabernacle; it may be fitted tightly, or draped loosely,[45] which looks better and is more tent-like. It must have an opening down the middle, so devised that the door of the tabernacle may be opened without difficulty, or without injuring the veil. The conopaeum may be ornamented in any becoming way —either richly, for great feasts, with (real) jewels or embroidery; more simply, for ordinary use, with gold or silk braid, or galloon and fringe. Symbols of the Blessed Eucharist (the fish, the pelican, the basket of loaves, etc.), or sacred monograms[46] provide appropriate decoration.[47] As the conopaeum is viewed from a distance, bold patterns in the fabric and ornamentation are best. The designs used in upholstery textiles should, as a rule, be avoided.

The Colour of the Conopaeum

The colour of the veil may be always white (being the liturgical

[42] Exodus 40.   [43] R.R. V, i, 6.   [44] S.R.C. Index, p. 481.

[45] It should then be ample in size, the material used being twice the perimeter of the tabernacle. Loose veils are better unlined.

[46] A heart by itself (detached from the body of our Lord or our Lady) is not desirable (cf. S.R.C. 3492).

[47] There are excellent illustrations of different kinds of veiled tabernacles in Anson, *Churches,* p. 92.

colour of the Blessed Sacrament) or, better still, the colour of the Office of the day.[48]   Black is, however, excluded, and so on All Souls' Day and for Requiem functions a violet conopaeum is used.[49]   The ornamentation of the conopaeum may be of any suitable colour, but, obviously, the colour of the conopaeum itself (of the material) should predominate.

II.   GRADINES

The step or shelf at the back of the table of an altar is called a "gradine" or "halpas" (*gradus, predella, scabellum*).   Gradines came into use abroad at the Renaissance period (15th-16th century); in England few were used in pre-Reformation days. They grew larger and more numerous later.   The gradine may have originated as a support for a retable,[50] or may have been the shelf for the occasional display of relics or of church plate.   In Rome the gradine is not usual on the high altar.   S.R.C. 3759, allows the candles for Mass to be placed on a gradine, and 4322 refers to gradines "ubi candelabra collocantur" in connection with small electric lights.   The Instruction of the Congregation of the Sacraments on the custody of the Blessed Sacrament of 1938, speaks of fastening the tabernacle "in infimo gradu altaris."

Law

There is no law concerning the gradines.   The perfect altar is without gradines.   The use of one low gradine is tolerable.   In general, a gradine—*a fortiori* gradines—is undesirable for: (1) it often spoils the proportion of the altar, introducing a horizontal line into its composition which disturbs its harmony; (2) it detracts from the dignity and purpose of an altar, which is a stone of sacrifice, not an ecclesiastical dumb-waiter; (3) it encourages the overloading of the altar with unnecessary candlesticks and flower-vases.   In any case, the

[48] Cf. R.G. xviii, 1; S.R.C. 3035[10], and 9, Dec., 1947. "The sequence of colour [of the veil and frontal] brings out with a force beyond the power of words how our Blessed Lord on His altar and in His tabernacle identifies Himself with the feast of the saint, as the Head with the members of one mystical Body, of whose victory He is the sole origin and completion." (Webb, *The Liturgical Altar*, p. 50).
[49] S.R.C. 3562.
[50] See p. 182. Sometimes the gradine had its own little frontal (Rock, *Church of our Fathers*, I, p. 186).

rubrics[51] suppose the cross and candlesticks on the table of the altar,[52] and this entirely covered with cloths. A gradine is an abuse if it interferes with the due veiling of the tabernacle. If, on a special occasion, many extra candles, etc., are needed, e.g., at the Forty Hours' Prayer, the best plan is to use temporary movable gradines.

III. DOSSAL, RETABLE, REREDOS

The ideal altar—standing well away from the surrounding walls—needs no background other than the wall of the apse in which it stands. Frequently, however, an altar stands close to, or even against, the wall (e.g., in a side chapel), or—if it stands apart—a special background is built for it for ornament's sake. This may be: (1) a painting or sculpture, generally called an *altar-piece* (often this is a triptych); (2) a hanging of some rich fabric (tapestry, brocade, velvet, etc.), often embroidered with sacred images or symbols; this form of background is called a *dossal* (dorsal, dossell) and is suggested by C.S. I, xii, 13; (3) an ornamental band of screen of the same material as the altar (stone, metal, wood) built, like a gradine, across the entire width of the altar at the back of the table, or a frame enclosing decorated panels constructed at the back of the altar; this is called a *retable;* (4) finally, a large structure, usually built of the same material as the altar, richly ornamented (elaborately carved, sometimes bearing statues, etc.) forming part of the structure of the altar, or (the better plan) separated from it, standing apart or constructed against the wall at the back; this is called a *reredos.*

History

For over a thousand years the high altar stood apart, isolated, almost empty—its only background the decorated apse. On it, at the time of Mass, were placed the sacred vessels and the Gospel book. No cross appeared on it, nor lights on its table, before the 11th century. Reliquaries were the first things to be placed on the altar, from about the 9th century. This led (9th and 10th centuries) to the ap-

[51] C.E. I, xii, 11.
[52] If there is a permanent gradine it is better that it should continue right across the altar, behind the tabernacle, so that the candlesticks and cross may stand on it in a line, on the same plane.

pearance of a low, simply adorned, gradine as a support for these reliquaries. At first this was put on only on occasion, later it became fixed (from the 11th century). Sometimes a movable dossal (a painting, a metal or textile dossal) was used on great feasts. In the 13th and 14th centuries the gradine grew into the retable,[53] was made of the same material as the altar, and so became fixed on to it or to the wall behind it. It was the happy hunting-ground of artists, sculptors, etc., in which to exercise their art. The civory was edged out and became outmoded; the altar table grew longer; the glorification of the east wall became established. From the 14th to the 17th or 18th centuries was the period of the great reredos, which had ceased to be a mere ornament and had become the principal, completely dwarfing the altar itself and reducing it to insignificance. The altar became a mere base for extravagant structures with masses of turrets, niches containing statuettes, and all the rest. The "fine altar" meant a huge reredos, as later on it was to mean one with an elaborate, ornate fixed Exposition throne. The tabernacle often became a mere cubby-hole, scarcely distinguishable, in a great reredos. In the 11th and 12th centuries the retable was often made of precious metal; from the 13th century stone was much used (marble alabaster, etc.); from the 14th century it was often in wood (painted, carved, etc.).

Law

There are no rubrical prescriptions about the dossal, retable or reredos. It is permitted *provided that it does not interfere with the essential structure of the altar as prescribed by liturgical law.* Hence: (1) it must not prevent the cross and candlesticks from standing in a line, and on the same plane, at the back of the altar table, or on a gradine; (2) it must allow the tabernacle to stand free on all sides, so that it may be *entirely* veiled by the conopaeum; (3) it must not prevent the use of a civory or baldaquin over the altar, as the rubrics require. In addition, if the altar is one at which Pontifical Mass will be celebrated by the Bishop, there must be space between the tabernacle and the retable for the seventh candlestick and for the cross to stand before it.

[53] In the 14th and 15th centuries painted retables were much in evidence.

In its construction and ornamentation a retable or reredos should be in keeping with the style of the church and altar, and of such a character (dimensions, etc.) as not to detract or distract from, but to enhance, the sacred table which *is* the altar. For smaller altars especially, a textile dossal—which can be changed according to the liturgical season, or for special occasions—is very suitable. It can be made in colours that contrast with and emphasize the colour of the conopaeum and frontal.

IV. CURTAINS

C.E. I, xii, 4 speaks of beautiful hangings (*panni*) of silk or leather, or other becoming material, suitably ornamented, for the decoration of the church porch on great days, and (§ 5) of silken and other valuable curtains (*aulaea, cortinae*) to adorn the walls and tribunes of the church.

History

Two kinds of curtains were used in the church: (i) those hung around the altar civory (*tetravela*)—of which there is clear evidence from the 7th century[54]—and (ii) those hung to decorate the apse or walls (to which there is reference in the 5th century), or to close a door or window (*vela*). In the course of time the *tetravela* split up (when the civory began to disappear) into a dossal (the eastern end curtain), and side curtains on rods (riddels, costers), fastened to the wall or retable. Sometimes the riddels were affixed to posts (the relics of the back pillars of the civory) and these often carried lights, or figures of angels, on top. *Tetravela* were much in use in Rome in the 8th and 9th centuries and were used in Italy up to the 13th. They were employed in England in Anglo-Saxon times (6th to 11th centuries). In the 14th and 15th centuries side curtains at the high altar were in use in many countries—England, France, the Low Countries —and were sometimes prescribed by synodal law (e.g., in Germany). This use began to die out in the 16th century, but the curtains remained on in the Low Countries until later. They were restored in some places in France in the 17th and 18th centuries; and in England in the 20th century.

[54] E.g., *Liber Pontificalis* speaks of gifts of them made to basilicas by Popes Benedict II († 685) and Sergius I († 701).

Law

There is no law about curtains around the altar. Their purpose is dignified ornamentation, to secure greater quietness and privacy for the celebrant at Mass, and to create an atmosphere of special reverence for the altar—the "holy place." Hangings of beautiful fabrics behind the altar, in the sanctuary or around the church are highly decorative. They need to be of rich, heavy material, well lined (light material soon loses its shape and becomes shabby). Curtains supply a fine patch of colour, and, if the liturgical colours are used, they will express the spirit of the season or feast; they accord suitably with the liturgical decoration of the conopaeum and frontal (or, if contrasting colours are used, they enhance these), and supply a good setting for the altar. Curtains need to be full to drape gracefully. If patterned, the design needs to be a bold one, to be effective at a distance. The return to the use of textiles in churches—a dignified and beautiful decoration—is much to be desired. They improve acoustics and give warmth and homeliness to a church or oratory.

V. THE EXPOSITION THRONE

Whenever the Sacred Host is exposed in a monstrance it must be placed under some form of canopy as a mark of respect and honour.[55] If the altar—as the rubrics require—is surmounted by a civory or tester, no other canopy is needed for Exposition. For the Exposition of the Forty Hours' Prayer—and for any Exposition of special solemnity and lasting for some hours—it is the practice to erect a special throne above the high altar.[56] For shorter and less solemn Exposition (as at ordinary Benediction) no special throne is needed (provided, of course, that the altar is surmounted by a canopy); the monstrance is placed on the table of the altar[57] (the most sacred place in the church). Except in a church or chapel where there is continual or

[55] As a canopy is used over an altar, or as part of the throne of a bishop or king. A canopy is forbidden over images of relics (except those of the Passion). Cf. S.R.C. 2379[2], 2647, 2951[1].
[56] This is prescribed for the Forty Hours' Prayer by the Clementine Instruction (§ V). Cf. S.R.C. 3349, 3375.
[57] Cf. C.E. II, xxxiii, 24; R.R. X, v, 5; I.C. § xxxi. This eliminates the ugly and sometimes perilous practice of climbing a ladder with the monstrance in hand, or carrying it around to the back of the altar. It also recalls the link between the sacrifice of the Mass and the reserved Host.

quasi-continual Exposition, a permanent throne must *not* be erected over the altar. It is expressly forbidden[58] in the case in which it is so situated that the altar cross must be placed in it—for this is expressly prohibited,[59] and it nearly always does interfere with the correct position of the cross—or it prevents the tabernacle being properly veiled. As a throne above the altar is needed for only a subsidiary function (solemn Exposition) that rarely occurs, it is absurd to allow it to interfere with the essential construction of the altar and make it a fixed feature of this (as has been the common practice for the past two centuries). Besides, an empty throne permanently over the altar is meaningless, and tends to distract attention from the altar itself, the focal point of the church.[60]

Where, however, Exposition is perpetual, a permanent throne may be erected, but it should be built into the wall behind the altar, or in the reredos (when this is well back from the table of the altar)—so that it does not interfere with the cross or the veiling of the tabernacle —but not too far away from the altar itself, with which it should form a moral unity[61] (because of the dependence of Exposition on the sacrifice, and the symbolism of the altar, representing Christ).

Form of Temporary Throne

The temporary throne which may be needed for Exposition may be made of precious materials (gold, silver, marble, etc.) but as it should be easily movable it is generally made of lighter materials, e.g., of wood, or light metal, and textiles. It often takes the form of a miniature royal throne, with base and canopy (supported on a frame or on pillars), connected by a panel of some fabric (silk, velvet, brocade, etc.); or it may be, e.g., a miniature temple, the roof (forming the canopy)[62] being supported on four pillars. Generally the framework is gilded. The panel that forms the back is best white in colour,[63] but may be ornamented with gold or other colours, and with symbols of the Blessed Eucharist. The size of the temporary throne will, of

[58] S.R.C. 4268[4].   [59] S.R.C. 3576[3], 4136[2].
[60] At Exposition the throne itself is the focal point.
[61] S.R.C. 4268[5].
[62] As there should be a canopy over the Sacred Host, an open crown is not correct for the roof of the throne, unless, of course, there is a canopy over the altar itself.
[63] This is prescribed for the Forty Hours' Prayer (I.C. § 5).

course, depend on the dimensions of the altar and of the monstrance to be placed in it. The throne may have branches for candles fixed on each side of the base,[64] but this is undesirable and dangerous. The throne must not be illuminated within by electric light placed within it.[65]

Position of the Exposition Throne

The problem of the position of a temporary throne (as distinct from a mere stand for the monstrance) arises only when, in disregard of liturgical law, there is no canopy over the altar. The throne is best placed on a base, erected permanently or, better still, temporarily only, behind the tabernacle and the cross. This base must be of such a height as to raise the monstrance above the tabernacle, but should not itself—especially if permanently fixed—show above the top of the tabernacle. If there is no room behind the tabernacle for the throne, it may be placed on the tabernacle (granted that this has a flat top or a movable domed one),[66] though this is undesirable, for the tabernacle is an independent structure, the full veiling of which must not be impeded, and, in any case it does not seem becoming to make the tabernacle a base for anything (though placing the altar cross on it is not forbidden).[67] As far as possible the throne should be easy[68] of access, either from the footpace or by a suitable stairway at the back of the altar.

When the altar is not surmounted by a canopy, some form of throne is, strictly speaking, required even for a brief Exposition, but for such there is no law requiring the throne to be placed above the altar, it may be placed on it. There is no liturgical warrant for the use of a "thabor" (an elaborately ornamented stand, generally in metal, like a flat missal stand) on the table of the altar, and it is often inconvenient in use. Sometimes, however, it might be useful to raise the monstrance, thereby bringing the Sacred Host into greater prominence.

[64] S.R.C. 3780[4].   [65] Cf. S.R.C. 2613[5],4275.
[66] A new idea in U.S.A. (cf. *Liturgical Arts*, vol. I, p. 124) of a domed top that can be raised by rods and counter-weights so as to form a canopy seems somewhat too mechanical a device for such a purpose.
[67] S.R.C. 4136[2].
[68] Mechanical devices for raising the monstrance are forbidden (S.R.C. 3425; cf. 4257[3]).

CHAPTER X

The Adornment of the Altar

THE true, traditional, liturgical adornment of the altar springs from the very nature of the altar—from its importance as the focal point of the whole church,[1] from its dignity and sanctity as the consecrated stone of sacrifice and the symbol of Christ himself. The purpose of any adornment of the altar should be to concentrate attention on—not distract attention from—the altar itself, and what takes place on it; to enhance the beauty of the structure and emphasize its paramount place in the building. In the ornamentation of an altar—especially of the high altar—great care must be taken to respect the essential character of the altar, and maintain its dignity, its austerity, its holiness. The high altar is not a mere support for the tabernacle,[2] much less a pedestal for a statue, or a stand for candlesticks and flower-vases. Its adornment must be worthy of the awesome character of an altar, and nothing tawdry or pretty, artificial or sham (redolent of the properties of a theatre) should mar its sacredness. The adornment should be restrained and dignified, something that teaches by its beauty and its symbolism. It must be such as not to spoil the architectural proportions, the essential lines and features of the altar itself.

The ornamentation should also be graded, marking (1) the different liturgical seasons, differentiating in its simplicity or in its splendour between the degrees of festivity—the adornment of the altar must not

---

[1] P. 23.
[2] The tabernacle—despite its sacred contents—is, in relation to the altar, secondary. It is only an accidental addition to some altars, and no mention is made of it in the rite of the consecration of a church or altar.

Church of San Clemente, Rome, showing (i) the altar surmounted by its civory, (ii) *cancelli* (surrounding the choir), (iii) Gospel ambon, with the Paschal candle holder beside it, (iv) Epistle ambon (on the right)

suggest a perpetual feast; (2) the dignity of the celebrant of a function (e.g., a cardinal or bishop). Simple splendour would seem to be the ideal, even for the greatest festivals. "Many an altar loses its beauty precisely because of its expensive embellishment."[3] When the liturgical laws of the adornment of an altar are followed faithfully, then the maximum of majestic, dignified and austere beauty is attained.

The traditional permanent adornment of the altar consists of its canopy,[4] and its clothing (the altar frontal, frontlet, and altar cloths); its temporary ornamentation, of reliquaries and flowers.

I. THE ALTAR CANOPY[5]

According to liturgical tradition and the rubrics the structure of an

[3] *The Liturgical Altar*, Geoffrey Webb, p. 99.
[4] In this book the canopy is treated as part of the structure of an altar (pp. 142 *sqq.*), which it really is. So is the dorsal (pp. 181 *sqq.*), which may also be considered an adornment of an altar.
[5] C.E. I, xii, 13-14, 17; xiii, 3; xiv, 1.

altar is not complete unless it be surmounted by a canopy—as a mark of distinction and honour. There are two chief forms of this canopy: (1) the *civory* (*ciborium,*[6] *tegmen, tegurium*), cibory or civery, i.e., an edifice—in stone or metal or wood—consisting of four or more columns, united by an arcade or architrave, roofed (with either a domed, spherical or flat roof) and highly decorated, built over the altar. Familiar examples are Bernini's civory over the high altar of St. Peter's Rome (1633), and Bentley's civory over the high altar of Westminster Cathedral. This form of canopy is used over big altars in greater churches. Constantine erected a civory of gold and silver over the altar of the Lateran basilica in the 4th century.[7]

(2) The second form is called a *baldaquin*[8] (*baldachinum, umbraculum*) or *tester,* a smaller and lighter structure, of metal or, more commonly, of wood (carved or gilded), which is either hung over the altar (suspended from the roof by chains or metal bars) or is attached to the wall behind or to the reredos, bracket-wise, or is supported at the back on two posts or pillars so that it juts out over the altar like the canopy of a throne. This form of canopy over an altar dates from, possibly, the 14th century, and some authorities think it is derived from a bisected civory (its roof lifted off and raised, its pillars disappearing, or remaining as posts from which "riddels" or curtains surrounding the altar were often hung; or two of the columns of the civory disappearing, and the other two, the back pair, supporting the dais over the altar, as over a throne). The tester may be of carved wood, coloured or uncoloured, or it may take the form of a framework of timber (often gilded), lined with silk or brocade, or other rich fabric, with a hanging valance and/or behind, a hanging curtain[9] of the same material ornamented with gold braid or galloon, and with fringe or tassels. In this case the material may be of the colour of the day,[10] but as it is seldom practical to keep changing the cover of the

[6] The word is used in this sense since at least the 5th century; only from the 14th was it used for the vessel containing sacred Hosts. The term is derived from *kiborion,* the globular seed pod of the Egyptian water lily, or from *kibo(ta)rion,* a casket.
[7] *Liber Pontificalis* calls it *propitiatorium* and *fastigium.*
[8] So called from a rich textile, a kind of brocade, from Baldacco (Bagdad), with which it is sometimes ornamented.
[9] When the baldaquin is throne-like in appearance.
[10] As C.E. I, xii, 13, suggests.

canopy, it may be and usually is permanently of one colour. White or red is generally used, the former being appropriate for the altar where the Blessed Sacrament is reserved. When the baldaquin is of the throne kind, it is possible to change the textile that forms the back of it occasionally (using one curtain for ordinary days, a more ornate one for great feasts, a violet one in Lent, etc.).

History

The civory over the high altar is known since the 4th century.[11] Its origin is uncertain, but its use may have been influenced by the baldaquin (*propitiatorium*) over the Ark of the Covenant,[12] or the pagan usage of erecting a canopy over the statue of a god, or by the edifice sometimes erected over tombs, especially those of the martyrs. It was the practice also to have a canopy overhead as part of a throne, a mark of distinction and honour. The civory was a great feature of altars in the 7th, 8th and 9th centuries;[13] but from the 10th century its use (outside Rome, where it has been always retained) began to decline,[14] when large reliquaries made their appearance on or behind the high altar, and gradually displaced the civory. The practical purposes of the civory were: (1) to preserve the high altar from accident, dust, etc., and sometimes it was erected so that curtains might be hung around the altar; (2) to increase the dignity of the high altar[15]—giving majesty and amplitude to a small altar—and to concentrate attention on it as the focal point of the church. The civory is by tradition the chief ornamentation of an altar.[16] It was generally elaborately wrought and lavishly ornamented; from it hung lamps and jewelled votive crowns; around it were rich hangings, and on feast days it was garlanded with flowers; and, long before the cross made its appearance on the altar table (about the 11th century), a cross surmounted the civory or hung from its roof. The civory had its

---

[11] The oldest extant civory (9th century) is in the church of St. Apollinaris in Ravenna.   [12] Exodus 25.17 *sqq.*
[13] *Liber Pontificalis* mentions gifts of civories by popes and emperors to various churches.
[14] In England it was still in common use at the end of the 12th century.
[15] This was especially necessary when, as always in the early centuries, a very simple altar was the focal point of a spacious and lengthy church.
[16] For about a thousand years the altar itself remained a simple table—the stone of sacrifice. A canopy is always over an altar at which the Pope celebrates Mass.

symbolical *raison d'être* also, it was a traditional mark of reverence and honour,[17] emphasizing the royal dignity of the altar, and covering it and the sacred ministers, when they stand before it, as they and it represent Christ. The civory forms a beautiful and dignified setting for the altar, without any infringement of the inviolable sanctity and detachment of that sacred stone.

Law

The use of a canopy over an altar is certainly of obligation for the high altar of a cathedral[18] (this high altar being distinct from the altar of the Blessed Sacrament), and over every altar at which the Blessed Sacrament is reserved[19] (the high altar, in most churches).[20] When an altar is covered with a canopy, no other covering is needed for Exposition (and so the monstrance may be placed on a simple stand in an elevated position), or short Benediction (when the monstrance is best left on the table of the altar).

A civory may be made of any becoming material—of precious metals (gold, silver, etc.), or stone (marble, porphyry, etc.) as the medieval civory was made—or of wood, gilded or painted. A tester (sometimes) and a baldaquin use textiles as well. In size the canopy should cover the altar and the footpace and, in larger churches, the steps, so that the sacred ministers at High Mass are covered also.[21] C.E. (I, xii, 13) supposes the hanging canopy to be square in form, but legitimate usage allows any shape (oblong, round, oval). The canopy should be designed to suit the architecture of the church, and to fit in with its own background, and may be decorated with suitable symbols, etc.

On special occasions a civory may have a temporary decoration of curtains, or lamps, or garlands suspended from it.[22]

[17] As it is also the sign of jurisdiction over a throne. [18] C.E. I, xii, 13; xiii, 3; xiv, 1.
[19] S.R.C. 1966, 2912 (cf. Index of S.R.C. decrees, p. 442), cf. 3525[2]. The correct interpretation of the note added in the Index of S.R.C. to decrees 1966, 2912 (p. 35) seems to be that the obligation of a canopy over *all* altars has fallen into desuetude. For the visitation of the churches of Rome in 1904, St. Pius X prescribed this query: "Is there a hanging baldaquin, or one supported on columns, over the altar of the most Holy Sacrament?"
[20] A double reason for the use of a canopy.
[21] They, with the celebrant, represent Christ, as the altar does. In medieval England the size of a tester was, normally, not less than the square of the length of the altar.
[22] Cf. C.E. I, xii, 17; 14.

The pillars of a civory should all be set on the same level, and so placed that they will not hinder free movement at the altar, or impede ceremonial actions (e.g., the incensation of the altar). The roof should be high enough to escape, at least in great part, smoke from the altar candles.

The use of the altar canopy has always been maintained in the great churches of Rome.[23] In our own day its restoration in our churches has begun and is making good progress. The neglect of this correct—and indeed obligatory—ornamentation of, at least, the high altar in the 17th and 18th centuries (when its use was partly restored in France), and in the 19th also (with its "wedding-cake altars" ornamented [?] with great fixed exposition thrones),[24] shows a regrettable departure from tradition.[25]   The canopy should never be sacrificed in favour of a window behind the altar, or of an altar-piece (dossal). It enhances the beauty and magnifies the dimensions of the high altar.

II. The Altar Frontal

The true liturgical decoration of the altar and its oldest adornment is the frontal (*pallium, palla, paramentum, frontale, antependium*). It is so by liturgical tradition and by prescription of the rubrics.[26]   It consists of a piece of stuff (generally a textile) which covers the *entire* front of the altar (and the back also, if this be visible to the congregation) and, with the linen altar cloths, completes the traditional "clothing," of the altar. *Vestiunt altaria* says a rubric of the Roman Pontifical (Part I) at the end of the consecration of an altar; *vestiuntur altaria* repeats the Ceremonial (C.E. II, xxvii, 1). The General Rubrics of the Missal speak (§ XVIII) of the *paramenta altaris* being of the same colour as the vestments of the sacred ministers, and (§ XX) order the altar to be adorned with a pallium, of the colour of the day.

---

[23] It is used, too, in churches of the Byzantine, Syrian and Armenian rites.
[24] See p. 137.
[25] In an old Anglo-Saxon Pontifical (of Magdalen College, Oxford) is found a solemn blessing (with anointing of its columns and incensing) of the civory, that formed part of the rite of consecration of a church (cf. Rock, I, 16, 153).
[26] R.G. XVIII, 1; C.E. I, xii, 11, 16; xxix, 4; II, xi, 1, etc. P.R. *passim.* M.R., first rubric of Tit. I, II, III, IV.

History

The clothing of the altar is mentioned in the East from the 4th century and in the West from at least the 5th. *Liber Pontificalis* frequently mentions gifts of *pallia* from the popes of the 7th, 8th and 9th centuries to different churches.

The frontal was often made in purple and gold and ornamented with jewels, or with beautiful embroideries. Frontals from the 8th or 9th centuries were sometimes made of precious metals, movable plates of gold and silver. Probably the frontal has its origin in the early covering of all four sides of the altar, at first with linen, then (from the 4th century) with coloured textiles. In the course of time the frontal got broken up into the white linen cloths that clothe the table and two sides of the altar, and the coloured clothing of the front (and the back when visible). By the 13th century the frontal had reached its present form; and the sequence of colours—following those of the vestments[27]—was established in the 13th century; and codified in the Missals of 1570 (R.G. § XVIII) and 1604 (§ XX), and in C.E. of 1600 and P.R. of 1596. The use of the frontal began to decline in the 16th century and its neglect became widespread in the 17th—due probably, to a large extent, to the desire of the sculptors and painters of the Renaissance to display their skill (to do their worst) on the front of the altar, as well as on the retable.

The Meaning of the Frontal

The frontal—the altar's clothing—has a deep, symbolical value.[28] As the early linen clothing of the altar recalled our Lord's burial shroud, so the precious coloured fabric of the later frontal is to recall his royalty. At the ordination of a subdeacon,[29] the bishop in his charge to the candidate says "the cloths and corporals of the altar [which represents Christ] are the members of Christ, God's faithful people, with whom, as with costly garments, the Lord is clad, according to the Psalmist: 'The Lord reigns as king, robed in majesty'." The clothed altar with its beauty and changing colours is a symbol of

---

[27] C.E. added the use of gold and silver frontals.
[28] See the excellent article "Inspired Symbolism," by Geoffrey Webb in *Liturgical Arts*, Feb. 1942 (p. 32).
[29] P.R., Part I.

the Mystical Body—the whole Christ, Christ united with all his saints —it translates this doctrine into the language of colour and form. In addition to its symbolical value, the frontal—with its sequence of colours and its changing form and decoration—lends variety and new beauty to the altar, and helps to mark the degrees of festivity in the Church's liturgy. In presenting an unbroken coloured surface it also draws attention to the altar, as the focal point of the church, giving it architectural prominence.

Law

The use of the altar frontal is prescribed by the rubrics of C.E.[30] and of the Missal,[31] and is assumed in P.R. and in M.R. Because of its function as an adornment of the altar—although this is not its primary purpose, which is its symbolism—some liturgical writers maintain that its use is not obligatory, by custom, if the altar is itself made of precious material and highly decorative.[32] But if the frontal is not used, not only is its symbolism disregarded but the altar is without change of permanent adornment, degrees of festivity cannot be adequately expressed, nor can the liturgical changes of season or feast be fully indicated. Does not the unclothed altar depict Christ as permanently stripped of the members of His Mystical Body? The use of the frontal has been maintained in the great basilicas of Rome, and in greater churches of the Roman rite.

Material of the Frontal

C.S. (I, xii, 11) speaks of gold or silver *pallia,* or those made of silk, with gold artistically interwoven, of the colour suitable to the feast. The frontal is best made of some textile—because it is part of the clothing of Christ—brocade, tapestry, velvet, silk, damask, etc., richly ornamented with jewels, embroidery, apparels, etc.; or more simply for lesser days, or in small churches, with orphreys of silk, or with braid or fringe. Designs should be bold since the frontal is viewed from a distance. In the traditional Roman frontal the material is di-

---

[30] C.E. I, xii, 11, 16; xxix, 4, etc.
[31] R.G. XX; XVIII, 1.
[32] In such a case how are the abandonment and desolation of Good Friday to be expressed, or mourning at a Requiem function?

vided vertically into panels (generally five)[33] by narrow strips of braid; across the frontal (about one-fourth of its depth from the top) is a deeper strip, and the upper part of the frontal[34] above this is divided into twice the number of panels (normally ten) by braid or galloon (p. 146). The frontal may be adorned with woven or painted figures or scenes,[35] or with suitable symbols (e.g., of the Blessed Eucharist).

The Colour of the Frontal

Normally, the colour of the frontal will be that of the Office of the day. At an altar of Exposition of the Blessed Sacrament (unless this be of very short duration) it must be white.[36] For a solemn votive Mass it will be the colour of the Mass. At an altar where the Blessed Sacrament is reserved a black frontal may not be used on All Souls' Day or for a Requiem; instead a violet antependium is used.[37] The sequence of colours is not of strict obligation for a frontal, and so, for great feasts, a frontal of, e.g., cloth of gold or silver, or of a precious fabric in various colours, may be used. In poor churches even one double-sized frontal would suffice, with gold material on one side for feasts, and a violet fabric on the other for penitential days and Requiem functions; or two reversible frontals could be made, one white backed by violet, the other green backed by red.

Fixing a Frontal

The frontal must cover the entire front[38] of the altar. It may be fixed on to a wooden frame (telarium)—as C.E. suggests (I, xii, 11) —which slips into a groove under the table of the altar; or it may hang, by small rings, from a rod, supported on metal lugs in the front elevation of the altar. The rod and its attachment are concealed by a frontlet.[39] It is sometimes desirable to back a frontal with some heavy material, like strong canvas, to get it to hang well. The frontal should

[33] The number will depend on the size of the frontal; an uneven number is better.
[34] Called the *aurifrigium* or *aurifrisium*.
[35] A common ornament of mediaeval frontals was a picture of Christ surrounded by the Apostles or other saints. In the 15th century, scenes from the Gospels were often depicted.   [36] S.R.C. 1615[7], 2673.
[37] S.R.C. 3201[10], 3562, and Index Generalis, p. 357.
[38] And the back also, if this be visible to the congregation.   [39] See *infra*. p. 196.

be set well back from the front edge of the altar, so that when the priest stands at the altar he will not touch the frontal with his feet, nor with his left knee whenever he genuflects.[40]

The Frontlet

The frontlet, or super frontal (*frontale, frontellum, parura*), is an apparel or strip of material, extending the full width of the altar, and hung from a cloth laid on the table of the altar, or tacked on to the lowest linen altar cloth.[41] It serves to fill the gap between the edge of the altar table and the top of the frontal, and to cover the rod and rings on which this is hung.[42] It may be of the same material and colour as the frontal, or of a neutral or contrasting colour.[43] It is usually some 6 inches deep, and sometimes fringed. The frontlet made its appearance about the 14th or 15th century, and was at first attached to the frontal rather than to an altar cloth, but at one time it seems to have been an adornment of this cloth. Lace—especially of poor quality and inferior design—is not appropriate for a frontlet. It lacks colour, and is too trivial to adorn the stone of sacrifice or serve as a part clothing of Christ. On the ground of appearance the linen altar cloth should not overhang the altar table and replace a frontlet. The impressive, strong, unbroken block of colour made by and frontal and frontlet, covering the entire front surface of the altar, should not be broken into by an indeterminate and intrusive wobbly line of white, which immediately catches the eye and distracts it from the altar itself.

III. ALTAR CLOTHS

On every altar on which Mass is celebrated there must be three linen cloths[44] (*tobaleae, mappae, linteamina*).

History

From the earliest times a linen cloth was associated with the cele-

---

[40] The frontal may be blessed, using the formulary *Benedictio Tobalearum* found in P.R. (Part II) at the end of the rite of consecration of an altar.
[41] Or it may be clipped on to a metal band fixed on to the front edge of the table.
[42] The Roman type of frontal usually comes up to the level of the altar table and does not need a frontlet. The band that crosses this type of frontal sems to be a relic of a frontlet.
[43] And one frontlet could be used with several frontals.
[44] R.C. XX; *De Defectibus*, X ,1, 12; C.E. I, xii, 11.

bration of Mass and is mentioned in documents from the 3rd and 4th centuries. In the early centuries the one cloth, of white linen (and sometimes with it a coloured cloth, that later developed into the altar frontal), served as altar cloth, corporal and pall. Two ideas influenced the use of a cloth or cloths on the altar; the symbolism of the clothing of Christ, represented by the altar (later this was carried out chiefly by the frontal), and the symbolism of linen as a shroud for the Body of Christ (the "sindon" of the Gospel account of the burial and resurrection of our Lord).[45] Respect for the sacred Species also demanded that they should be laid on fair linen.[46] In due time the original cloth broke up into the frontal, the altar cloth itself (covering the table and sides of the altar), the corporal (an extra cloth used at the time of Mass only), and the pall.[47] At first the altar cloth was used only during the time of Mass,[48] being spread by the deacons at the beginning of the service, and removed after it. Later (from about 1000) the cloth(s) was left on the altar permanently. The number of altar cloths varied very much at different periods and in different places. At first there was only one linen cloth. Rome had adopted the use of three cloths by about the 8th or 9th century, but two were also in use there even as late as the 15th or 16th century. The use of three cloths is mentioned in *De Defectibus*[49] of the Roman Missal (which dates from the 12th or 13th century), and is prescribed in the *Ordo Missae* of John Buckard (1502), in C.E.[50] (1600) and in the General Rubrics of the Missal[51] (1604). Linen was the material prescribed for the altar cloths, yet mention is also sometimes made of the use of silk and other precious fabrics. The Anglo-Saxons were fond of purple, and sometimes dyed their cloths that colour, or used a purple cloth under the white one. At first the altar cloth was plain, but from about 1000 it began to be ornamented. The chief adorn-

---

[45] Cf. the third prayer of the blessing of a pall, and corporal (R.R. IX, ix, 5).
[46] Cf. the use of linen in the divine worship of the Old Law (Exodus 25 *sqq.*).
[47] Originally the altar cloth was turned up to cover the *oblata;* the corporal was also so used (cf. the second prayer used in the blessing of an altar cloth and of a corporal—R.R. IX, ix, 4, 5).
[48] This happens now in the aliturgical synaxis of Good Friday.
[49] X, 1, 12. The use of three cloths arose, probably, to provide against the accidental spilling of the Precious Blood, that it might be soaked up by the cloths and not reach the altar or ground.
[50] I, xii, 11.
[51] R.G. XX.

ment, for many centuries, was a band of coloured material, richly embroidered, across the top of the front face of the altar (the frontlet, or *aurifrisium*).[52]   In more recent times a less suitable and less worthy adornment has come into use, i.e., lace, generally of inferior quality and poor design.

Law

The table of an altar on which Mass is celebrated is to be covered with three linen cloths, the top one being long enough not only to cover the table but also the two sides down to the ground[53]—this cloth, with the frontal, making up the full clothing of the altar. For the two under-cloths one cloth, folded in two, may be used. In the case of a "stable" altar (p. 152), it suffices if the two under-cloths cover the actual portable altar (or altar stone) that is inserted in its table. An extra cloth is desirable for Benediction to save the permanent altar cloth from wax droppings from the candles (if these be placed on the table of the altar). The altar cloths must be of linen or hemp,[54] not of cotton or other inferior material—for both practical and symbolical reasons—and a fairly heavy linen, of not too fine a weave, is most suitable. It is better when the front edge of the cloth is flush with the edge of the altar table and does not overhang it.[55]   If a fold does hang down (replacing a frontlet),[56] it may be adorned for feast days with embroidery, etc.   Lace over a coloured fabric is tolerated.[57]   The ends of the cloth at both sides may also be suitably adorned for greater days, e.g., with orphreys, as in the Middle Ages.   The cloths must not be kept in place by frames or mouldings, or clasps of wood or metal;[58] they can be fixed—if necessary—on to studs at the back of the table; or have a rod running through a hem on the back edge of the cloth, and allowed to fall over the table at the back, so that its weight sustains the cloth; or by lead weights sewn on to the back edge of the cloth. An altar cloth before use is to be blessed. The form of blessing is in R.R. IX, ix, 4.

---

[52] See p. 196.   [53] C.E. I, xii, 11; R.G. XX; S.R.C. 4029[1].
[54] S.R.C. 2600, 3868.
[55] An overhanging fold is bad in appearance (p. 196); also it frays and gets soiled easily.   [56] P. 196.
[57] S.R.C. 3191[5].   [58] C.E. I, xi, 11, 16; S.R.C. 4213[1], 4253.

IV. Relics and Reliquaries

Relics (*reliquiae, lipsana*) of the saints or of the beatified are of two classes, primary (i.e., the body of the saint, or part of the body or bones) and secondary (i.e., things sanctified by immediate and close contact with the saint, e.g., the clothes he wore, things he used in life, the instruments of his torture, in the case of a martyr).[59] Certain primary relics are notable (*insignes*),[60] i.e., the body, head, arm, forearm, heart, tongue, hand or leg of a saint, or that part of the body in which a martyr suffered, provided it be entire and not small. The relative veneration of real relics of saints is approved by the Church;[61] and public honour in a church may be given to the relics of canonized saints,[62] provided that these have been officially declared genuine relics by a cardinal, or the Ordinary of the place, or other person appointed by the Holy See to authenticate relics.[63]

History

From the earliest times the bodies (bones or ashes) of saints— especially of martyrs—have been treasured and honoured, and have been given liturgical veneration since the 4th century. While bodies were broken up from that time, or even earlier, into small relics in the East, Rome did not approve of the removal of bodies, nor of their dismemberment, until about the 7th or 8th century. Relics were first under altars, then inside altars of tomb formation (from the 6th century), then on altars—at first temporarily (from the 9th), later permanently (from the 11th)—and over and behind altars (in caskets, etc.). Small relics were buried in the table of the altar from the 9th century or earlier.

Relics were preserved in reliquaries (*thecae, lipsanothecae, capsae, capsellae*)[64] often made of precious metals, elaborately adorned with jewels, etc. These reliquaries were of varied forms, not only urns, caskets or coffers, but also miniature sarcophagi, churches, castles,

[59] Things that merely touched primary or secondary relics are not themselves relics in the true sense and may not be exposed for public veneration.
[60] C.J.C. 1281, § 2.
[61] C.J.C. 1255, § 2; 1276.
[62] C.J.C. 1281, § 1; 1283, § 1; 1287, § 1. Relics of the beatified may be exposed for public honour only where their Mass and Office are allowed by the Holy See.
[63] C.J.C. 1283, § 1.
[64] And C.E. I, xii, 12, speaks of *tabernacula*.

towers, etc., cylinders of crystal, and especially crosses.   Often nowadays small relics are preserved in an oval-shaped monstrance of metal,
or gilt wood, or some other becoming material, with a triangular base,
and furnished with a handle at the back, to enable the relic(s) to be
presented to the people to kiss.   The relic itself is fastened to the back
of the reliquary, covered with white or (for martyrs) red silk, and is
labelled with a piece of parchment giving the name of the saint whose
relic it is.   The front of the reliquary is glazed, and is covered with a
veil, when the relic is not exposed for veneration.   The reliquary is
firmly sealed at the back with sealing wax bearing the seal of the
prelate who authenticated the relic.[65]   Several relics may be placed
in the same reliquary; but any relic of the Passion (e.g., a piece of the
true Cross) must have its own special reliquary[66] (at least when exposed for veneration).

Law

Relics of canonized saints may be exposed on the high altar—between the candlesticks,[67] not on the tabernacle, nor before its door[68]
—or at a side altar, or on a stand or table in a convenient place, for
the veneration of the faithful. Two lights (lamps or candles[69]) must
burn before a relic thus exposed for public honour. The reliquary
must not be placed on a pall,[70] nor should it be canopied.

When relics are not exposed for special veneration they should be
kept—veiled—in a locked aumbry, labelled *Reliquiae* or *Relics,* in the
church,[71] or in a side chapel, or even in the sacristy. In the appendix
to the Roman Missal there is the Mass of a special feast of all the
relics possessed by any diocese, celebrated by concession of the Holy
See, in some dioceses, on November 5.

Reliquaries as an Adornment of the Altar

For the adornment of a large high altar, on great days, C.E. I, xii,

---

[65] There is a special blessing for a reliquary in R.R. IX, ix, 8.
[66] C.J.C. 1287, § 2; S.R.C. 2647, 2854, 4186[1].
[67] Cf. C.E. I, xii, 12. A relic of the Passion is placed in the centre of the altar—a
more honourable place—but must not impede the altar cross.
[68] S.R.C. 2613[6], 2740[1], 2906.   [69] *Lumina* says S.R.C. 2067[9], 3029[13] (cf. 3204).
[70] S.R.C. 2689[3].
[71] Near the altar is a becoming place, because of the traditional connection of relics
with altars.

12, speaks of reliquaries, placed between the candlesticks; and the *Ritus* of the Missal (IV, 5) gives directions for the incensation of these relics, whenever the altar is incensed. Such relics would, ordinarily, be small primary relics, encased in the ordinary monstrance-shaped reliquary, or, sometimes, in busts of saints, made in silver or other precious materials. Reliquaries are not used for the adornment of the altar in seasons of penance,[72] or at a Requiem function; nor may relics be unveiled when the Blessed Sacrament is exposed for veneration.[73]

V. Flowers

The use of flowers for the temporary decoration of an altar is widespread in the Western Church and is recognized by liturgical law.

History

In the early centuries flowers were used to adorn the tombs of the martyrs and, later, the *confessio,* where the body of a saint was enshrined. From the 4th century (e.g., in the writings of SS. Jerome, Augustine, Paulin) there are references to the use of flowers in the church and around (not on) altars. Garlands were hung on the walls, on columns, on doors, and adorned the civory and the ambos. Sometimes, too, they were used symbolically (e.g., the dropping of red rose leaves during the Sequence on Whit Sunday). Flowers and sweet-smelling herbs were scattered on the church floor. St. Charles Borromeo (1584) speaks of ornamenting the church doors with foliage; and there is mention of vases of flowers—not, on, but behind the altar—in the 14th century.

It seems that artificial flowers were first made by nuns in the 13th century, and it was they who first used flowers *on* altars. The practice was adopted by the Mendicant Orders, and then by smaller churches in the 16th century. Greater churches (cathedrals, collegiate and monastic churches) do not, as a rule, use flowers on the high altar at all.

Law

The rubrics of the Missal dealing with the celebration of Mass, of

[72] C.E. II, xx, 3. But a relic may be exposed—better away from the high altar—even during these seasons, on the feast of the saint whose relic it is.
[73] S.R.C. 2365[1], 2779. I.C. § IV.

the Roman Ritual which treat of the reservation of the Blessed Sacrament, and of the Clementine Instruction[74] are totally silent about the use of flowers. C.E. (I, xii, 3, 12, 14, 16) in describing the adornment of the church on *very great* feasts, when the Bishop pontificates solemnly, speaks of ornamenting the doors and the civory with flowers and foliage, and says vases of flowers ("studiose ornata") *may* be used on the altar. It also declares that it is becoming to decorate the *confessio* with flowers and foliage. C.E. also speaks of flowers and leaves strewn on the path of the Bishop entering his diocese, "as a sign of joy,"[75] on the streets over which the Blessed Sacrament will pass in the Corpus Christi procession,[76] and all around the place where the Bishop carries out the Mandatum, or Washing of the Feet, on Maundy Thursday.[77] The *Memoriale Rituum*[78] allows flowers to be used at the Mass on Candlemas Day, Maundy Thursday and Holy Saturday in small churches, if this be the local custom. The restored rite of Easter Eve (§ 29) speaks of the altar being adorned with flowers for the first Easter Mass. The Instruction of the Cardinal Vicar for the churches of Rome (issued in 1932) allows the use of flowers in churches with restraint (*sobrie*).

As flowers on the high altar are a sign of joy and festivity they are excluded on Good Friday and at Requiem functions,[79] and on penitential days, when the vestments are violet[80] (some authors make an exception for *Septuagesima,* and *Gaudete* and *Laetare* Sundays).

Artificial Flowers

C.E. I, xii, 12, permits the use of artificial flowers if they are made of silk. Liturgical writers interpret this ruling as permitting such flowers if they are made of worthy and not tawdry materials, and when natural flowers are not available. In his Instruction for the churches of Rome (1932) the Cardinal Vicar stated: "Artificial flowers (of whatever material, cloth, bronze, brass, earthenware) are for-

[74] Dealing with the Forty Hours' Exposition.
[75] C.E. I, ii, 2.   [76] C.E. II, xxxiii, 2.
[77] C.E. II, xxiv, 3.
[78] M.R. Tit. I, IV, VI. It also speaks of flowers at the "Altar of Repose" on Maundy Thursday (IV, 1).
[79] Cf. C.E. II, xxv, 2; xi, 1; M.R. Tit. V.
[80] Cf. C.E. II, xiii, 2; xviii, 1; xx, 1. M.R. Tit. II, III. The Church *tolerates*

bidden. They must be removed at once from churches and oratories, and from altars, and they may not be placed there for any reason whatsoever. For the decoration of churches and altars a sober display of fresh flowers and plants . . . may be used." While plants seem admissible *around* an altar (provided they do not obstruct ceremonial movement there) they are undesirable on it, and contrary to tradition, which favours cut flowers.

Vases

If flowers are used to decorate the altar it is desirable that vases of becoming material, and good but simple[81] design, be used; e.g., vases of silver or of good quality glass. They should be of sufficient size to have dignity, and not appear trivial; they ought to have wide necks to allow air to the flowers and permit their proper arrangement. When possible, flower-vases should be kept off at least the greater part of the table of the altar,[82] being placed at the back, between the candlesticks (as M.R. directs). They must never be placed before the door of the tabernacle,[83] nor on it, nor before the cross.

The Use and Abuse of Flowers

The indiscreet use of flowers—especially on the high altar—has become a widespread abuse. When an altar is continually cluttered up with flower-vases, flowers cease to adorn, and lose their symbolical value as a mark of special joy and festivity. They introduce on the altar accessories (such as stands for vases and flower-pots) which often hide its beauty and spoil its lines and proportions, and sometimes overshadow the liturgical furnishings. Often the use of plants on stands around the altar, on the altar steps, etc., impedes ceremonial movements in the sanctuary. To turn the altar—the awesome stone of sacrifice—into a stand for flower-vases betrays an ignorance of liturgical principles and traditional correct usage, and sometimes results in a vulgar and costly display. The money often spent on flowers would

wreaths at a funeral (S.R.C. 3804[6]); prescribes a wreath (*corona*) on the corpse of a child who died before the use of reason, "as a sign of bodily integrity and virginity" (R.R. VII, vii).
[81] Vases are entirely subsidiary on an altar.
[82] Cf. R.G. XX.
[83] S.R.C. 2067[10]; cf. 2613[6], 2740[1].

be much better spent on what the Church *orders* for the adornment of the altar and for the honour due to the Reserved Sacrament. The correct use of flowers is regulated by an appreciation of what the altar is, and of the liturgical principles that govern its proper adornment, by good taste and by common sense. These demand that flowers on altars[84]—especially the high altar—be used *with the greatest restraint.* Flowers are not a permanent decoration of an altar—they are not ordered, they are merely permitted because of usage—it is supposed that they may be used, on occasion, to mark a special degree of joyous festivity, and they are an entirely subsidiary decoration.

Some Practical Points about Flowers

(1) The quality of the flowers is much more important than their quantity; a few vases (two, or at most four) of well-arranged, suitable flowers is the ideal. Only large flowers are suitable for a high altar, they have dignity and can be seen even at a distance, and they should be flowers that last well when cut and do not exhale a heavy perfume. (2) It is becoming when the colour of the flowers is in harmony with the liturgical furnishings (the colour of the Office); sometimes a complementary colour looks well. Flowers of one colour only are usually best, to avoid a blurred effect at a distance. (3) The artistic arrangement of flowers is a special art; use long-stemmed, fresh flowers, very loosely arranged, with plenty of suitable foliage; avoid overcrowding the vase. (4) Some flowers need puncturing of the stems to allow of a fuller intake of water; some, too, are best in bud, as they bloom quickly in water.

Flowers in church should speak to us by their fresh beauty and their symbolism of their Maker—of His craftsmanship and goodness, and of His other perfections. They should enhance the beauty of the altar and its setting, not distract attention from it or disfigure it.

[84] More liberty—but not licence—is permissible at mere shrines.

CHAPTER XI

Furniture of An Altar

1. THE ALTAR CROSS

THE cross, with the figure of Christ, is the chief, and should be the predominant, thing on the altar. It is essential for the celebration of Mass.[1]

History

The altar cross as we know it now did not appear on the altar itself for the first millennium of the Christian era. The first representations of the cross in a church date from the Constantinian Peace (4th century) and were depicted on the walls (usually in the apse), painted or in mosaic. From the same period a cross—without a staff[2] was sometimes carried in procession, either as a secular emblem (e.g., the labarum of Constantine), or as a religious one (e.g., the cross carried when St. Augustine landed in Kent, 596). From the 4th century also a cross was sometimes hung from the roof of the altar civory or from a corona. While crosses were carried in the Papal cortège—each at the head of a section of those taking part from the different quarters of Rome—in the liturgy of *Ordo I* (8th century), the first clear mention of a cross at the head of a procession in Rome[3] is at the coronation of Charlemagne (800), who presented such a cross to Pope Leo III (795-816). After that time the use of a cross at the head of a pro-

---

[1] C.E. 1, xii, 11, 12, 16; R.G. xx; R. II, 2.
[2] Such a cross is now used at the funeral of a child (R.R. VII, vii).
[3] There are earlier references in England (cf. Rock, *Church of Our Fathers*, II, p. 184).

cession became commoner, and a cross was also carried before the Pope. This latter practice spread to archbishops, and was fairly general about the 11th century. At first there was no figure of Christ on the cross; then (from about the 6th century) he was depicted with the cross, but in triumph; and finally (from the 8th century) on the cross, shown however, not in suffering, but clothed and as a triumphant conqueror.[4]   Only in the 11th and 12th centuries did the practice begin of displaying our Lord unclothed and suffering on the cross.

Before the 11th century the cross, for Mass, was not placed on the altar. The processional cross was often used and was fixed, during Mass, behind the altar or at its side, or held there by a server. In the 11th century the cross, as we now know it, began to make its appearance on the table of the altar. Innocent III (1216) speaks of this as the Roman usage of his time, and by the 13th century it was the general practice, but does not seem to have been universal until the 16th. Only then did the cross become part of the permanent furniture of an altar.

Burchard's *Ordo* (1502) supposes a cross on the altar for Mass, and so do the rubrics of 1570 Missal. It was definitely prescribed by C.E. (1600), by R.G. (1604) and by the Constitution *Accepimus* of Benedict XIV in 1746.

Many of the earlier crosses were made of precious materials—of gold and silver, ornamented with jewels, ivory, enamel, etc. St. Charles Borromeo († 1584) supposes the altar cross to be a movable one, made in gold, or, at least, gold-plated, even in parish churches, for greater days; and he allows gilded wood for its base only in poorer churches, otherwise he prescribes that the base be of precious metal.

Law

The cross—a crucifix[5]—is essential for Mass. It should be a large cross[6]—large in proportion to the size of the church and altar, with the figure of the Crucified overtopping the candlesticks[7]—clearly visible to the priest and the people.[8] This cross is not only an orna-

---

[4] See p. 105.   [5] C.E. I, xii, 11; R. I, 2.
[6] In 1900 S.R.C. issued a warning about this; and at the visitation of the churches of Rome in 1904 (under St. Pius X) small crosses were eliminated.
[8] Benedict XIV in 1746 and S.R.C. 2621[7].   [7] C.E. I, xii, 11.

ment, but an object of veneration—in the course of Mass it is often saluted and is incensed, and nine times the celebrant is directed to look up at it—and so must not be dwarfed by huge candlesticks, or great statues, much less hidden by flowers. The altar cross should command attention by its size and position—it is not an accessory, but the principal thing on the altar—and honour by its beauty.[9]

Material

C.E. supposes the altar cross to be made of the same metal as the six candlesticks (e.g., gold, silver, bronze, gilded copper) and of the same design, and this is the common practice. But a wooden crucifix—with the figure in wood or of another material (e.g., ivory) is traditional and quite permissible. In fact, it seems preferable, not only aesthetically, but also because of the references in the liturgy to the wood of the cross (e.g., in the Preface of the Cross, in the liturgy of Good Friday).

Position

The cross must be so placed as to be clearly visible to all at Mass— as far as this is possible. Its normal place is between, and in line with, the candlesticks on the altar—either on the table, or on a gradine if there is one running across the full width of the altar. If there be a tabernacle, the cross stands behind it—the figure of the Crucified standing out above it—not on it.[10] If there is a fixed throne for Exposition over the altar—which, normally, is not permissible[11]—the cross may *not* stand in it.[12] When a seventh candlestick is used at a pontifical Mass, this will take the normal place of the cross, which will then stand in front of the extra candlestick.[13] The altar cross may also be hung; this practice, too, is traditional, and is sometimes more convenient.

[9] It is to be *opere praealta,* says C.E. (I, xii, 11).
[10] As the tabernacle ought not to be made a stand for anything, and as it is to be fully veiled, the decision of S.R.C. 4136[2]—permitting the cross on the tabernacle —must be interpreted as meaning that a large crucifix may be fixed to the apex of the dome of the tabernacle, or stood on a ledge in the wall above and behind the tabernacle (cf. Webb, *The Liturgical Altar,* p. 55).
[11] See p. 184.
[12] S.R.C. 3576[3], 4136[2]. It must not even seem, from a distance, to stand in it.
[13] C.E. I, xii, 12.

If the altar-piece (painting, sculpture) or reredos has as its chief figure that of Christ on the cross, and this is clearly visible, an altar cross may be dispensed with.[14]   A small image of Christ crucified in the altar-piece, or a small cross placed as an ornament on the top of the dome of the tabernacle, will not do as a substitute for the altar cross;[15] nor will a stained-glass window, behind the altar, depicting the crucifixion suffice.[16]

Blessing of Cross

The blessing of the altar cross is not prescribed,[17] but it is, obviously, desirable.[18]   The correct formula of blessing is not (it would seem) that for a "cross,"[19] which means a cross without the figure of the Crucified, but the blessing of an image.[20]

II. The Altar Candlesticks

At an altar at which low Mass is celebrated there should be "at least two candlesticks with lighted candles";[21] at an altar where solemn Mass and other functions take place there are to be six candlesticks.[22]

History

Lights were used for cultual purposes,[23] as a mark of respect, at Mass, probably since Apostolic days. Mass without a light was forbidden by Leo IV in the 9th century, Leo V in the 10th century, and Gregory VII in the 11th. *Ordo I* (8th century) speaks of seven candles carried before the Pope at solemn Mass and set beside the altar, and the *Ordo* of St. Amand (8th or 9th century) speaks of two placed behind the altar. At first all candlesticks for ceremonial use were carried and during Mass were set down, temporarily, not on the

[14] S.R.C. 1270[2].
[15] S.R.C. 1270[1], 2621[7].
[16] Cf. S.R.C. 4191[4].
[17] S.R.C. 2143[1].
[18] The cross is included among the *ornamenta altaris* that are blessed by the bishop at the end of the consecration of a church or altar (P.R. Part 2).
[19] R.R. IX, ix, 13.
[20] Ibid. 15. Cf. S.R.C. 3524[4].
[21] R.G. § XX; cf. *De Defectibus*, X, 1.
[22] C.E. I, xii, 11.
[23] See p. 63.

altar, but beside it or behind it (between the altar and the people), or were held by servers. Only after a thousand years or more when the inviolability of the altar was fading from memory, the civory was falling into desuetude, and relic shrines and retables were invading the table of the altar, did the cross and candlesticks find their way on to it; and then, at first, only temporarily, during a function. It was probably in the first half of the 11th century that the practice began, in some places, of setting a candlestick, or candlesticks, on the altar table. Innocent III at the end of the 12th century, Durand in the 13th, speak of two candlesticks placed beside the cross at Mass. This usage was widespread—but not universal—in the 15th and 16th centuries.

The number of candles used around the altar at Mass varied greatly from century to century and from place to place, and for different days. For certain votive Masses, for symbolical reasons (e.g., seven candles for a Mass of the Holy Spirit) three, five, seven, twelve and even twenty-four candles were sometimes lit. Innocent III (in 1195) testified that, even at the Pope's stational Mass, there were only two candles on the altar; but by the middle of the 13th century seven had made their appearance, on the table of the altar, at a solemn papal Mass, at least on great days. At low Mass there was sometimes only one light,[24] oftener two. Burchard in his *Ordo* (1502) directs the server to carry to the altar, for low Mass, two candles, light them, and place them on the altar; and, at the end of Mass, extinguish them and carry them back to the sacristy. The seven candlesticks, for great altars, were reduced, probably for symmetry's sake, in the 15th century to six; and these often remained permanently on the altar from the 16th century. C.E. (1600) fixed the number of candlesticks for great churches at six;[25] and R.G. XX (1604) directed at least two candlesticks to be on the altar for low Mass.

Single candlesticks were in use from the 5th or 6th century. At first they were squat in appearance, but from the 13th century their height was gradually increased. It became exaggerated in the 17th century.

[24] Illustrations from, e.g., MSS. of the 15th century often show one candle, on the altar or held by a server.
[25] A seventh is used for certain pontifical Masses (C.E. I, xii, 12).

Candlesticks were often made, in great churches, of precious metals and were of marvellous workmanship.

Law

Altar candlesticks are to follow the traditional pattern of a foot, a stem with a knob, and a pan or bowl—sufficiently large to catch falling wax—with a pricket[26] or socket for the candle. Because of the trouble from falling wax, it is useful to have a smaller movable pan (of metal, porcelain or glass) which can be easily set into the permanent bowl. Branch candlesticks, or bracket candlesticks hung on the wall near the altar, are not permissible for Mass.[27] In design and ornamentation the altar candlesticks should be in keeping with those of the church and altar. Their size will depend on the proportions of the altar and cross; they should not overshadow the cross, and those nearest the cross must not exceed the base of the cross in height.[28] The six candlesticks are placed in a line with the cross, on the table of the altar, or on a gradine.[29] C.E. directs that the candlesticks at each side of the cross increase in height, rising in echelon from the two sides towards the centre, making the cross the focal point; but this prescription is not strictly binding,[30] and the candlesticks may all be of the same height. Naturally, smaller candlesticks, and of simpler design, are used at side altars.

The altar candlesticks may be made of any becoming material. C.E. (I, xii, 11) suggests, for great churches, silver[31] or bronze, or gilded copper; and it supposes that more beautiful, higher and more striking candlesticks are used on great festivals than on lesser days. Well-designed wooden candlesticks, gilded, look well, and are preferable to brass, which, after all, is a modern, tawdry substitute for gold. For penitential days and Requiem functions candlesticks of ebony, or of dark timber (e.g., mahogany, dark oak), are very becoming. On such occasions the altar candlesticks are not to be draped with black

[26] "Many awkward problems would be solved if chandlers and candlemakers would treat prickets as normal [rather than sockets] . . . Prickets take candles of any thickness, without paring or packing, and save infinite trouble in cleaning out candle-ends from sockets." (Anson, *Churches*, p. 113.)   [27] S.R.C. 3137[1,4].
[28] C.E. I, xii, 11.   [29] S.R.C. 3759.
[30] Cf. S.R.C. 3035[7] (and Index Generalis, p. 56).
[31] Silver is excluded on Good Friday (C.E. II, xxv, 2).

or violet cloth.[32]   Six candlesticks are the normal number for the high altar; two suffice for side altars.   As the six large candles are, normally, used only for solemn functions, it is usual to put two smaller candlesticks on the high altar for low Mass.   These should be removed after Mass.[33]   A seventh candlestick is used at certain Masses celebrated by the Bishop of the diocese; this will stand in line with the six candlesticks, and is usually a little higher, with the cross set before it.[34]

If extra lights are desired, for greater splendour, on a special occasion, they should not (for Mass or the liturgical Divine Office) be put on the altar, but may be set around the sanctuary—a practice which is traditional.   For example, standard candlesticks[35] or tall candelabra may be used.

The rubrics of the Missal[36] prescribe that a candlestick be placed on the Epistle side of the altar—it is generally a bracket candlestick, fixed to the wall of the sanctuary—with a candle, which is to be lighted, at low Mass, from the Consecration until after the Communion.   If there is an established legal custom of not lighting this "Elevation candle" the custom may be continued, but even then the Ordinary may order the rubric to be observed.[37]

This practice arose in the 12th to 13th century because of the desire of the people to see the Sacred Host when elevated. The candle was then often held by the server.   It is a substitute, at low Mass, for the torches carried at solemn Mass.   It is useful, too, in indicating to a new arrival in church or, passer-by, what part of the Mass is going on.

CANDLES

Candles used for cultual purposes must be real wax,[38] because of traditional usage and because of the symbolism attaching to wax.[39] Oil lamps may not be substituted for them.[40]

If pure beeswax candles are difficult to obtain, those with some ad-

[32] Cf. S.R.C. 3266.
[33] The ideal is to keep all candlesticks (except the six) off the sacred table of the altar, except during the time they are actually in use.
[34] C.E. I, xii, 12.   [35] P. 213.
[36] R.G. XX; R. VIII, 6.   [37] S.R.C. 4029[2], 4141[6].
[38] C.E. I, xii, 11; De Defectibus, X, 1.
[39] See the prayers used at the blessing of agnus deis (cf. *Praeconium Paschale*).
[40] S.R.C. 3173.

mixture of vegetable fats may be used, but (a) for the Paschal candle, and for at least two of those that burn during Mass, wax "saltem in maxima parte" must be used; (b) for all other candles that burn *on* the altar beeswax "in greater part or to a notable extent" should be used.[41] Non-wax candles are not allowed on the altar, or within its immediate ambit.[42] Normally, the candles are of white[43] (bleached) wax. Yellow (unbleached) wax candles are used for Requiem functions, for Tenebrae and on Good Friday.[44] Thick candles are desirable, to avoid their bending or spilling wax; thin wicks are necessary in them when they must burn for a long time (e.g., at Exposition). Coloured and ornamented candles are not forbidden, but, traditionally, they are the special privilege of the Pope's chapel. They are used in some places for Candlemas, and at certain functions (e.g., to offer to the officiating prelate at the consecration of a bishop). Real, not fake, candles should be used in altar candlesticks. While dummies ("souches," imitation candles of painted metal, having inserted in them a candle butt [!], supported by a spring) are tolerated,[45] they are most undesirable, and, as an unworthy pretence, are condemned by liturgical authorities.[46] The quality of the candles at any function is much more important than the quantity.[47] The blessing of candles for church use (R.R. IX, viii, 1) is not prescribed except at Candlemas—but it is very desirable.

If an extra candle is used on the table of the altar to read, where the light is insufficient, the candlestick used must not[48] resemble the hand-candlestick of a prelate,[49] and the candle need not be wax, though it is more becoming if it is.

[41] S.R.C. 4147. The official interpretation of this decree is: (i) for England and Wales, the Paschal candle, the two candles for low Mass, the six for high Mass, and the candles that are obligatory for Exposition and Benediction must contain at least 65 percent of genuine beeswax; and all other candles placed on the altar at least 25 percent wax (Bishops of England and Wales, Dec. 4, 1906). (ii) For Ireland, the Paschal candle and the two principal candles on the altar for Mass must contain at least 65 percent beeswax, and all others used on the altar 25 percent (Bishops of Ireland, Oct. 1905). (iii) For U.S.A., see Collins, *The Church Edifice*, p. 123. [42] Cf. S.R.C. 2865, 3063, 3173, 3376[3], 4257[5].
[43] C.E. I, xii, 11. [44] C.E. II, x, 2, 4; xi, 1, 7; xxii, 4; xxv, 2.
[45] S.R.C. 3448[13].
[46] It is, obviously, an abuse to burn candles of proper length at Benediction, and use up candle ends for the adorable Sacrifice.
[47] For the correct number of candles to burn at Mass, see O'Connell, *Celebration of Mass*, p. 250; at Exposition or Benediction, *Ceremonies of the Roman Rite Described*, pp. 231 sqq. [48] S.R.C. 2578[3]. [49] See *infra*, p. 217.

III. Other Candlesticks

Besides the candlesticks used on the altar, the liturgy uses (1) standard candlesticks, (2) the Paschal candlestick, (3) processional candlesticks, (4) torches and lanterns, (5) the hand-candlestick of a prelate.

1. *Standard Candlesticks*

Standard candlesticks (*funalia, candelabra magna*)—either those that take a single large candle, or those that take a number of candles —figure very early in the list of church equipment.

The emperor Constantine, in the 4th century, gave seven great bronze candlesticks to be set before the high altar of the Lateran in Rome; and four were placed before the tomb of St. Peter. The number seven may have been inspired by the seven golden candlesticks of the Apocalypse.[50] These great candlesticks are mentioned in the liturgical books, either as sources of extra necessary light (e.g., on Christmas Eve at Matins),[51] or for greater splendour at solemn Mass, especially when celebrated on great days, when candles in six or seven[52] large candlesticks may be placed on the balustrade of the chancel.[53] Two candles in standard candlesticks, standing in the sanctuary, may, when necessary, replace the torches that are carried at the private Mass of a bishop, for the Consecration and up to the Communion.[54] The Clementine Instruction (§ VI) speaks of two such candlesticks in use before the Blessed Sacrament exposed. Standard candlesticks, for use on great days, in the sanctuary are, then, a traditional, dignified and appropriate adornment and sign of festivity in churches. The same kind of candlestick—in wood or iron painted black—is suitable for use around the coffin or catafalque at exequial functions.[55]

2. *The Paschal Candlestick*

This candlestick is a tall, ornate candlestick, to hold the Paschal candle after its blessing on Easter Eve until Ascension Day.

[50] 1.12; 2.1.   [51] C.E. II, xiv, 3.
[52] Possibly C.E. means that six would be used normally; seven when seven candles burn on the altar for pontifical Mass of a feast, sung by the Ordinary.
[53] C.E. I, xii, 20. At one time these were probably lighted in honour of the triumphal cross often represented on the chancel arch.   [54] C.E. I, xxix, 7.
[55] Altar candlesticks should not be used for this purpose (cf. R.R. VII, i, 19).

History

The ceremony of blessing and singing the praises of a great candle —representing the Risen Christ—goes back to the 4th century in many places outside Rome. It had become part of the liturgy of Rome by the 6th century, and in that century and the 7th spread throughout the Western Church; and the great Paschal candlestick can be traced back to the 5th century. It was an immense, single candlestick, wondrously wrought in gold, silver, ivory, bronze, gilded iron or precious marbles; and richly adorned. Its traditional place is on the spot where the Gospel is sung at Mass (on the north side of the chancel); and, often, it was attached to the Gospel ambon. Sometimes, however, it was placed in the rood loft.

Law

The Paschal candlestick is to be a single, great tall one (*magnum condecens*),[56] in gold or silver, or gilded iron or wood, or other becoming material, suitably and richly adorned. It is to contain a wax candle (at least 65 per cent pure wax)—which may be adorned with flowers—at least sufficiently large to burn, at the times prescribed,[57] until Ascension Day. This great candle symbolizes the Risen Christ, and recalls the pillar of fire of the Old Testament (Exodus 13, etc.). The Paschal candlestick is to be placed on the ground (*in plano*), ordinarily on the Gospel side of the chancel.[58]

3. Processional Candlesticks

In the liturgy candles are carried in a procession, at its head—generally at the side of the cross—or before, or at the side of, the Sacred Host, as a mark of honour.

History

Candles were carried in procession long before they were used on the altar. Lights used to be carried before the Roman emperor, and be-

[56] C.E. II, xxvii, 1; M.R. VI, i.
[57] See *Ceremonies of the Roman Rite Described*, p. 334.
[58] C.E. II, xxvii, 1; M.R. VI, i; S.R.C. 2890[2].

fore the higher officials of the Roman Empire. This mark of respect was passed on to the bishops, when they became civil dignitaries, from the 5th century. *Ordo I* (8th century) and the Gregorian Sacramentary (6th century) mention the seven candles carried in the papal procession, for solemn Mass, on great days. Two candles accompanied the Gospel book for the singing of the Gospel from about the 6th century. Candles were sometimes carried on the arms of the processional cross; and, from at least the 3rd century, were borne in funeral processions.

Law

There is no special rubric about processional candlesticks. They ought to be simple in design,[59] tall—to be easily seen at the head of a procession—and light in weight, since they have to be carried, sometimes for quite a long time.

4. *Torches and Lanterns*

Torches (*funalia, intorticia*) are mentioned in the rubrics for use at solemn Mass[60] (or low Mass with special solemnity), and in processions of the Blessed Sacrament.[61] In Rome a torch usually consists of four long candles stuck together, with their four wicks giving a large flame. Usually, however, torches are made resembling candlesticks without a base, in metal or in gilded or painted wood. A good height is about 3 feet 9 inches. The usual number of torches for Mass is two or four; on a very great occasion six, or (at a pontifical Mass) eight at most.[62] In processions of the Blessed Sacrament four or six—eight at most in the great processions of Corpus Christi and the Forty Hours' Prayer—are used.

For outdoor processions swinging glass lanterns, fixed to staves by means of U-shaped brackets, are sometimes used. No mention is made of them in the rubrics.

[59] Sometimes they are designed like the six altar candlesticks, since originally it was the portable candlesticks that found their way to the altar table.
[60] R. VIII, 8. C.E. I, xii, 20; xxix, 6; II, viii, 68; xi, 7. Cf. S.R.C. 3059[8].
[61] I.C. § xx.
[62] At a Requiem Mass—even pontifical—four only, with candles of unbleached wax (C.E. II, xi, 7).

Ambone

Corona

Hanging Pyx

Bugia

Pax

Legile

Bacile

Faldstool

Catafalque
covered with Pall

5. *The Hand-candlestick*

A special form of hand-candlestick (*palmatoria, scotula, bugia*) is used as a mark of peculiar honour to their rank, by cardinals, bishops, and certain lesser prelates (e.g., Protonotaries Apostolic, Domestic Prelates).

History

The use of the hand-candlestick seems to be comparatively modern. No mention is made of it in the *Ordines Romani* (8th-14th centuries), nor by any liturgist before the 14th century. Presumably, its use was at first merely practical, to afford light to a prelate to read in a badly lighted place. The Pope does not use this candlestick.

Law

The bugia is like a candlestick for domestic use—low and with a wide pan to catch falling candle-grease—but with a long handle. It is made in silver;[63] but a cardinal sometimes uses one of gold or gold-plated, on a great occasion. It is not used on Good Friday; and prelates do not use it, normally, in presence of a superior.

IV. THE ALTAR COVER

When the altar is not in use, it is customary—there is no general law about it—to cover the table with a coloured cloth (*vesperale, stragulum*). It should be made of a strong material that will prevent dust reaching the linen altar cloth. Green is the correct colour, but any colour—except black—is permissible. It should not, however, be a colour that will clash with the frontal or the conopaeum. Violet is a becoming colour in penitential seasons. As this cloth is not a liturgical ornament, but just a protection against dust, it should be very simple in design and inconspicuous. It is best when it covers the table only of the altar, and does not hang over in front, partly covering the frontal or frontlet. It must be entirely removed, not merely rolled back, for sacred functions.[64]

---

[63] C.E. I, xx, 1.
[64] S.R.C. 3576[2], C.E. II, i, 13, 15, seems to refer to this cloth and permits it on the altar during Vespers, except during the incensation of the altar.

RÉSUMÉ

THE PERFECT ALTAR

To sum up the liturgical law regarding an altar—the perfect altar may be thus described: it is a consecrated altar, standing clear of its surroundings, with no reredos—or with one that does not interfere with the correct structure of the altar, the full veiling of the tabernacle, the proper position of the cross—and no fixed exposition throne. It is fully clothed with its frontal and altar cloths, and surmounted by a canopy (civory, baldaquin or tester). If the altar has a tabernacle, this will be entirely detached and fully veiled by its conopaeum. The altar cross will be such as to be clearly visible in all parts of the church. Such an altar would be the ideal altar from the liturgical point of view.

PART III

CHURCH FURNITURE

THE CREDENCE

History

The credence[1] (*credentia, fenestella*) is a table standing, normally, on the Epistle side of the sanctuary, to hold certain requisites for Mass and other functions. It is mentioned in C.E. I, xii, 19, 22, and in R.G. XX. The original form of credence was a niche in the wall—it was often part of the *piscina*[2]—hence the rubric of the Missal calls it *fenestella* (a little window). A separate table came into use at least in the 13th century, but does not seem to have been common in England before the 17th.

Law

The credence may be made of any becoming material and in a style suited to the church in which it is used. Normally it is made of wood; and, as it is not a liturgical ornament, but purely utilitarian, it ought to be simple in design and light in weight, so as to be easily movable. It should be higher than a table for domestic use, say 3 feet or 3 feet 4 inches, with a surface measuring at least 2 feet by 1 foot 8 inches; while for a big function a larger table, or tables, will be needed. A shelf underneath is often very convenient. In a small sanctuary, and where high Mass is seldom celebrated, the console or niche form of the credence is convenient and traditional; and it can

---

[1] The name seems to be derived from the practice of testing at this table (which was also a kind of sideboard) food and wine destined for persons of high rank, to see that it was not poisoned. The person who did the *praegustatio* was called *credentiarius*.
[2] See p. 88.

be designed to be quite an architectural feature of the sanctuary.

For episcopal functions the credence—which should be a large one —must stand away from the wall, as the attendants of the bishop (*familiares*) take their place behind it,[3] when not occupied. For such functions a second credence is often used on the Gospel side of the sanctuary, near the throne. As the credence is regarded as a continuation of the table of the altar, it is to be covered with a white linen cloth hanging to the ground all around on feast days,[4] but covering only the actual table on Good Friday.[5]

PRIE-DIEU

The liturgical use of a prie-dieu or kneeling-desk (*genuflexorium*) is for a prelate kneeling before the Blessed Sacrament, or before the high altar.[6]   When used by a cardinal, anywhere,[7] or by a "greater prelate" in the place of his jurisdiction, it is covered over with a large veil, of red silk for a cardinal, of green cloth for other prelates. For all, on penitential days or at Requiem functions, the colour is violet. An *undraped* prie-dieu is used for higher prelates outside the place of their jurisdiction,[8] and for certain lesser prelates[9] (e.g., a Protonotary Apostolic); and it is undraped, even for "greater prelates," on Good Friday.[10]

A prie-dieu, when used for prelates, is furnished with two cushions,[11] one to kneel on, the other under the prelate's arms.   Their colour will be that of the veil of the prie-dieu.

A draped prie-dieu, with cushions, is allowed for royal personages[12] attending a function. By custom, it is allowed—undraped and uncushioned[13]—for other lay people, either because of their rank or for a special occasion (e.g., for the bridegroom and bride at the Nuptial Mass).

[3] C.E. I, xi, 12; xii, 19.
[4] C.E. I, xii, 19.
[5] C.E. II, xxv, 2.
[6] C.E. I, ii, 5; xii, 8; xv, 5; xxx, 1.
[7] Cf. S.R.C. 2621[10].
[8] Cf. S.R.C. 367, 2011[2].
[9] S.R.C. 4154[10].
[10] C.E. II, xxv, 9; xxvi, 1.
[11] See p. 225.
[12] Cf. S.R.C. 1738, 2621[10].
[13] Cf. S.R.C. 1808[3].

LECTERN

The Ceremonial mentions the use of a lectern or reading-desk (*legile, pulpitum*) to hold the book for the singing of the Gospel at high Mass (II, viii, 45), of the Lessons at Matins (II, v, 5; xiv, 6) and on Holy Saturday (II, xxvii, 13), for the Maundy (II, xxiv, 4) and for the *Praeconium Paschale* on Easter Eve (II, xxvii, 1, 13). A lectern is also used for the chanting of the Passion in Holy Week. Lecterns are of three kinds. The earliest one was a stone or metal reading-desk (*lectorium*) fixed to the edge of an ambo (p. 79), or forming part of the ambo. The second form is the fixed choir lectern —a solid structure in stone or metal[14] (sometimes double-faced, with a rest for the book on each side), which is a fixture in a cathedral or monastic choir and is used by the chanters at the Divine Office. The third form is the portable, folding lectern—made of two X frames (wooden or metal), of uneven length, connected together by a bar in the centre, and joined at the top by a piece of strong cloth or leather. As one arm of the frame is longer than the other, when the arms are linked together by cloth or leather, they present a sloping surface on which the book is laid. Lecterns were used at quite an early period. A very common form is the eagle one, in which the reading-desk is the back of an eagle[15] with outstretched wings. This form—for the fixed lectern—has been very general since the 13th and 14th centuries.

Law

There are no rubrical directions about the form of the lectern. The portable one is best when made in wood, the lower part of the book-rest being some five feet or so high. On festival days for the singing of Epistle and Gospel, for the Mandatum and the *Praeconium Paschale,* the lectern is completely covered with a veil[16]—a long strip of cloth of gold, or of silk, of the colour of the Office, bordered with galloon or braid, and with a fringe at each end. The lectern is bare at Matins, and for the Lessons on Holy Saturday. If used at a Requiem function, it may be bare, or covered in black or violet cloth.[17]

[14] In this form the book-rest generally revolves on a pivot.
[15] Sometimes it was a pelican.
[16] C.E. *in loco.*
[17] Or even silk (S.R.C. 4172[1]).

The veil serves as an ornament and as a protection for the binding of the books placed on it.

CARPETS AND CUSHIONS

CARPETS

On great days C.E. (I, xii, 16) directs that "all the lower steps of the altar be covered with a large and beautiful carpet (*tapete*) that, as far as possible, they may be more conspicuous than the rest of the sanctuary, which is covered with green cloth (*pannus*). If such a carpet be not available, let the footpace at least,[18] which is nearest the altar, be covered with some carpet." The idea of the Ceremonial seems to be to attract attention to the altar as the focal point of the church. Just before (I, xii, 10), it had said that "all the floor of the sanctuary, up to the lowest step of the altar, ought to be suitably covered with a green textile" (*panni*). Even the footpace of a side altar should be carpeted.[19] The sanctuary floor and altar steps are uncarpeted for Requiem functions,[20] and on Good Friday.[21] As a mark of honour the steps of the bishop's throne are carpeted;[22] and a strip of carpet may be used before the celebrant's seat,[23] when the Bishop is not present.[24]

Green is the correct colour for the sanctuary carpet—violet for the footpace and altar steps at penitential functions—it is a colour that does not distract attention unduly, and it will not clash (in most of its shades) with the frontal and other altar furnishings. For festal occasions any fine carpet may be used, of any colour, or of mixed colours. A patterned carpet is, normally, more practical than a plain one (on which every stain shows clearly). The design should be one suitable for a church, with nothing profane; and with no sacred symbols to be trod upon.

CUSHIONS

A cushion (*cussinus, pulvinus, pulvinar*) is mentioned in the litur-

---

[18] Cf. S.R.C. 3576[1].
[19] C.E. I, xii, 16.
[20] In this case a strip of carpet (black if Blessed Sacrament is not present, otherwise violet) is used on the footpace, and under the faldstool.
[21] C.E. II, xxv, 1.
[22] C.E. I, xiii, 3.
[23] Cf. C.E. II, iii, 4.
[24] S.R.C. 2079[7].

gical books for (1) kneeling on, genuflecting on, (2) as a support for the missal, (3) as a support for the cross on Good Friday.

1. *Kneeling Cushion*

Apart from a special infirmity, only prelates[25] may, ordinarily, use a cushion for kneeling on at any function. C.E. mentions it[26] for a bishop kneeling at a prie-dieu or faldstool, or for genuflecting on[27] (e.g., at *Et incarnatus* of the Creed, during its recitation by the celebrant). It is used for the Bishop's undraped throne at Tenebrae,[28] and for his stall at Compline.[29] The canon-celebrant at Vespers, or Matins, or Lauds, may have a cushion at his seat, when the Bishop is absent.[30] The celebrant for the prostration on Good Friday may —even though not a prelate—use a cushion.[31]

Silk is the usual material for the covering of cushions—generally square or oblong in shape—by prelates; cloth or leather for anyone not a prelate. The correct colour for a cardinal is red, for a bishop and other prelates, green; for all, violet[32] at a penitential function.[33] Cushions for kneeling on should be plain, or very simply ornamented with braid and never with sacred symbols.

2. *The Missal Cushion*

Since the 13th century there has been mention of a cushion—or two cushions, one at each corner of the altar—as a support for the missal when in use. Possibly its use arose out of the need to treat with respect some of the beautifully bound missals. The rubrics (R.G. XX, and C.E. I, xii, 15) speak of this cushion, and C.E. gives as an alternative the missal-stand,[34] which is now almost universally used. R.G. give no material or colour for the cushion, but C.E. says it is to be (at least for a bishop) of silk of the colour of the Office. The missal

[25] S.R.C. 4268[9] (Cf. 2532[2]).
[26] C.E. I, ii, 5; xii, 8 *et passim*.
[27] E.g., C.E. II, i, 12.
[28] C.E. II, xxii, 17.
[29] C.E. II, iv, 1.
[30] C.E. II, iii, 4; vi, 5. S.R.C. 2027[1], 2079[7], 4172[2].
[31] M.R. v.
[32] Even on Good Friday (M.R. v).
[33] The cushions used for a celebrant at the faldstool are of the colour of the Office (p. 244).
[34] See p. 227.

cushion may also be covered in cloth or leather, and is stuffed until stiff with some fabrics like wool or down. A good size is about 16 inches by 10 or 12 inches. The cushion may be adorned with galloon or cord, and with embroidered religious emblems; and finished off at the corners with tassels.

3. *Cushion for the Cross*

The cushion on which the cross is laid after its unveiling on Good Friday is described by C.E.[35] as a large cushion of violet silk velvet, trimmed with gold; while M.R. calls it "pulvinar violaceum nobile."[36] A veil of white silk, adorned with violet silk, is laid over the cushion.

THE MISSAL AND MISSAL-STAND

THE MISSAL

History

The missal gradually reached its present form, between the 9th and 12th or 13th centuries, by combining with the early sacramentary (which contained only the texts needed by the celebrating bishop or priest), the readings from the Lectionary, the chants from the Gradual and the rubrics from the *Ordines* (8th-14th centuries). The first printed missal appeared in 1474, and the first official edition was issued in 1570 by St. Pius V, following the Council of Trent (1545-1563). Since then there has been a typical edition published in 1604, 1634, 1884, 1900 and 1920.

Law

There are no rubrics about the missal. Modern missals are usually well printed and well bound. The best colour for the binding is dark green, which will not clash with the altar frontal or tabernacle conopaeum of any colour. C.E.[37] supposes the books used at Mass, or the Divine Office, to be covered in a detachable cover of the colour of the Office. The missal should not be too heavy, since it has to be carried about, often by a small boy. The text should be so printed—as it is in

[35] C.E. II, xxv, 3, 22.
[36] M.R. v, i.
[37] I, xii, 15; II, iii, 4.

the best editions—as to avoid: (1) turning the page at an inconvenient moment, especially for the sung parts of the Mass (e.g., during a Collect or Preface); (2) too many cross-references; each date should have, at all events, the three prayers of the day (which are always needed for, at least, a commemoration). The missal must have the necessary regional or religious Order supplements. It should be equipped with strong ribbon markers, well fastened to their holder; at least eight are needed, and preferably eleven (two of each liturgical colour, and a neutral colour for the Preface).

THE MISSAL-STAND

The rubrics suppose a cushion used as a support for the missal,[38] but it has been superseded almost everywhere by a missal-stand, which C.E. (I, xii, 15) mentions as an alternative. Such a stand has been in use since at least the 13th century. The Ceremonial supposes it made in silver, or in wood, well designed and of good craftsmanship (*affabre elaboratum*). Brass is undesirable for a missal-stand: it is garish and too heavy. The best form seems to be a stand supported in the centre by one pillar on a round base.[39] It will need to be stoutly made and well balanced, so that the heavy book will not overturn it easily. It should be of a good height[40] and the ledge for the book should be deep (at least 2½ or 3 inches) and strong. In some places it is customary to cover the missal-stand with a veil of the colour of the vestments. This usage—recalling the missal cushion, the veil of the ambon and the Roman practice of vesting liturgical books—is a laudable one. The stand should be uncovered on Good Friday and for a Requiem Mass.

ALTAR CARDS (CHARTS)

These are cards containing some of the prayers from the Order of Mass to aid the memory of the celebrant.[41] They first came into use about the 16th century—in the beginning one only was used (*tabella*

---

[38] See p. 225.

[39] This form takes up the minimum of space. There are no legs to slip off the altar or intrude on to the corporal.

[40] Most stands are too low, and force the priest to bend down over the book when reading from it.

[41] R.G., XX (cf. *De Defectibus*, X, 1; and R.R. I, n. 11).

secretarum), sometimes in triptych form. Later (in the 17th century) the two side cards were added. Higher prelates do not use charts, they use a *canon episcopalis.* The charts are generally framed and glazed, though for small side altars cards covered in mica, or some similar material, are quite good. The frames may be of any material or design that is suitable for altar use, but as the cards are no part of the liturgical ornamentation of the altar, they ought to be as simple[42] and inconspicuous as possible. They should not be too large—so that the middle one is heavy to move and covers the crucifix, or tabernacle, unduly.[43]　More ornate cards may be used for great feasts; for penitential days or Requiem functions cards in dark, plain frames are most suitable. If the cross or gradine against which the cards are often placed is too far away the cards should have struts to support them independently. The cards should be clearly printed, in bold type, and not unduly illuminated, so that they can be read without difficulty. The contents and order of the prayers on the middle card vary. Perhaps the best arrangement is to follow, as far as possible, the proper order of the prayers—(*a*) in the left column it is possible to put *Aufer a nobis, Oramus, Gloria, Munda cor meum* and *Jube,* and the Creed, (*b*) the centre of the card, which is largely covered by the chalice, might well be reserved for the *Qui pridie* with the words of consecration in capitals, and the blank spaces filled with a simple vignette;[44] (*c*) in the right column the Offertory prayers, *Suscipe sancta Trinitas, Commixtio* and *Placeat.*[45]　The three prayers before Holy Communion are unnecessary (and indeed so is *Commixtio*)—the celebrant has them in the missal open beside him, if he needs to read them. In large churches there might well be three sets of cards: (1) for High Mass, with the incensation prayers added[46] (the prayer *Accendat* being on the right-hand card); (2) for low Mass of the living; (3) for Requiem Mass (omitting *Gloria, Jube,* Creed and the first prayer before Communion). Altar cards need an *imprimatur.*

[42] When they are over-ornate they are often illegible.
[43] If the tabernacle has a deep base, it may be possible to make the middle card low, so that it remains below the level of the tabernacle door, and need not be moved each time this is opened.
[44] A picture of the crucifix is quite superfluous.
[45] As *Placeat* is a tricky prayer to remember, it might be well to put it at the right-hand top corner, where it won't be covered by the veiled chalice.
[46] Or perhaps these are better on a separate card.

ALTAR CRUETS

The rubrics[47] speak of glass cruets (*ampullae vitreae, urceoli*) to contain the wine and water needed at Mass, and which are placed on a small dish or tray (*pelvicula, parvum bacile*).

History

From the 4th century there are references to large cruets (*amae, amulae, etc.*)—often made of precious metals, of amber, onyx, etc., jewelled and enamelled—to receive the offerings of wine made at Mass by the people in the early liturgy, and to hold the large quantity of wine needed when the faithful received Holy Communion under both kinds. When this practice was abolished (about the 13th century) the present practice of small twin cruets was introduced. From that time glass was used for them, and they were often marked—from the 14th century—sometimes, in rubies (for the wine) and topaz (white, for the water)," "A" for the water cruet and "V" for the wine one.

Law

The cruets ought to be made of clear white glass, so that the wine and water may be plainly visible. Cruets made of precious metals (gold, silver) are tolerated,[48] but are not desirable. For great days it is becoming to have glass cruets mounted only in gold or silver, with the upper part of clear glass, free of metal,[49] so that the contents of the cruets can be plainly seen. The best form of cruet is a simple glass one, with a wide opening so that it can be easily cleaned. The pouring lip should be so made that it will be easy to pour from it a *small quantity* of water (such as the priest pour into the chalice at the Offertory of Mass). Glass spouts to the cruets are undesirable; it is almost impossible to keep them clean. Handles are unnecessary. The cruets may have loosely-fitting glass stoppers; hinged lids are inconvenient in use. The tray on which the cruets stand may be made of any becom-

[47] R.G. XX; R. VII, 4, 9, 10; C.E. I, xi, 10.
[48] S.R.C. 3149. They should be clearly marked "A" and "V."
[49] If there is any base metal near the mouth of the cruet it becomes stained with verdigris.

ing material (glass is the easiest to keep clean). There should be a different (glass) dish or tray[50] to receive the water that is poured over the priest's fingers at the Lavabo. The use of a small spoon to convey a little water to the chalice—nowhere prescribed and undesirable—is not forbidden.[51] If it is used, it should be open and shallow, so that it can be easily kept clean.

THE SACRING BELL

The rubrics prescribe a small bell (*parva campanula, tintinnabulum*)[52] for use within the church at sacred functions.[53] It is called the "sacring bell."

History

The ringing of the little bell at Elevation of Mass came into general use in the 13th century; after the introduction (at the end of the 12th century) of the ceremony of the elevation of the Sacred Host. Ringing the bell at the *Sanctus,* as a warning of the approaching Consecration, came in somewhat earlier. The warning used to be given by the big bell in the church tower; or, more often, by a medium-sized bell specially for the purpose, situated in a little bellcote built for it, on the peak of the gable of the church. It was called the "Sanctus bell" and was sometimes rung by a bell-pull in the sanctuary, or through a nearby window, by the Mass server. Ringing the little bell at Mass is not mentioned in Burchard's *Ordo* (1502), nor in Pius V's Missal (1570), but it is prescribed in Clement VIII's Missal (1604) at the *Sanctus* and Elevation. Ringing the bell, as a warning of the approach of the Communion time, at *Domine, non sum dignus,* and shortly before the Elevation,[54] came in later in certain places, and spread gradually. In some places the bell is also rung at the "little Elevation" at the end of the Canon. The rubrics mention the ringing of the bell only at low Mass, but S.R.C. in 1922 (D.4377) ruled that it was also to be rung at pontifical, solemn and sung Masses, unless

---

[50] It must not take the form of the *bacile* (p. 243), used for prelates (S.R.C. 4100[4]).
[51] S.R.C. 3064[4].
[52] In the Middle Ages the terms *nola* and *squilla* were also used.
[53] R.G. XX; R. VII, 8; VIII, 6; C.E. I, xxix, 6; M.R. *passim.*
[54] This latter usage was approved by S.R.C. in 1922 (S.R.C. 4377).

some other signal (e.g., the silver trumpets at the solemn papal Mass) was used.

Law

What the rubrics envisage is a small, single-tongued bell, and the correct kind of bell is a simple hand-bell, in silver or bronze, with one tongue. It ought to have a good tone, and, for a large church, a robust one. Chiming bells, a carillon—used in some places since the 15th century—are not forbidden, but are less correct and cause distraction. Indian gongs are not allowed.[55] The sacring bell—unlike the large church bell—is not blessed.

LAMPS

Faithful to a very old tradition the Ceremonial of Bishops (I, xii, 17) directs that lamps, in uneven number, burn in churches for cultual purposes, for ornament and for symbolical reasons. These lamps are to burn especially before the altar of the Blessed Sacrament and before the high altar. It is becoming that they be hanging lamps, containing a number of lights, three, at least, before the high altar, not less than five before the Blessed Sacrament[56] (three of which, at least, are to burn all day). One lamp may be placed before other altars; and, on the great festivals, be lighted at least during Vespers and solemn Mass. If there is a *confessio* a lamp is to burn before it, where this is the custom. Lamps may also be hung from the civory of altars.

History

From the Constantinian Peace (4th century) lamps were lit in churches not only to give light, but for greater splendour and for symbolical reasons. Then came the cultual use of lamps, to honour that before which they burned, the altar (from the 4th century, especially in the Eastern Church), images, relics, and around the tombs of the martyrs. The lamps hung from the altar civory, or were fixed into *coronae*, or set in standards. There were little lamps of terra-cotta; and big lamps made of various metals, some of them of elaborate

[55] S.R.C. 4000[3].
[56] This rubric is interpreted as of obligation only in great churches, but it indicates the direction of the ideal practice for any church.

design. They were fed with olive oil or with wax, and both these materials were among the things that the faithful in the early Church used to present—with the bread and wine—at the Offertory of the Mass.

Law

Church lamps are best made in silver, or silver gilt, but any suitable material (e.g., bronze) may be used. They are usually suspended on chains or pulleys, but may also (in a small church or chapel) be placed in brackets fixed to the side walls,[56a] or may be supported on suitable stands. The style of the lamp container may be in keeping with the style of the church; and the size of the lamp should be in proportion to the place where it burns. A simple design is best, so that the lamp may be easily cleaned. Because of its symbolism the flame of the lamp should be visible. Oil lamps should not be placed on or over altars,[57] for cleanliness' sake.

THE BLESSED SACRAMENT LAMP

Before the Blessed Sacrament reserved in the tabernacle at least one light (at least three in greater churches) is to burn continually.[58]

History

From the 11th century a light burned in cathedral and monastic churches before the Sacred Host reserved on Maundy Thursday for the Good Friday liturgy; and lights accompanied the Blessed Sacrament on that day in its journey to the "place of repose," or when it was taken to the sick. There is no evidence of a perpetual lamp before the reserved Sacrament until the second half of the 12th century. During the 13th and 14th centuries the practice gradually spread. Synodal legislation made the use of a perpetual lamp obligatory in some places in the 16th century; and a reply of S.R.C. (D.31) in 1593, about the Blessed Sacrament in a small non-parish church, orders this. With the publication of the Ceremonial in 1600, and the official edition of the Roman Ritual in 1614, came the first general law for the Western Church.

[56a] S.R.C. 3576[4] (cf. 2033).
[57] Cf. S.R.C., 4035[6].
[58] C.E. I, xii, 17; R.R. V, i, 6.

Law

The lamp before the Blessed Sacrament must be within the sanctuary and before—not on or over—the altar;[59] nor should it be over the carpeted footpace or steps, because of the risk of falling oil. It should be so hung as not to impede a view of the altar cross, or of the image of the Titular of an altar placed above it.[60] The glass of the lamp that burns before the tabernacle should be white (the colour of the Blessed Sacrament), but coloured glass is tolerated.[61] This lamp should be fed with olive oil, or a mixture of this with pure wax.[62] Where olive oil is not available the Ordinary may allow the use of other oils—vegetable oils as far as possible.[63] Only as a last resort—because of the symbolism of olive and wax—may the Ordinary permit the use of electric light for the Blessed Sacrament lamps.[64] The continual watchful care that is needed to keep an oil lamp perpetually alight is a symbol of the assiduous devotion of the guardian of the sanctuary.

THE PROCESSIONAL CROSS

The true liturgical cross, the forerunner of the altar cross, is the processional cross; i.e., a crucifix fitted with a (detachable) staff for carrying in a procession. There are various kinds of processional cross, e.g., the prelatical cross (carried before the Pope and before his legate, or before a metropolitan in the place of his jurisdiction),[65] the capitular cross (carried at the head of a Chapter of Canons), the parochial cross (the ordinary processional cross of a parish church).

History

The first form of processional cross was the *crux stationalis,* carried before the Pope (possibly from the 5th century) as he went to officiate

[59] S.R.C. 2033, 3576[4], 4035[6].
[60] This is one good reason for not having lamps too big.
[61] S.R.C. 3576[5]. By Roman usage the vessel which contains the oil—usually glass, but sometimes metal—is so lowered into its container that only the lighted wick appears.
[62] R.R. V, i, 6; S.R.C. 4205.
[63] R.R. V, i, 6; S.R.C. 3121, 4205, 4230, 4334.
[64] S.R.C. Mar. 13, 1942; Aug. 18, 1949.
[65] C.E. I, iv, 1; xv, 2.

at the stational liturgy. This use of the cross as a mark of special dignity spread to papal legates (from the end of the 12th century) and to archbishops (in the 11th and 12th centuries), and this usage was authorized by the popes in the 13th and 14th centuries. A cross was carried at the head of different sections of the clergy and people in the stational processions in Rome (e.g., in *Ordo I*);[66] and at the head of the papal procession itself after Charlemagne's gift (in 800) to Pope Leo III of a beautiful cross for this purpose. In medieval England a processional cross of wood, painted red and without the figure of Christ, was used in Lent for processions; and one of crystal from Easter morning until Ascension Day. At first the processional cross bore no figure of the Crucified. From the 11th or 12th century the figure was generally added, but crosses without it were in use in the 14th.

Law

The processional cross is now carried at the head of a sacred procession[67] (i.e., a procession of clergy preceding a vested celebrant), or —as a personal privilege—before a metropolitan in the place of his jurisdiction.[68] The cross in a sacred procession represents the altar,[69] and is normally accompanied by lights as a mark of respect.

The processional cross is usually made of silver, or tubular metal plated with gold or silver. It may also be made in wood. It is a crucifix, i.e., bears the image of the Crucified. The staff is usually of wood —the cross should not be unduly heavy—and with one or two knops or bosses. It should be detachable from the cross, since this is used without the staff at the obsequies of a child, or when accompanying a priest going to give Extreme Unction.[70] As the cross should be clearly seen in a procession, it must be tall (say some 6 feet 8 inches). For the Way of the Cross the Roman custom is to use a plain, wooden cross painted black. There is no obligation to bless a processional

[66] 8th century.
[67] R.R. X, i, 5; cf. C.E. I, ii, 4.
[68] This cross has only one transom or cross-piece; the double cross-bar belongs to heraldry only.
[69] S.R.C. 4198[16].
[70] R.R. VII, vii, 1; VI, ii, 2.

cross,[71] but it may be blessed—by any priest, if blessed without solemnity—with the *Benedictio Imaginis.*[72]

THE PORTABLE CANOPY

The portable canopy has two forms, large (*umbraculum, baldachinum*)[73] and small (*umbella, ombrellino*). It is used as a protection and as a mark of honour (replacing the canopy of the altar and throne).

It is used to carry over: (1) the Blessed Sacrament in a procession[74] (being first so used on Maundy Thursday and Good Friday, and from the 14th century in other processions); (2) a Cardinal Legate at his solemn entry into the place of his legacy, or the bishop of the diocese for his first solemn entry into his cathedral or other church of his diocese[75] or at visitation (there are references to this use from the 12th century, at first for the Pope only).

The canopy may not be carried over relics or images *in procession,*[76] but is tolerated for relics of the Passion.[77] A fixed canopy is allowed, for protection and honour, over an image in its place on the exterior of the church (since the 12th century), or inside (from the 14th).

Forms of Canopy

The large canopy is either collapsible, sustained by four, six or eight poles,[78] or fixed rigidly on a frame (in some places since the 17th century). The former type is more difficult to carry well, but it is more graceful when properly carried, and is easier to store. The canopy is usually made in silk or other rich fabrics (cloth of gold or silver, brocade, etc.) ornamented with sacred symbols, edged with a valance, gold or coloured fringe, etc. For use in uncertain weather the exterior part (the roof) should be made of stronger, waterproof ma-

[71] S.R.C. 2143.
[72] R.R. IX, ix, 15.
[73] C.E. I, xiv, 1.
[74] C.E. II, xxiii, 13; xxv, 31; xxxiii, 5, 8; R.R. V, iv, 10, 12; M.R. Tit. IV and V; I.C. § xix.
[75] C.E. I, ii, 2, 4; S.R.C. 2951[1].
[76] S.R.C. 2379[2], 2647, 2951[1], 2808.
[77] S.R.C. 2647.
[78] C.E. I, xiv, 1.

terial; the interior should be white[79] (for the Blessed Sacrament). The canopy should not be too heavy, that it may be easily borne.

The smaller canopy (used for carrying Viaticum to the sick in Rome from the 5th century; earlier, carried over the Pope) is a large white umbrella—surmounted by a cross or a symbol of the Blessed Sacrament—with a long handle, jointed in the middle, so that the *umbella* can be bent and carried directly over the head of the priest bearing the Blessed Sacrament. It is used in less solemn processions of the Blessed Sacrament (e.g., when moving It from one altar to another, or in carrying Viaticum publicly to the sick), or, even in a solemn procession, when lack of space prevents the use of the large canopy.

INCENSE AND THE THURIBLE (CENSER)

INCENSE

Incense (*thus, thymiama, olibanum*), a mixture of aromatic resinous gums and spices, is used in the liturgy of high Mass, at solemn Lauds and Vespers, at Exposition of the Sacred Host, at funerals, at certain consecrations and blessings, and in processions.[80] It is used to add splendour and solemnity to the rite; as a mark of honour to sacred persons and things; as a symbol of sacrifice, of adoration and of prayer;[81] as a sacramental, to hallow persons and things, and as a demonifuge.

History

At first the use of incense was eschewed by Christians because of its association with pagan worship, but in the 4th and 5th centuries it began to be used at funerals and in the translation of relics. From the 4th century also it began to be used in churches, in fixed thuribles— stood or hung before altars and images—but principally, it would seem, as a deodorant. Its first ritual use (from about the 6th century) seems to have been the carrying of it in processions—as a mark of honour—before the Pope and before a Bishop (as it used to be car-

[79] For relics of the Passion red may be used; but violet on Good Friday (S.R.C. 41972).
[80] Grains of incense are inserted in the Paschal candle, and in the "sepulchre" of a consecrated altar.
[81] Cf. Psalm 140.2; Apocalypse 5.8, 8.3.

ried before civil dignitaries in Rome), and before the book of the Gospels (from the 7th century). About the 9th and 10th centuries, outside Rome, arose the practice of incensing the altar (derived from the 7th-century Gallican rite of the consecration of an altar) and of incensing persons. These usages were not adopted in Rome until the 12th century. The incensation of the *oblata* (bread and wine) at Mass dates from the 11th century; and by the 12th the Roman rite used incense at the Introit, for the Gospel book, and at the Offertory. In *Ordo XIV* (14th century) the use of incense at Mass is exactly as it is today. Incensation at solemn Lauds and Vespers dates from the 13th century.

Law

The rubrics of the Ceremonial[82] order the use of pure incense (*thus purum, olibanum*) of a sweet savour. Other sweet-smelling gums may be added, but in lesser quantity. The modern synthetic chemical products which sometimes go by the name of "incense" should be avoided. Unpowdered incense will give fumes which last longer than those given off by powdered incense.

THE THURIBLE (CENSER)

The thurible or censer (*thuribulum, incensorium, thymia[ma]terium*) is a metal bowl, to hold lighted charcoal, with a perforated cover actuated by a chain, sustained by three chains which end in a ringed disk.

History

The censer was probably derived from the chafing dish that used to be carried (in the 4th century) in processions, in order to light candles from it, if necessary. At first the censer was a kind of brazier[83]—on a base or on legs—both fixed,[84] and hanging. Later (from about the 9th century) it developed into the portable, swinging thurible we now know. Gradually it became more elaborate in design, and was sometimes made in precious metals and even jewelled. At first the cover

[82] C.E. I, xii 19; xiii, 3.
[83] Such a censer is still used at the consecration of a church bell.
[84] Some of the fixed censers were made as silver cranes, the incense being put in through a hole in the back of the bird, and the smoke issuing from its beak.

was spherical with geometrical piercing; later it received complete architectural treatment, and the most intricate "Gothic," "Rococo," and other style censers were made. In the 14th century especially ornate and complicated censers were in use in many places.

Law

No rubric deals with the form of the censer. The better ones are made in silver, or are silver-plated. For practical purposes the censer should not be unduly heavy, and a simple design is best; if over-ornate it is difficult to clean. There should be no protruding ornament, which gets caught in the chains. The three chains which support the thurible are usually about three feet long and terminate in a convex disk, to which a large ring is attached that serves as a handle. A sliding ring— embracing the three chains—which slips down over the cover, and holds it fast, is a desirable addition. The interior of the censer is fitted with a movable iron (or other fireproof) container—with a handle— into which the burning charcoal is put.

THE INCENSE-BOAT

The incense is presented in a container (*acerra, navicula*) which is boat-shaped, with a base on which it stands. At first a square or cylindrical metal box was used for the incense, but the boat-shaped container made its appearance at the Gothic period (13th-14th centuries) or even earlier. There is mention of a spoon from the 10th century.

The incense boat is made of the same material and design as the censer. It may have one or two openings (according as only one half the cover or both halves open); the base should be quite flat, and possibly weighted, so that the whole thing is well balanced and will not overturn easily when laid down. The spoon should be flat and shallow, and not too short, otherwise it slips into the incense.

THE PAX-BREDE

The pax or pax-brede[85] (*instrumentum pacis, tabula pacis, osculatorium*) is a tablet or disk bearing a sacred image, with a handle at

85 Also "osculatory," "pax-board."

the back, which is used to convey the kiss of peace[86] to certain persons during the Liturgy.[87] The pax is kissed by the celebrant, assistant priest or subdeacon (as the case may be) before being taken to the person who is to receive the pax. C.E. (I, xxix, 8) points out that the kiss of peace is transmitted from the Sacrifice of the altar.

History

The accolade, or kiss of peace—in sign of Christian unity and brotherly love—was a very early feature of the Liturgy (from at least the 2nd century). In the 13th century, in England, began the practice of sometimes not giving the kiss of peace by actual embrace, but transmitting it by some holy object (a relic, an image, a consecrated paten).[88] This usage was adopted by Rome in the 15th century. In course of time came the special instrument—the pax-brede—for conveying the kiss. It was made, in varying forms, of precious materials (gold, silver, ivory, etc.), beautifully adorned (chased, enamelled, jewelled). Sometimes it was made of wood, overlaid with a precious metal, or having a religious image painted on it.

Law

There is no rubric about the form of the pax-brede. It is usually a plaque—of any shape, square (say 4 inches), oblong (say 3 by 4 inches), oval or round—made of gold or silver, or silver-plated metal, or ivory, etc. It bears, in relief or chased, some sacred image, e.g., the crucifixion, *Agnus Dei* (very appropriate) or an image of our Lady, of the Titular of the church or the Patron of the place. The pax is fitted with a handle—which acts as a strut at the back, to enable it to stand—by which it may be presented to a person to kiss (p. 216).

FUNERAL FURNITURE

For exequial functions the mortuary chapel (p. 15) of a church should be equipped with trestles to support a coffin, a catafalque, a hearse cloth or pall, and standard candlesticks.

The rubrics of the Ceremonial (II, xi, 1; xxxviii, 24, 25), and of

[86] Cf. O'Connell, *Celebration of Mass*, p. 542.
[87] R. X, 3. C.E. I, xxiv, 6, 12; xxix, 8; xxx, 2.
[88] This is no longer allowed (S.R.C. 416).

the Roman Ritual (VII, iii) suppose a dead body to be borne to the church on a bier (*feretrum*) or feretory.[89] There the coffin is laid on a stand or on trestles, covered over with a pall, and candles set around it. On the same bier it is borne to the grave later. For an exequial function when the body is not present, a catafalque (a board, generally shaped like a coffin, set on a stand or trestles) replaces the coffin[90] (C.E. II, xi, 10-13; R.R. VII, v).

History

From the earliest centuries—certainly from the 4th century—a dead body was borne to the church before burial, sometimes in an open coffin, sometimes wrapped in a shroud or in a hair shirt; accompanied by lights as a mark of respect, and also as a symbol of the faith of the dead man and of the Christian hope of eternal happiness. In the church the bier was set on a platform (*krabation*) and lights placed around it. In the course of time arose the practice of erecting over the coffin (or catafalque) of persons of high rank or great wealth a kind of civory, a lofty arched framework of wood, or metal, with four or six posts, roofed (sometimes two storeys high), and fitted with prickets for a multitude of tapers. From it hung flags and representations of the arms of the dead person. This towering structure received the name *castrum doloris* (p. 216). It is still used at an exequial function for a pope or bishop, or other personage, but the corpse may not now be under a canopy.[91] Up to quite modern times, many persons were buried in the church itself, and the Absolution *absente corpore* was carried out at the actual tomb.[92]

[89] In connection with funerals the rubrics use the following terms: *castrum doloris* (hearse), C.E. II, xi; P.R. Part III; *feretrum* (bier, feretory), C.E. II, xi, xxxviii; R.R. VII, iii; *lectus* (funeral couch—bier), C.E. II, xxxviii, xi, *lectica* (catafalque), C.E. II, xi, 11, 12; R.R. VII, v, 1; *tumulus* (catafalque—grave). R.R. VII, v, i; iii, 13. "Hearse" in English has many meanings (the Oxford English Dictionary gives nine). In the Liturgy it means: (1) the harrow-shaped triangular frame used for the fifteen candles of Tenebrae; (2) *castrum doloris;* (3) a car for carrying a coffin.

[90] The simplest form of a substitute is a black cloth, spread before the altar, or before a bishop's throne or faldstool, for the Absolution (C.E. II, xi, 10, 12; xxxvii, 2).

[91] S.R.C. 3500[1].

[92] That is, probably, why R.R. VII, v, speaks of carrying out the Absolution (*absente corpore*) *ad locum tumuli.*

Law

For an exequial service the coffin or the catafalque is to be placed in the middle of the church,[93] not in the chancel, whatever the rank of the deceased person. In larger churches it will be, usually, in the special mortuary chapel.

Around the coffin or catafalque, or on it, may be put the insignia (coat of arms, decorations, etc.) of the dead person. By the coffin of a cardinal or bishop is placed his pontifical hat (which is later hung over his tomb): when the body is absent, his white linen mitre replaces the hat. For a priest a biretta, and a black or violet stole, may be laid on the coffin.[94]

Flowers on or around the coffin are contrary to the spirit of the rubrics (which prescribe[95] a crown of flowers, or sweet-smelling leaves, on the head of a child who dies before reaching the use of reason, as "a sign of his (her) integrity of body and virginity"). S.R.C.[96] in reply to a query from the Patriarch of Goa (India), said the use of flowers on the bier in Goa might be "tolerated." Flowers are excluded in some places by local law. It is forbidden to hang (artificial) wreaths on the walls of a church.[97]

THE FUNERAL PALL

A pall (*panus emortualis*) or hearse cloth is used to cover the coffin in the church, or over a catafalque.

History

From the earliest centuries there was a practice of covering the bier (and the body in its open *arca*) with a cloth, and of laying cloths on the tombs of the martyrs. In the Middle Ages—in England—friends of the dead person brought pieces of rich material ("palls"), sometimes of cloth of gold, to place over the corpse. These palls were often black—with a broad white or coloured cross on them—but they were also green, blue, red or russet. After the obsequies they were re-

[93] C.E. II, xxxviii, 25; R.R. VII, iii, 4.
[94] Cf. R.R. VII, i, 12, 13; S.R.C. 4228.
[95] R.R. VII, vii, 1.
[96] S.R.C. 3804[6].
[97] S.R.C. 3909.

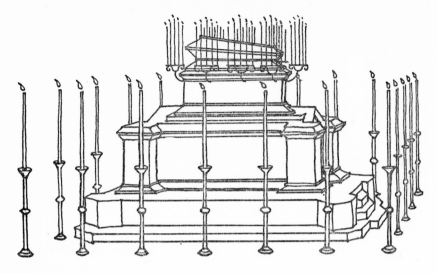

Castrum Doloris

garded as gifts to the church, and were made into vestments, frontals, etc.

Law

The pall is to be black[98] in colour and made of velvet, or cloth, or (for a prelate) silk.[99] It may be soberly[100] ornamented (by tradition) with gold or yellow braid, or galloon and fringe, but violet (as a modern mourning colour) is now preferable. A white cross on the pall is not used in Rome, but it is not forbidden. A white pall is forbidden,[101] except for children who died before reaching the use of reason. The national flag may be laid over a coffin, and this is the usual practice if the dead person was a member of the armed services. An altar frontal may not be used as a pall.[102]

FUNERAL CANDLES

Lighted candles are carried in the procession bearing a corpse to

[98] S.R.C. 4165[5].
[99] C.E. II, xxxviii, 12, speaks of a black silk, or at least woollen, cover for the funeral couch of a bishop.
[100] S.R.C. 4165[5].
[101] S.R.C. 3035[11], 3263, 4397[7].
[102] R.R. VII, i, 19.

the church, and candles are placed around the coffin (or the catafalque) and lighted for any part of the obsequies.[103]

History

Light is a symbol of faith, hope, grace, life eternal, and is also a mark of honour, and so from the earliest times lights accompanied a corpse and were placed around it. Candles for the purpose were supplied by the family of the deceased and became the property of the church where the obsequies were held.

Law

The number of lights is not fixed. Four[104] or six candles of unbleached wax, in tall standard candlesticks are generally used. It is becoming if these candlesticks are made in wrought iron or wood, painted black; or they may be of mahogany or some other dark-coloured material. The candlesticks used on the altar may not be used around a coffin or catafalque.[105]

THE BACILE

A special form of ewer and basin—which C.E. calls *bacile* and *buccale*,[106] or *pelvis* and *urceus argenteus*[107]—is used for the ceremonial washing of hands of a cardinal, bishop and some lesser prelates.[108] This ewer and basin (a kind of deep tray, with a hump in the middle to keep the ewer steady) is made of silver, or metal silver-plated; or, for a cardinal, of gold or silver-gilt (p. 216). With it goes a small salver (*lanx*) on which are carried the towels.

THE FALDSTOOL

The faldstool is a portable, folding chair, with arm rests, but no back (or a very low one), used by prelates at liturgical functions (p. 216).

History

The faldstool (*faldistorium*) resembles the curial chair used by the

[103] R.R. VII, i, 10; iii, 1, 4. Cf. C.E. II, xxxviii, 11, 13.
[104] Cf. C.E. II, xxxviii, 13.
[105] Cf. R.R. VII, i, 19.
[106] C.E. I, xi, 12.
[107] C.E. I, xii, 19.
[108] S.R.C. 4154, (§§ 10, 27).

ancient Romans, and seems to have first come into use as a bishop's chair about the 8th century, when the bishop preached from it on the footpace, instead of from his throne. The faldstool is used instead of a throne by the Bishop of the diocese pontificating in the presence of a superior, and by an abbot in his monastery pontificating in the presence of a "greater prelate." The Bishop also uses the faldstool for functions that require a movable seat (e.g., at ordinations, or consecrations). It is used for all pontifical functions by a bishop outside his diocese, by a titular bishop and by certain high prelates who have pontifical privileges (e.g., a Protonotary Apostolic of the first or second category).[109] A faldstool is also used to kneel at by prelates, instead of a kneeling-desk.[110]

Law

The faldstool is usually made of metal or wood,[111] and may be suitably adorned (inlaid, etc.). As it should be portable it must not be too heavy. The seat is normally made of leather or strong cloth. It is furnished with two cushions, one for sitting on and one on which the prelate kneels. When used as a seat the faldstool is covered to the ground on all sides with a silk cover—trimmed with galloon or fringe —a kind of caparison, of the colour of the vestments used at the function[112] (including black for a requiem service).[113] When used as a kneeling-desk there is no covering (Roman usage), and the cushions will be of red silk (violet, for penitential days) for a cardinal, of green cloth (violet, for penitential days) for a bishop[114] or protonotary.

[109] S.R.C. 4154, (§§ 6, 27).
[110] C.E. I, xii, 8; cf. S.R.C. 2471⁶.
[111] By Roman usage a faldstool used as a kneeling-desk is made of wood gilt.
[112] C.E. I, xii, 10.
[113] C.E. II, xi, 1.
[114] C.E. I, xii, 8.

Directives for the Building
of a Church[1]

PRINCIPLES

THE Christian church, a house of God, is a sacred place filled with the divine presence (even apart from the Holy Eucharist), a place where the people of God assemble, and that for several purposes:

First and above all, to celebrate the re-presentation of the redeeming Sacrifice of our Lord.

Secondly, to partake of the fruits of Christ's redeeming Sacrifice in the holy sacraments.

Thirdly, to hear the preaching of the word of God.

Fourthly, to render homage and adoration to the presence of our Lord in the eucharistic Bread.

Fifthly, to engage in various non-liturgical devotions.

The Christian church building, however, serves not only as the assembling place for the Christian community, whether for liturgical or non-liturgical worship; it is also a place for individual private devotion.

2. Such being the character and the purposes of the Christian church edifice, it bears a distinction of incomparable dignity.

It is, firstly, in a unique way "the tabernacle of God among men" (Apoc. 21:3), the place where by His mercy His people may surely find Him; it is our Father's house (Luke 15:17); it is the *"basilica,"* the palace of the King.

Secondly, this house of God is the holy place in which the Church, the Mystical Body of Christ, is formed and upbuilded, and hence the visible edifice is a symbol of this Mystical Body.

---

[1] Composed by the Rev. Theodore Klauser, Rector Magnificus of the University of Bonn, by order of and in cooperation with the Liturgical Commission established by the Catholic bishops of Germany. This originally appeared in *Orate Fratres,* Dec., 1949, and is reprinted here with the permission of The Liturgical Press, Collegeville, Minn.

Thirdly, this house of God is the place in which the eternal union of God with His people in life everlasting is anticipated, and therefore the Christian church edifice is rightly regarded as the heavenly Sion descended upon earth.

3. These various purposes which the church building must serve present a peculiar problem in its construction. The eucharistic Sacrifice requires an arrangement of space different from that required by the administration of the sacraments of baptism and penance; the requirements in the administration of these sacraments differ from those which preaching demands; and differences appear again as between preaching and eucharistic adoration, as between eucharistic adoration and community worship, as between community worship and private devotion. It is the task of the architect to find a solution of the problem which will best satisfy these several purposes of the church edifice.

4. The services of Christian worship, the eucharistic Sacrifice, the administration of the sacraments, the preaching of the word of God, adoration of the eucharistic Christ, these are not rendered in precisely the same way in all churches throughout the world. In the course of the centuries divers methods have developed, the so-called "liturgies" or "rites." By far the most important of these are the Roman and the Byzantine rites, the former in the bishoprics of the West and the latter in those of the East.

While agreeing in all essentials, the Roman and the Byzantine rites have features that are definitely distinct. Therefore the church edifice in which the Roman liturgy is to be celebrated cannot be exactly like one which serves the Byzantine liturgy.

5. The church edifice today is intended for the people of our times. Hence it must be fashioned in such way that the people of our times may recognize and feel that it is addressed to them. The most significant and the most worthy needs of modern mankind must here find their fulfilment: the urge toward community life, the desire for what is true and genuine, the wish to advance from what is peripheral to what is central and essential, the demand for clarity, lucidity, intelligibility, the longing for quiet and peace, for a sense of warmth and security.

CONCLUSIONS

1. The several parochial buildings, church, school, parish library and charity bureau and hospice, rectory and janitor's dwelling, should not, except in case of necessity, be erected apart from each other in separate localities.

The ideal which should be desired is a juxta-position of these several units so as to form one *"domus ecclesiae,"* a parish center where the close interrelation of temple and priesthood, of Eucharist and charity, of sacraments and education would be visibly expressed.

2. It is not desirable that the church edifice, except in cases of necessity, be located directly on a street filled with the noise of business and traffic, even though the people of our times who are so immersed in earthly things do greatly need a distinct reorientation of their mind toward God on high. It would be a commendable thing if the people assembling for divine worship might traverse a zone of quiet, a bordered fore-court, a formal atrium, and so be inwardly disposed and attuned to the divine atmosphere of the sacred interior.

3. It would be a mistake to plan the exterior structure in its outlines and spatial proportions, in its structural members and its decoration, according to the style of the profane architecture of the time and of the surroundings: lest the attractiveness of the church building be merely that of this world. It is a mistake also to point out to the public the direction to the church by means of showy sign-boards along the way.

Our effort should be no doubt to express by the exterior appearance of the building the supernatural, the divine character of the worship that transpires within—and yet to adapt the edifice in harmony with its surroundings.

4. In planning the entrances to the church building the chief considerations should not be simply protection from wind and weather and the orderly coming and going of the congregation.

The portals of the church, and especially the main portal, should by their impressive design suggest to the faithful the symbolism of church portals as representing the gates of heaven.

5. The plans for the interior of the church should be determined

chiefly by the requirements for the eucharistic Sacrifice; not, as one sometimes finds, primarily for the sake of devotion to our Lord's eucharistic Presence so that spatial arrangements are made to serve chiefly for adoration and contemplation. This latter procedure is incorrect, because in the gradation of purposes that of eucharistic adoration is not the first in order.

The problem presented by this gradation of purposes can best be solved by a spatial arrangement which provides areas for eucharistic adoration and for the administration of the sacraments of baptism and penance distinct from that which is required for the eucharistic Sacrifice. These several areas could then be given their appropriate architectural treatment.

6. It is a mistaken, although a widespread notion, that the altar should be placed in the midst of the congregation, and that therefore the circular form of edifice is the only satisfactory one.

The Christian church building is intended primarily for the celebration of the eucharistic Sacrifice. This holy Sacrifice is, according to the mind of the Roman liturgy, an action: above all the action of Christ, our High-priest, and of His representative in the priestly office; but it is also the action of the entire Christian community. Climactic moments in the action of the congregation are the acclamations before the preface, the *Amen* at the end of the Canon, as well as the offertory and communion processions, of which the former now rarely appears in our day. The concurrence and concord of these actions suppose a spatial arrangement directed toward the altar, so that there is exchange of address and response between sanctuary and nave, between priest and people, and processional movement to and from the altar. The ideal therefore is a church building arranged with regard to these wishes of the Roman liturgy: direction toward the altar, opposite positions of priest and people, provision for orderly procession to and fro: while at the same time the altar must not be too far removed from the farther end of the nave.

7. The altar has a meaning from earliest times as a station from which earth looks up to heaven. In the Christian religion the altar is, according to its purpose, the sacrificial and banquet table of the people of God, and at the same time the place of God's eucharistic advent

among us. Since at the Consecration in the Mass our divine Lord becomes present upon the altar, it is, even without the tabernacle, Christ's throne on earth. And since the altar is His throne, the faithful from patristic times saw in the altar a symbol of Christ Himself, for the throne symbolizes the person of the Ruler. Therefore it is evidently incorrect to fashion the altar as a mural console as though its purpose were merely or chiefly to serve as a pedestal for tabernacle and crucifix, for candelabra and reliquaries, for painted altar-pieces or groups of statues.

In the well planned church interior the altar should appear with greatest prominence as the most sacred object, the very center and heart of the entire environment. This will be made evident by its isolated placement, its relative elevation, accessible from all sides, well proportioned, excellent in the given material, monumental in the measure which the edifice demands, situated in right perspective, at the most lightsome point, and surmounted by a baldaquin or canopy.

8. Whenever it is possible the venerable tradition according to which the main axis of the building proceeds from west to east, with the altar at the eastern end, should be retained.

The significant and beautiful symbolism contained in this eastward direction would profitably be restored in the consciousness of the faithful, and thus the eastward placing of our churches revived. Various evidences seem to show that in days to come the ancient custom will be restored whereby the position of the priest is at the farther side of the altar, facing toward the people, as is still the case in the old Roman basilicas. This alteration of the present custom apparently corresponds to the widely felt desire for a more distinct expression of community oneness at the table of the Lord. The rule of eastward direction would not thereby be infringed; for the ideal goal in this orientation is God our Father and His only-begotten Son; and their divine light is regarded as rising and enthroned in the East, like the sun in the natural firmament. Now, this theophany, this appearance of God among us, takes place upon the altar, and hence the eastward direction in our churches is not toward the extreme eastern wall but toward the altar. Thus both priest and people are rightly turned toward the altar.

9. Yet it is not desirable in churches of great size to place the altar invariably near the extreme end of the building as was done in some churches here and there in ancient times (the one-area church).

More in accord with the general tradition would be, in larger churches, a rectangular, or semicircular, or polygonal sanctuary (choir) evidently distinct from the nave (the two-area church).

10. The terminal wall of the sanctuary should not be pierced by windows, lest the clear vision of the altar be obscured. Nor should the terminal wall be adorned with figured paintings that bear no direct relation to the eucharistic Sacrifice or to the theme of the liturgical year.

The architecture and the decoration of the sanctuary should be so designed that the eye will not be distracted but rather drawn to the altar and to the action of the eucharistic Sacrifice. Where figured paintings or mosaics adorn the sanctuary, these should represent ideas drawn from the Canon of the Mass, i.e., from the *Sursum corda* to the final doxology. In all cases the representation should not be of historical events but of static motives.

11. It would be unfortunate if the interior of the church were planned in such way that the congregation would lack the feeling of oneness, of family union in the rendering of divine worship. On the other hand it would be a mistake to plan the entire space in such a way that nowhere would there be left a quiet corner for private prayer.

Where possible, it would be ideal to provide a larger area for the large Sunday and feast-day congregations, and also another distinct and smaller one for the lesser number on workdays, so that in both cases there would be the feeling of a well-knit community, with still some provision of retired spaces for private devotion.

12. The highly desirable concentration of the whole interior upon the altar may be considerably disturbed by side altars, the stations of the Way of the Cross, confessionals, poorly placed lighting fixtures and benches and chairs, all of which may distract the gaze of the faithful from the sanctuary.

Everything really superfluous should be eliminated, and such details as are indispensable should be placed as inconspicuously as possible, perhaps in a lower chapel. Whatever must remain in the main area should be so designed and placed as not to interfere with the lines converging upon the altar.

13. The sacristy should be located quite near to the sanctuary and not, as in ancient times, alongside the facade of the building.

But there should be some way of passage from the sacristy to the entrance of the church so that on Sundays and feast-days there may be a festive approach of the clergy to the altar through the midst of the congregation, and furthermore so that the entrance chant, the Introit, may again be rendered as of old.

14. The vast interiors of cathedral churches and of churches in pilgrimage places and in our great cities have made it necessary that preaching be done not from the sanctuary but from an elevated pulpit usually located almost about the center of the nave and to one side, or again, fixed to a side wall. This example set by large churches has been adopted rather generally and without equal reason, and with the pulpit so placed the preacher is turned away from part of the congregation.

Preaching, according to the liturgy, that is, preaching which is in organic relation to the eucharistic Sacrifice, should be primarily an extension and explanation of the two readings which announce the word of God. Therefore, like the Epistle and the Gospel, the sermon should, wherever possible, issue forth from the sanctuary, that is, from a lectern or an ambo located near the sanctuary rail.

15. The choir or *schola cantorum* has a well defined liturgical task to fulfill, namely, to lead the congregation in prayers and hymns and acclamations, to alternate with the congregation in the responsorial chants, and to represent the congregation now and then. Therefore it is a mistake to locate the choir in a high gallery to the rear of and out of sight of the congregation.

In a church which adheres to the strict rules of the liturgy, the choir is placed at the forward end of the congregation and next to the sanctuary. If the high gallery is retained at all it may serve as the location for the organ. The function of this instrument is not to furnish solo pieces during the mis-called "pauses" in the sacred action, but rather to support the chant of the choir and the congregation, and occasionally to accentuate the spirit of festivity before and after the divine service. (The gallery would also be the proper place for a polyphonic choir and for an orchestra, which latter of course is never permitted in a truly liturgical service.)

16. In the sacrament of baptism we are born anew as children of God and we are incorporated into the Church, the Mystical Body of Christ. It is a deplorable fact that this full significance of baptism, so fundamental a truth in the ensemble of our faith, does not receive sufficient emphasis in our modern parochial life, and accordingly the baptismal font is usually one of the most neglected objects in the furnishings of our churches.

The baptismal font, which should be of imposing design and proportions, should be located in its own distinct area near to the entrance of the church. This area should be, according to venerable ecclesiastical tradition, in circular or polygonal form. The text of the rite of baptism also suggests this architectural treatment. For at the decisive moment in this ritual ceremony the baptised person appears not as an active agent in the process, but as the passive recipient of the divine mysterious action. Such being the case, the appropriate architectural form here is not the rectangular space, which is symbolic of an active process, but rather a circular space, the axis of which is vertical and suggestive of a passive experience.

17. It would be a mistake to arrange and decorate the interior of the church in such way as to create the atmosphere of a comfortable and cozy bourgeois residence; and a mistake also to wish to imitate the poverty of a proletarian dwelling.

The church interior should be neither bourgeois nor proletarian. It should bespeak forcibly the grandeur of God which surpasses all earthly measure, so that it may exalt the worshiper above the sphere and atmosphere of his daily private life; and yet, it must still leave one with the friendly feeling of "the goodness and kindness of our Savior" (Titus 3:4).

18. It would be a mistake, and it is one that is often made in our times, to entrust the decoration of the church, in painting and sculpture, in the designing of its furnishings, above all in the artistic treatment of the main portal, of the sanctuary, the altar, the baptismal font

and the pulpit, to the arbitrary action of a transient pastor or of a donor, or to the risk of mere haphazard.

In our efforts to erect an exemplary church edifice it is necessary to work out not only a structural plan, but also a well thought out plan of artistic expression which will be theologically and pedagogically correct. Such a plan will recognize that the decorative scheme of the finished house of God should present to the view of the congregation an ensemble of the theme of our holy faith, not in a fragmentary way, but with a certain completeness and in significant proportions and with right placing of accent.

19. In the planning of new churches there is often a desire to fix the dimensions at the maximum that financial resources and the ground area permit. It is a mistake to imagine that a larger church is necessarily a finer one.

There is an optimum size which should be kept in mind. That optimum is attained in a church in which the priest at the altar may be seen and may be heard without mechanical aid from the farthest reaches of the congregation, and in which the distribution of holy Communion to all the faithful may be accomplished without disrupting the holy Sacrifice of the Mass. This optimum size should never be exceeded except in extraordinary cases such as a cathedral church or a pilgrimage church which must of course be of larger dimensions.

20. It would be a mistake to provide for a church of average size a sanctuary of large dimensions sufficient to accommodate all the clergy of a cathedral chapter; and a mistake also to reduce the size of the sanctuary to such degree that the altar steps reach nearly to the sanctuary rail.

The dimensions of the sanctuary should be in proper proportion to those of the entire building, the area between the altar steps and the sanctuary being of such width and depth that the ceremonies of solemn high Mass may proceed in good order and harmony.

21. It would be a mistake to fill the church unnecessarily with pews to such degree that they would extend forward almost to the altar rail and sideways to contact with the outer walls.

There should be center and side aisles of sufficient width, and space enough about the church entrances and before the altar rail. Thus there will be no unseemly crowding at Communion time, and on certain occasions processions may take place with ease, such as the entrance procession on Sundays and feast-days and processions of Candlemas day and Palm Sunday.

A serious responsibility rests upon those who are entrusted with the task of church building. The result of their work will determine whether or not succeeding generations of the faithful will love this house of God with a true familiar feeling, and whether they will come joyfully or reluctantly to the sacred action of community worship. Therefore the planning of a new church edifice needs to be thought out with earnest conscience and with great care.

BIBLIOGRAPHY

Amicis, P. de: *Caeremoniale Parochorum* (1948).
———— *Il Ceremoniale Completo* (3 vols., 1903).
Anson, Peter F.: *Churches, their Plan and Furnishing* (1948).
Bartoli, L.: *L'Arte nella Casa di Dio* (1950).
Battistoni, A.: *La Fractio Panis e la Messa Romana* (1941).
Bayart, P.: *Les Divins Offices* (1948).
Bishop, E.: *Liturgica Historica* (1918).
Bliley, N. M. (O.S.B.): *Altars According to the Code of Canon Law* (1927).
Brannach, F.: *Church Architecture* (1932).
Braun, J. (S.J.): *Der Christliche Altar* (1924).
———— *I Paramenti Sacri* (1914).
Callewaert, C.: *De Missalis Romani Liturgia* (1937).
———— *Sacris Erudiri* (1940).
Caroe, A. D. R.: *Old Churches and Modern Craftsmanship* (1949).
Cavanaugh, W. T.: *The Reservation of the Blessed Sacrament* (1927).
Collins, H. E.: *The Church Edifice and its Appointments* (1953).
Comper, J. N.: *Further Thoughts on the English Altar* (1953).
———— *Of the Atmosphere of a Church* (1947).
———— *Of the Christian Altar* (1950).
Corblet, J.: *Histoire du Sacrament de l'Eucharistie* (2 vols., 1885).
Costantini, Celso (Cardinal): *Arte Sacra e Novecentesimo* (1935).
———— *L'Instruzione del S. Offizio sull'Arte Sacra* (1952).
———— *Nozioni d'Arte per il Clero* (1909).
Costantini, Celso (Cardinal), e Giovanni (Archbishop): *Fede ed Arte* (3 vols., 1945-1949).
Cours et Conférences des Semaines Liturgiques (1912-1937).
Cox, J. C.: *English Church Fittings, Furniture and Accessories* (1933).
Croegaert, A.: *Les Rites et Prières du S. Sacrifice de la Messe* (3 vols., 1948).
Dix, Gregory: *A Detection of Aumbries* (1942).
———— *The Shape of the Liturgy* (1943).
Feldhaus, A. H.: *Oratories* (1927).
Herdt, P. J. B. de: *Praxis Pontificalis* (3 vols., 1904).
Hope, W. H. S.: *English Altars* (1899).
Maffei, E.: *La Réservation Eucharistique* (1942).
Malherbe, G.: *Le Mobilier Liturgique* (1927).
Many, S.: *De Locis Sacris* (1904).
Martinucci, P.: *Manuale S. Caeremoniarum* (4 vols., 1911-1915).
Miscellanea Liturgica Mohlberg (2 vols., 1948-1949).
Moretti, A.: *De Sacris Functionibus* (4 vols., 1936-1939).
Morris, Joan: *Modern Sacred Art* (1938).
Munier, A.: *L'Eglise* (3 vols., 1925-1926).
———— *Un Projet d'Eglise au XXe Siècle* (1933).

255

Nabuco, Joachim: *Pontificalis Romani Expositio* (3 vols., 1945).
New Churches Illustrated (1936).
Ochsé, Madeleine: *La Nouvelle Querelle des Images* (1953).
O'Connell, J.: *Celebration of Mass* (3 vols., 1940-1942).
────── *Directions for the Use of Altar Societies and Architects* (1936).
Perardi, G.: *La Dottrina Cattolica, Il Culto* (1938).
Pilkington, R.: *La Chiesa e il suo Arredamento* (1937).
Post-War Church Building (edited by E. Short) (1947).
Pugin, A. W.: *Glossary of Ecclesiastical Ornament and Costume* (1868).
Régamey, R. R. (O.P.): *Art Sacré au XXe Siècle* (1952).
Reinhold, H. A.: *Speaking of Liturgical Architecture* (1952).
Righetti, M.: *Storia Liturgica* (4 vols. 1945-1953).
Rock, D.: *Church of our Fathers* (1903-1904).
Rosengarten, A.: *Handbook of Architectural Styles* (1927).
Roulin, E. (O.S.B.): *Nos Eglises* (1938).
────── *Vestments and Vesture* (1931).
Sadlowski, E. L.: *Sacred Furnishings of Churches* (1951).
Schuster, I. (Cardinal, O.S.B.): *The Sacramentary* (4 vols., 1924-1926).
Scott, Gilbert: *Mediaeval Architecture* (2 vols., 1879).
Soenens, F.: *Les Edifices du Culte* (1923).
Stappen, Van der, J. F.: *Sacra Liturgia* (4 vols., 1912).
Tamagnone, G.: *Il Decoro della Casa di Dio* (1950).
Vavasseur-Haegy: *Les Fonctions Pontificales* (2 vols., 1932).
────── *Manuel de Liturgie et Cérémonial* (2 vols., 1925).
Vismara, E. M.: *Le Funzioni della Chiesa* (2 vols., 1934).
Webb, Beresford: *Exploring Old British Churches* (1948).
Webb, Geoffrey: *The Liturgical Altar* (1939).
Weber, E. J.: *Catholic Church Buildings* (1927).

ENCYCLOPEDIAS

Catholic Encyclopedia.
Catholic Encyclopaedic Dictionary (D. Attwater).
Catholicisme (1947—).
Dictionnaire d'Archéologie Chrétienne et Liturgie. (1924-1954).
Dictionnaire de Droit Canonique. (1924—).
Dictionnaire Pratique de Liturgie Romaine (1952).
Ecclesia (1928).
Enciclopedia Cattolica (1949-54).
Liturgia (R. Aigrain) (1941).

PERIODICALS

Ami du Clergé, L'.
Art Sacré, L'.
Art d'Eglise, L'.
Bulletin Paroissial Liturgique.
Clergy Review.
Downside Review.
Ephemerides Liturgicae.

Irish Ecclesiastical Record.
Liturgy.
Liturgical Arts.
Maison Dieu, La.
Paroisse et Liturgie.
Pax.
Questions Liturgiques et Paroissiales, Les.
Révue Bénédictine.
Vie et Les Arts Liturgiques, La.
Worship (formerly *Orate Fratres*).

INDEX

Active participation of worshippers in
the Liturgy, 9, 12, 25, 49, 51, 134,
158, 161
Adornment, see Ornamentation
Altar, 133 sqq.
  additions to, 171 sqq.
  adornment, 187 sqq.
  Blessed Sacrament, 18, 159, 165,
    166, 171-173, 231, 232, 233
  clothing, 49, 138, 167-168, 192-196,
    196-198
  consecration, 23-24, 143, 144, 145,
    148, 149, 152, 154, 155-156, 167-
    168, 169
  construction, 142 sqq.
  definition, 139-140
  dimensions, fixed altar, 155-156,
    portable altar, 156
  "fixed," 140, 143 sqq., 165
  focal point of a church, 23, 24-25,
    27, 48, 77, 114, 136, 158, 165,
    187, 190, 194, 224
  forms, 141
  furniture, 205 sqq.
  history, 133 sqq., 138
  ideal, 138, 218
  kinds of, 140
  lighting, 63 sqq.
  material, 142 sqq.
  portable, 153-154
  position, 6, 23-24, 25, 135, 157 sqq.
  sacred character, 138, 167-168, 187
  sanctity, 167-168
  sepulchre, 148, 149, 152
  side, 164 sqq.
  "stable," 152-153
  steps, 158, 162-163
  supports, 144-145
  symbolism, 14, 27, 48, 49, 139-140,
    142, 143, 164, 167, 168, 193, 194
  table, 138, 143, 144, 155
  title, 61, 152, 153, 165, 169-170
  unity, 14, 48
  unencumbered, 168
  visible to worshippers, 24, 25, 158
Altar cover, 217

Altar stone, 134, 140, 152, 154, 156
Ambo, 79-80
Ambry for Holy Oils
  in baptistery, 126
  in church, 87
Anointing
  door posts, 6, 7
  walls of church, 6, 7
Antependium, see Frontal
Architect, Church, 49 sqq., 58
Architecture, styles of, 4, 23, 42, 44, 51
Art, Sacred, 28 sqq., 43, 44, 47, 52-53,
  56, 97, 106
  Christian tradition and, 43 sqq.
  Church's control, 38, 53 sqq.
  clergy and, 55
  commissions on, 29, 34-35, 38, 52, 56
  degraded, 35, 39, 47, 54, 98
  Faith and, 52, 55
  "laws," 29, 32 sqq., 45, 59
  liturgical, 30, 34
  modern, 23, 35, 36-37, 39, 41, 42,
    43, 44, 46, 47, 51, 98
  purpose, 31, 33, 53, 54
  social character, 35
  subsidiary, 34
  unworthy, 35, 38-40, 56, 98
Artist, Christian, 52 sqq., 58
  and his patron, 55 sqq.
Aspersory, 83
Aureole, 103, 107

Bacile, 243
Baldaquin, 189 sqq.
  Baptismal Font, 123, 125 sqq.
Baptistery, 26, 122 sqq., 126
  decoration, 61, 124
  focal point of a church, 23-24, 48,
    122
  position, 24, 27, 49, 124
Beauty in church, 9, 23, 31, 34, 35, 42,
  43, 50, 53, 59, 188, 204
Bedroom
  over the altar, 159
  over a church, 18

259

ILLUSTRATIONS

With the exception of those of the altar in the College of St. Robert Bellarmine, Heythrop, Oxfordshire, England, of Blessed Sacrament Church, New Rochelle, N. Y., of St. Patrick's Cathedral, New York, and of the Chapel of the College of New Rochelle, N.Y. — selected by the author—the illustrations which follow have been selected by Professor Francesco Montana, Head of the Department of Architecture of the University of Notre Dame.

In certain of them there is to be found an incidental infraction of a rubric, of the kind that is fairly common, as when, for example, the stipites of the altar are so disposed as to make it somewhat awkward for the Bishop to consecrate it; or the altar is placed against the wall of the sanctuary, thereby preventing his proceeding around it in accordance with the rubrics of the rite of consecration; or the tabernacles are not duly veiled; or the canopy is either omitted or not duly expressed; or the baptistry does not open directly into the nave of the church, as the baptismal rites demand.

These illustrations have been chosen for the purpose, not necessarily of presenting models for imitation, but rather of showing the freedom that is granted by the Church to pastors and architects in meeting the requirements of sound worship.

Plates 1 and 2:

St. Ann's Church
Normandy, Missouri

Murphy and Mackey, Architects

Photos by Hedrich-Blessing

Reredos in stained glass
designed by Emil Frei

Plate 3:

Church of the Resurrection
of Our Lord
St. Louis, Mo.

Murphy and Mackey,
Architects

Photo by Hedrich-Blessing

Plate 4:

Church of the Resurrection
of Our Lord
St. Louis, Mo.

Murphy and Mackey,
Architects

Painted reredos by
Emil Frei

Photo by Hedrich-Blessing

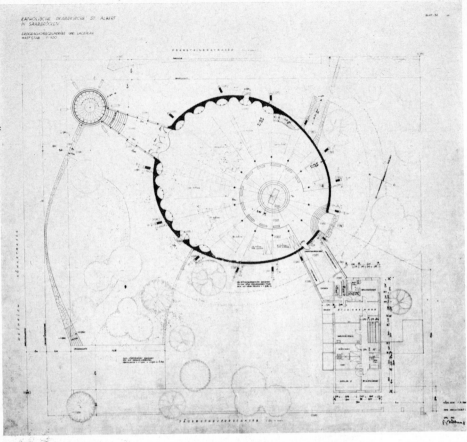

KATHOLISCHE PFARRKIRCHE ST. ALBERT
IN SAARBRÜCKEN

ERDGESCHOSSGRUNDRISS UND LAGEPLAN
MASSSTAB 1:100

Plate 5

Plate 6

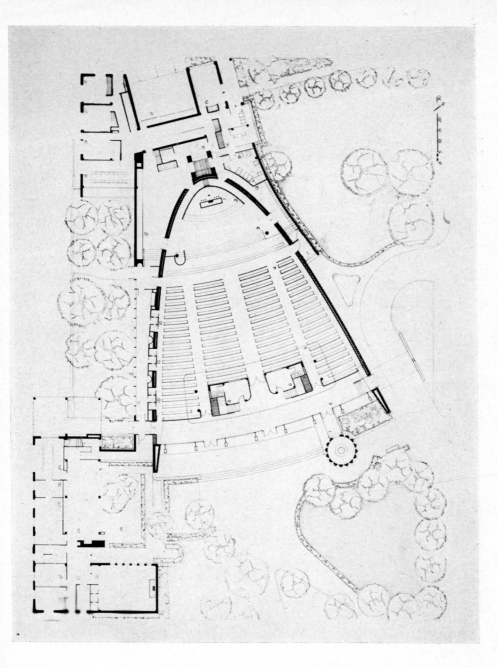

Plate 7: Above, plan of the Church of the Resurrection of Our Lord, St. Louis, Missouri. Murphy and Mackey, Architects.

Plate 5: Plan of St. Albert's Church, Saarbrucken, Germany. Dipl. Ing. Gotter Bohm, Architect.

Plate 6: Model of Church of Christ the King, Seattle, Washington. Paul Thiry, Architect. Photo by Charles A. Pearson.

Plates 8 and 9: Church of Christ the King, Seattle, Washington. Paul Thiry, Architect.

Plate 10:

Church of Christ the King,
Seattle, Washington

Paul Thiry, Architect

Photos by
Charles A. Pearson

Plate 11

Plate 12

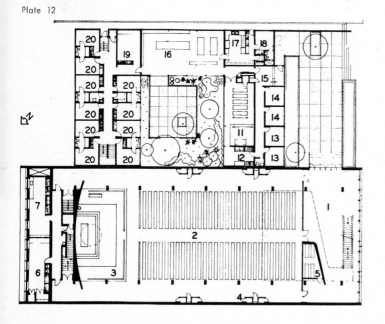

LEGEND

1. NARTHEX
2. NAVE
3. SANCTUARY
4. CONFESSIONAL
5. BABY CRYING RM
6. PRIEST SACRISTY
7. BOYS & WORK SACRISTY
8. BAPTISTRY
9. CHOIR BALCONY
10. ORGAN RM
11. CHAPEL
12. SACRISTY
13. MUSIC RM
14. PARLOR
15. VESTIBULE
16. LIVING DINING RM
17. KITCHEN
18. HOUSEKEEPER
19. WORK RM
20. BED RM

FIRST FLOOR
FIRST FLOOR PLAN

0   50   100FT.

Plates 11, 12 and 13:

Interior views and plan, Corpus Christi Church, San Francisco, California

Mario J. Ciampi, Architect

Photos by Rondal Partridge

Plate 14: Above, Saint-Andre de Messei, Flers, Normandy, France. M. Meurice, Architect. Photo by Fl. Thierry

Plates 15 and 16: Below and right, St. Matthias Church, Berlin-Schoenberg, Germany. Photos by Foto Hasse

Plate 17:

St. Peter's Church
Kirkwood, Mo.

Murphy and Mackey,
Architects

Photo by
Hedrich-Blessing

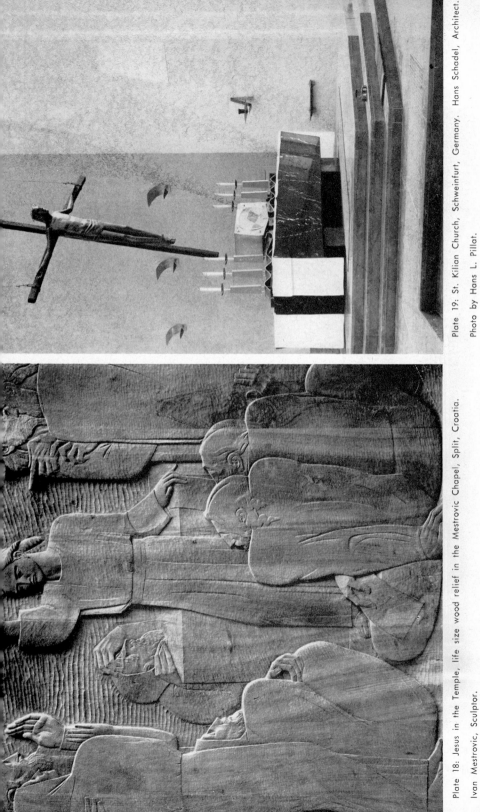

Plate 19: St. Kilian Church, Schweinfurt, Germany. Hans Schadel, Architect.

Photo by Hans L. Pillat.

Plate 18: Jesus in the Temple, life size wood relief in the Mestrovic Chapel, Split, Croatia.

Ivan Mestrovic, Sculptor.

Plate 20: Altar in the College of St. Robert Bellarmine, Heythrop, Chipping Norton, Oxfordshire, England.
Designed by Alfred Bartlett.

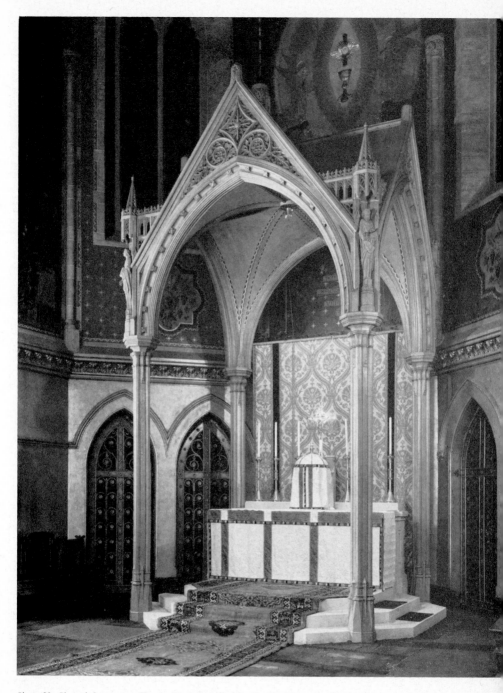

Plate 21: Blessed Sacrament Church, New Rochelle, N. Y. Furnishings by Rambusch.

Photo by F. S. Lincoln.

Plates 25 and 26: Above and lower right, Church of St. Anselmo, Rome.

Plate 27: Above, right, Chapel of the Ursuline Convent, New Rochelle, New York.

Liebfrauenkirche, Trier, Germany.
Altar and Sanctuary restorations by
Rudolf Schwarz. Plate 28: Left, Main
Altar; Plate 29: Below, Plan; Plate
30: Right, Reservation Ciborium.

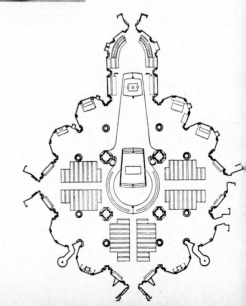

Plate 31: Above, Baptismal font in St. Quirin Church, Neuss, Germany. Hein Minkenberg, Sculptor. Photo by Christliche Kunst.

Plate 32: Left, Baptistry, St. Peter's Church, St. Louis, Missouri. Murphy and Mackey, Architects. Photo by Hedrich-Blessing.

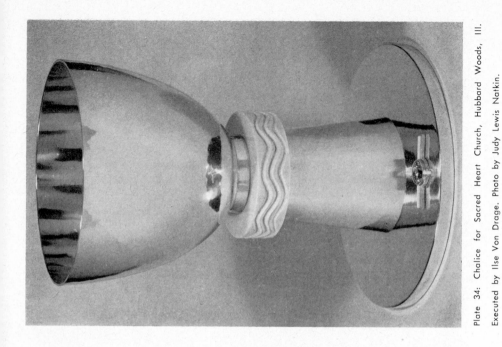

Plate 34: Chalice for Sacred Heart Church, Hubbard Woods, Ill. Executed by Ilse Von Drage. Photo by Judy Lewis Natkin.

Plate 33: Ciborium for Sacred Heart Cathedral, Salina, Kansas. Dunstan Pruden, Silversmith.

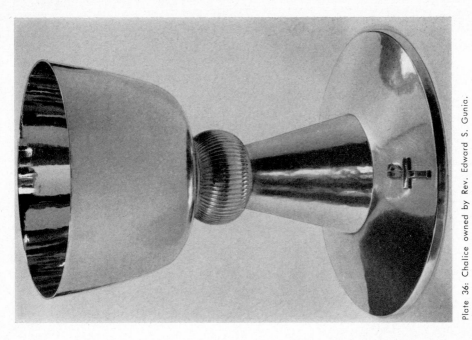

Plate 36: Chalice owned by Rev. Edward S. Gunia.
Executed by Ilse Von Drage. Photo by Judy Lewis Natkin.

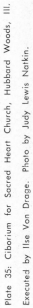

Plate 35: Ciborium for Sacred Heart Church, Hubbard Woods, Ill.
Executed by Ilse Von Drage. Photo by Judy Lewis Natkin.

Vestments designed and produced by
Sister Mary Augustina Flueler,
Stans, Switzerland.

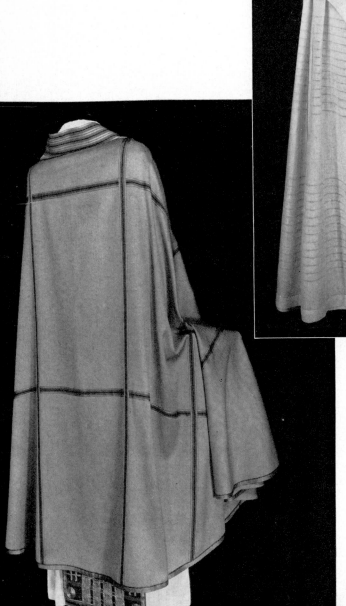

Plate 37: Above, Alb is of
handwoven linen.

Plates 38 and 39: Chasuble, left,
is of Romanesque form, and the
Dalmatic, right, is body length
with wide and very long sleeves.
The basic material for both is
handwoven silk of cherry-red
color. The trimmings are Turkish-
green, black and red, and the
embroidery is gold on a dark
green base.

Plate 40: Tabernacle in the Ciborium of Liebfrauenkirche, Trier, Germany.

Plate 41:

Corpus of rolled sterling silver sheet, by Louis Feron, in chapel of Bellarmine College, Plattsburg, New York. Figures painted by Pierre Bourdelle.

Plate 42:

Crucifix cast in aluminum, St. Mark's Church, Burlington, Vermont. Charles Umlauf, Sculptor.

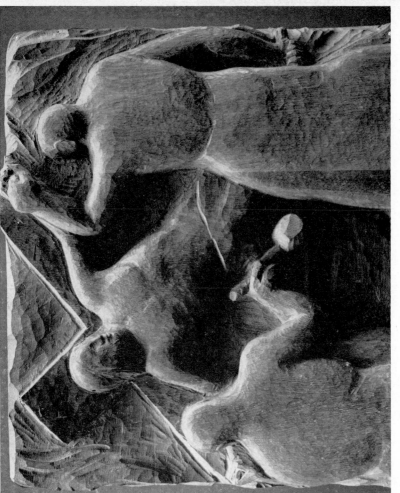

Plate 43: Above, Wood Station of the Cross, Corpus Christi Church, San Francisco, California. Mario J. Ciampi, Architect. Photo by Rondal Partridge.

Plate 44: Left, Man of Sorrows. Charles Umlauf, Sculptor. Photo by Koen Photo Service.